History
of
Lincoln COUNTY
GEORGIA

By:
Clinton J. Perryman

**Southern Historical Press, Inc.
Greenville, South Carolina**

This volume was reproduced from
An 1933 edition located in the
located in the publishers private Library

All rights reserved. No part of this publication may be reproduced,
stored in a retrieval system, transmitted in any form, posted
on to the web in any form or by any means without
the prior written permission of the publisher.

Please direct all correspondence and orders to:

www.southernhistoricalpress.com
or
SOUTHERN HISTORICAL PRESS, Inc.
PO BOX 1267
375 West Broad Street
Greenville, SC   29601
southernhistoricalpress@gmail.com

Originally published: Georgia, 1933
ISBN #978-1-63914-005-3
All rights Reserved.
Printed in the United States of America

TABLE OF CONTENTS

CHAPTER I	BACKGROUND OF LINCOLN COUNTY	PAGE 1
CHAPTER II	FIRST AND EARLY SETTLERS	PAGE 4
CHAPTER III	THIS SECTION DURING THE AMERICAN REVOLUTION	PAGE 7
CHAPTER IV	THE REVOLUTION--CONTD.	PAGE 10
CHAPTER V	THE REVOLUTION--CONTD.	PAGE 14
CHAPTER VI	THE CREATION OF LINCOLN COUNTY	PAGE 17
CHAPTER VII	ORGANIZATION OF LINCOLN COUNTY	PAGE 21
CHAPTER VIII	HOMES, OCCUPATIONS AND CUSTOMS OF EARLY SETTLERS	PAGE 26
CHAPTER IX	OTHER PHASES OF LIFE AMONG THE EARLY RESIDENTS	PAGE 29
CHAPTER X	CHURCHES OF LINCOLN COUNTY	PAGE 32
CHAPTER XI	LINCOLNTON	PAGE 47
CHAPTER XII	THE COUNTY TO THE WAR BETWEEN THE STATES	PAGE 50
CHAPTER XIII	THE COUNTY IN THE WAR BETWEEN THE STATES	PAGE 54
CHAPTER XIV	A HISTORIC RAID AND RECONSTRUCTION	PAGE 61
CHAPTER XV	PROGRESS OF THE COUNTY SINCE THE WAR	PAGE 65
CHAPTER XVI	LINCOLN SOLDIERS IN THE WAR WITH SPAIN AND IN THE WORLD WAR	PAGE 73
CHAPTER XVII	MISCELLANY	PAGE 81

CONTENTS CONTINUED

BIOGRAPHICAL SKETCHES:

Ashmore, Thomas P.	Page 98
Ashmore, Otis	100
Boykin, James Hamilton	104
Clarke, Elijah	107
Crawford, William Beall	111
Crawford, Thomas Remson	113
Curry, Jabez Lamar Monroe	115
Dooly, John	119
Dooly, Thomas	120
Dooly, John Mitchell	121
Dunaway, Ben Hill	126
Florence, Dr. Loree	126
Hogan, James Robert	127
Hogan, William Ambrose	128
Hogan, Luther Rice	130
Hudson, James Thomas	131
Humphreys, Ralph Wilbur	133
Lamar, Peter	135
Lamar, LaFayette	135
Lyon, Richard Francis	136
Murray, Thomas Walton	138
Perryman, Minnie Thaddeus	139
Smalley, Welcome Talmadge	141
Strother, Adolphus Erastus	140
Tutt, William Duncan	141
Ward, Lavilla A.	142
Ware, Nannie	143
Zellars, Peter	143
APPENDIX A	145
APPENDIX B	149

PREFACE

While deeply appreciative of the confidence of the Grand Jury in choosing him to prepare a history of Lincoln County, yet it was with some reluctance that the author accepted the responsibility. In the preparation of this work, he knew that he would be largely a pioneer, with only here and there a traveled path, which would require much time, research and labor, but his sense of patriotic duty and his love for his county prevailed and he entered wholeheartedly into the undertaking. At times, his work has been arduous, his progress slow, and he has been frequently interrupted by his official duties, but, on the whole, it has been pursued with pleasure. Accuracy has been his aim, and, to that end, he has sought information from all known available sources, realizing that absolute perfection is unattainable. That it may have imperfections, no one is more conscious than he, but he hopes that they may be overlooked by a generous public. While no compensation is provided for preparing the history, yet, if it helps to inspire the present generation, and those who come after them, to a greater pride in and a deeper love for their county, or if it contributes to elevate Lincoln to her rightful place among the sister counties of the State, he feels that he shall have been repaid and that his efforts shall not have been in vain.

He expresses his gratitude to Miss Ruth Blair, State Historian, to Miss Mary R. Mullen, State Librarian of Alabama, to Hon. William A. Slaton, of Washington, Ga., and to his many friends in Lincoln County, and elsewhere, for the valuable assistance given him. He desires especially to acknowledge the kindness of his departed friend, Hon. Marion L. Felts, of Warrenton, Ga., for the use of a number of his books bearing on Georgia's history, and for his warm words of encouragement. Authors and authorities quoted are acknowledged in connection with the quotations.

The author is a native of Lincoln County, and he loves her with an ardent devotion. With her are associated his fondest recollections and sweetest memories. His life is interwoven with that of her people.

Lincolnton, Ga.
June 1, 1933

This author located in Thomson, McDuffie County, Ga., since writing this history. As the cemetery at Lincolnton, Ga., is about full, he leaves it entirely with his family as to whether he shall be buried there or in Thomson, unless he should alter his views. April 2, 1938.

Thomson, Ga.   C. J. Perryman, Author

CHAPTER I

BACKGROUND OF LINCOLN COUNTY

CHAPTER I.
BACKGROUND OF LINCOLN COUNTY

The territory that is now Lincoln County was included in the lands ceded by the Creek and Cherokee Indians in 1773 from which Wilkes County was later created. While little is known of the frequency and extent of the occupancy of this section by the Indians, except that trading posts were established along the Savannah River; that there are a few ancient graves supposed to contain their dead; and that some local places are still identified by Indian names --Cherokee Hill and Cherokee Creek, it may be safely assumed that the vast forests, the abundance of game, the streams teaming with fish and the topography of the country made it congenial to their habits and customs, and that it was one of their favorite resorts in their nomadic life.

Fortunately, it is not left to the imagination to picture this region before it was touched by the hand of civilization. William Bartram, a botanist of Philadelphia, traversed it from Little River to Broad River, in 1776, and published an interesting description of it in his book, THE TRAVELS OF WILLIAM BARTRAM, p. 263 (Reprint Edition). He says: "I arose early next morning and continued my journey for Fort James.* This day's progress was agreeably entertaining, from the novelty and variety of objects and views; the wild country, now almost depopulated, vast forests, expansive plains and detached groves, then chains of hills whose gravelly, dry, barren summits present detached piles of rocks, which delude and flatter the hopes and expectations of the solitary traveller, full sure of hospitable habitations, heaps of white gnawed bones of ancient buffalo, elk and deer, indiscriminately mixed with those of men, half grown over with moss, altogether, exhibit scenes of uncultivated nature, on reflection, perhaps, rather disagreeable to a mind of delicate feelings and sensibility, since some of these objects recognize past transactions and events, perhaps not altogether reconcilable to justice and humanity.

"How harmonious and sweetly murmur the purling rills and fleeting brooks, roving along the shadowy vales, passing through dark subterranean caverns, or dashing over steep rocky precipices, their cold, humid banks condensing the volatile vapors, which falling coalesce in crystalline drops, on the leaves and elastic twigs of the aromatic shrubs and incarnate flowers! In these cool, sequestered, rocky vales, we behold the following celebrated beauties of the hills, fragrant sweet shrub, blushing pink rhododendron, delicate philadelphus modrus, which displays the white wavy mantle, with the sky-robed larkspur, perfumed lily, and flame azalea, flaming on the ascending hills or wavy surface of the gliding brooks. The epithet fiery, I annex to this most celebrated species of azalea, as being expressive of the appearance of its flowers, which are in general of the colour of the finest red lead, orange and bright gold, as well as yellow and cream colour; these various splendid colours are not only in separate plants, but frequently all the varieties and shades are seen in separate branches on the same plant; and the clusters of the blossoms cover the shurbs in such incredible profusion of the hill sides, that suddenly opening to view from dark shades, we are alarmed with the apprehension of the hill being set on fire. This is certainly the most gay and brilliant flowering shrub yet known; it grows in little copses or clumps, in open forests as well as dark groves, with other shrubs and about the bases of hills, especially where brooks and rivulets wind about them: the bushes seldom rise above six or seven feet in height, and generally but three, four, and five, but branch and spread their tops greatly; the young leaves are but very small whilst the shrubs are in bloom, from which circumstances the plant exhibit a greater show of splendor."

On page 56 of the same volume, Bartram describes his travels, in 1773, through the southwestern and western portion of what was later Wilkes County, and of the forests he says: "Continuing some time through these shady groves, the scene opens, and discloses to view the most magnificent forest I had ever seen. We rose gradually a sloping bank of twenty or thirty feet elevation, and immediately entered this sublime forest. The ground is perfectly a level green plain, thinly planted by nature with the most stately forest trees, such as the gigantic black oak, tulip poplar, black walnut scaly bark hickory, beech, elm, sweetgum, whose mighty trunks, seemingly of an equal height, appeared like superb columns. To keep within the bounds of truth and reality, in describing the magnitude and grandeur of these trees, would, I fear, fail of credibility; yet, I think I can assert, that many of the black oaks measured eight, nine, ten, and eleven feet diameter five feet above the ground, as we measured several that were above thirty feet girt, and from hence they ascend perfectly straight with a gradual taper, forty or fifty feet to the limbs; but below five or six feet, these trunks would measure a third more in circumference, on account of the projecting jambs, or supports, which are more or less, according to the number of horizontal roots that they arise from: the tulip tree, sweetgum, and beech were equally stately."

Trees of the same kind grew in this section, and still grow here, though not in an original state, but it is not probable that the black oaks equalled in magnitude those described by Bartram, else he would have noted the fact. As to the others mentioned, from the few, evidently of that era, which were scattered here and yonder up to two decades ago, they were equally large and stately. White oaks, from statements of aged residents and from tradition, were lords of the forest here, they grew larger and were more majestic; but, though some of lesser dignity remain, time and progress apparently have destroyed all these mighty monarchs of that distant period--save one. This lofty giant, dense in limb and foliage, with its one hundred twenty feet of height, its one hundred feet of circular spread, its seven feet of diameter four feet above the ground, --the admiration of every lover of trees,-- standing, in solitary beauty and grandeur, on what is known as the Dozier Hotel lot, in Lincolnton, is a silent witness to the tragedy of change and a mute reminder of departed sylvan glory.

The chestnut and the chinkapin were common trees of that era, and could be found in some sections as late as forty years ago, especially on or around Graves Mountain, while in the southeastern portion of this territory, now known as the Agnes and New Hope sections, was a forest of several thousand acres of long-leaved yellow pine, with a narrow strip extending to Savannah River above the mouth of Little River. These shapely pines, like stately columns, ranging from one and a half to six feet in diameter twenty four inches from the ground, and with a distance of thirty to sixty feet to the limbs, were unsurpassed for symmetry and quality by any other of their kind in America. In them were the best and most enduring lumber and shingles, but in an undeveloped country and in a purely agricultural age their value was not and could not be appreciated. Much of this forest was destroyed at the first in clearing the land for farming, and later it was constantly reduced to supply local demands for lumber. About a decade and a half ago, the last large tract--approximately four hundred acres-- was sold, and it was immediately converted into lumber. All that remains of this forest to connect the present with that distant past, besides a few widely scattered trees, is a lone fifty acre tract, and when that is gone, unless science discovers a way, the like will not be seen again; for these trees do not reproduce in the same quality. Their reproduction, while retaining the long leaf, are short and scrubby and entirely worthless for lumber.

In this vast wilderness, besides the common game animals, such as the rabbit, the squirrel and the o'possum, which are still native here, deer were numerous, and venison was not a rare diet with the early settlers; but the clearing of the forests, the continuous development of the country, the increasing population, pressed them into narrower and narrower ranges till, at last, those escaping the hunter's rifle migrated to more congenial regions. Wild turkeys, too, were plentiful, and a few could be found here as late as half a century ago, but, in the main, like the deer, being restricted in area and decimated by the hunstman, they gradually sought other haunts and finally disappeared.

Such was the country that met the gaze of the pioneer as, filled with wonder and admiration at the varied scene, he began to subdue the wilderness and to impress upon it the stamp of civilization.

*Fort James was located at the confluence of Broad and Savannah Rivers. McCall's HISTORY OF GEORGIA, (Reprint Ed. 1909, p. 261).

Note: The common names of the trees and flowers, furnished by the author's friend, Mr. W.A. Slaton, of Washington, Ga., have been used in lieu of the botonical names used by Bartram in his description of the country.

CHAPTER II

FIRST AND EARLY SETTLERS

CHAPTER II
FIRST AND EARLY SETTLERS

With the signing of the treaty with the Indians, the "Ceded Lands" were opened for settlement. Land courts were established to issue grants, for a reasonable sum, to those desiring to settle in the new territory. These Courts were held at Dartmouth, afterwards Petersburg, situated a short distance above the confluence of Broad with Savannah River, in what is now Elbert County, and at Wrightsboro, situated in what is now McDuffie County.

From the records of these Courts, the original of which is on file in the office of the Clerk of the Superior Court of Greene County, and a typwritten copy of which, furnished by Mr. James A. LeConte, of Atlanta, Ga., to Mr. Boyce Ficklen, Sr., of Washington, Ga., is on file in the office of the Ordinary of Wilkes County, it is shown that in 1773 the following grants were made to lands in what is now Lincoln County.

"Benjamin Mosley, North Carolina, Bute County, a wife and 7 children, 2 boys and 5 girls between 15 years and 5 months old. 100 acres on Soap Creek at a place called burchers Cabbin.

Patrick Maclemurray, South Carolina, a wife 1 son & 2 daughters, the son 5 years old, the daughters younger. 100 acres on Soap Creek joining 100 acres of the lower side reserved for Benjamin Mosley, no more planting land being there, the 100 acres Major Cheivers, a free negro now lives on sd. Ck.

"Lieutenant Thomas Waters, South Carolina, 11 negroes. 200 acres on Savannah River near Fishing Creek bounded southerly on land of Bryan Ward.

"Jesse Pugh, North Carolina, a wife and 6 children, 5 sons and 1 daughter from 16 to 2 years. 100 acres on North side of Little River below Maclemurray's old place, including spring.

"Lieutenant Edward Keating. Twenty four negroes. 300 acres on Savannah River below Fishing Creek, joining William Duloney's upper line where one Gustavous now lives.

"William Dean, South Carolina, a wife and one son aged 10 months. 100 acres on Savannah River whereon one Nail lives, above lands petitioned for by Mr. Edward Keating.

"Nathan Abney, a wife and 2 children, one boy 3 years old, a girl 4 months old, and 1 negro. 100 acres on Savannah River opposite an island containing about 10 acres near Douglasses Island, including said Island of 10 acres.

"Hugh Middleton, S. Carolina, a wife, 4 sons & 2 daughters, from 11 years to 9 months old and 10 negroes. 300 acres at Pistol Creek adjoining the lower line & Savannah River, including a place formerly surveyed for Gideon Chivers.

"Thomas Lamar, Jr., a wife & 1 son 4 years old. 100 acres on Fishing Creek at a place whereon Semore cut a parcell of logs.

"John Dooly, So. Carolina, a wife and 3 sons from the ages of 4 to 1 year of age, and three orphan nephews from the ages of 19 to 10 years old. 250 acres on Savannah River at Lee's old place, and 250 acres adjoining same.*

"Jacob Patten, a wife, 7 daughters & 6 negroes. 100 acres at Pistol Creek upon Trading Path 5 miles from ye river.

"Henry Kennedy, a wife, a son & 4 daughters. 50 acres at a place called High Hill fork, a mile above the Upper Trading Path,
Soap Creek."

"John Armstrong, a wife 2 sons and 2 daughters from 13 to 4 years old. 150 acres at a spring running into Soap Creek at O'Neal's Path.

"Alexander Mills, South Carolina, a wife 5 sons & 2 daughters from 16 to 4 years old. 150 acres on Pistol Creek 2 & 1/2 miles above the mouth at a flat rock on the upper side of the Creek.

"Randal Barden, South Carolina, a wife, a son and a daughter from the ages of 17 to 7 years old. 250 acres on a branch of Pistol Creek about 3 miles from Savannah River in lieu of a place entered.

"Hugh Middleton. (Family already given). 150 acres adjoining below 300 acres allotted himself on Pistol Creek. Savannah River.

"Edward Keating. 150 acres on Savannah River joining the upper line of 300 acres granted and to include an Island opposite the 300 acre tract.

"Ward Taylor, South Carolina, a wife 3 sons & 2 daughters from the ages of 11 to 3 years. 150 acres on Soap Creek about 3/4 of a ;mile above the Lower Trading Path.

"Stern Simmons, South Carolina, 100 acres on Soap Creek about 2 miles above the Cherokee Road on both sides of the middle fork where one Casey lived."

In 1774, the following grants were made:

"Ebenezer Low, himself only, North Carolina. 100 acres on Little River above the Cherokee Ford.

"James Maclemurray, South Carolina, himself only. 100 acres resigned by Patrick Maclemurray on Soap Creek."

Most, if not all, of these grantees located on the allotted lands, and are the first settlers of whom there is an authentic record.

After January, 1775, no other Land Courts, dealing with the lands in this territory, were held under the jurisdiciton of the Province of Georgia. This was doubtless due to the resentment, now glowing at white heat throughout all the Colonies and this Province, against the oippressive measures of England, and which turned the attention of the people to their liberties rather than to the settlement of the country. In fact, in January of 1775, the first Provisional Congress was held in Savannah, over the protest of the Royal Governor, James Wright, and from then events moved so rapidly that in June of the same year the Province of Georgia renounced British rule and created a Council of Safety to govern its affairs. In January, 1776, Governor Wright was arrested and made a prisoner. However, on June 7, 1777, on Sept. 16, 1777, on Jan. 23, 1780, on Feb. 17, 1783, and on Aug. 1, 1783, the General Assembly off the State of Georgia passed Land Acts making provision for grants to the unsettled lands. (Marbury & Crawford's DIGEST OF GA. LAWS, pp. 316-330). There were, doubtless, few, if any, settlements in this territory during the period of the Revolution, for in the Act of 1780 it is stated, "The rich and healthy lands in Wilkes County, and elsewhere in this State remain unsettled to the great detriment to the commerce and strength of the same*****And to the end, That every encouragement may be given to induce men to come from other States to settle lands in Wilkes County under this Act, shall not be compelled to serve in the militia, in any other way or place but in defending the same during the term of two years." Following the Acts of 1783, numbers of Carolinians and Virginians, with a few from other States, settled in Wilkes County under Head-right Land Warrants granted by the Land Courts, those settling in what is now Lincoln County being mostly from North and South Carolina, with a few from Virginia.

The names of the early settlers of this section, including some of the original settlers to whom other grants were issued, may be found in the records of land grants in the office of the Ordinary of Wilkes County and in the office of the Ordinary of Lincoln County, though all who received land grants, especially in Wilkes County, did not settle here. (See Appendices A & B).

*John Dooly was originally from North Carolina. His residence in South Carolina must have been short.

CHAPTER III

THIS SECTION DURING THE AMERICAN REVOLUTION

CHAPTER III
THIS SECTION DURING THE AMERICAN REVOLUTION

This Section Patriotic. In no other section of the country were the people more loyal to the colonies in their opposition to the oppressive measures of England than in what was later Wilkes and Lincoln Counties. The Declaration of Independence, on July 4th, 1776, found them prepared both in heart and mind to receive it with enthusiasm, and willing to sacrifice their lives and fortunes, if need be, to maintain its principles. They were Revolutionists to the core, and the tocsin of war never sounded on more patriotic ears. Though not participating in any of the battles of the Revolution till the war was transferred to the south, their ardor, in the meantime, found expression, in common with the other Patriots of the Province, in overthrowing the royal government and in preparing for the conflict, and in the notable service of helping to subdue and bring to terms of peace the hostile Cherokee Indians whose murderous and savage raids, incited by British agents and Tories, had been for several years the constant dread of the white settlements.

Leaders. There were two outstanding leaders of the Patriots in this section, Elijah Clarke and John Dooley, both of whom were residents of Wilkes County, which, at this time, had been created by the Georgia Legislature. Dooley lived in the area which later became Lincoln County, while Clarke did not reside in it till after the war. Both were fearless and capable and had the unbounded confidence of their followers. The part played by Wilkes County during the Revolution revolves largely around their names.

Another leader of promise was a brother of John Dooley, Captain Thomas Dooley, also a resident of what is now Lincoln County, but he was killed in a skirmish with the Indians near the Oconee River, on July 22, 1776, while returning from Virginia with a band of recruits for the continental brigade in Georgia. This was his only engagement, but he fought with courage, determination and an unconquerable spirit, being murdered by the Indians while trying to defend himself with the butt end of his own gun after having been shot down.

Military Activities. Defeated in their efforts to subjugate the Northern colonies, the British, in the latter part of 1778, transferred their major military operations to the South with the hope of conquering South Carolina and Georgia. Favored with superior numbers, and with no strongly fortified places to take, their progress in Georgia was rapid. With the capture of Savannah, on December 29, 1778, and Augusta, in January, 1779, by

Colonel Campbell, the State, for a time, was completely in the hands of the enemy.

Campbell established a post at Augusta, and placed it in command of Colonel Brown, a Tory, notorious for his cruelty and brutality, while he advanced into Wilkes County. Many families, taking their remaining stock of cattle and such other property as could be easily removed, fled into South Carolina and encamped, where they were saved from bitter hardships and dire want by the generous hospitality of the inhabitants; the others remained on their farms or repaired to the forts according to the degree of danger.

Establishing his headquarters in Augusta, Campbell at once set about making his triumph secure. Armed bands went out and overran the country. Property was stolen; the people were harrassed and intimidated; and the torch was applied to many of the homes of those who had fled to South Carolina. It looked as if Georgia was conquered.

Campbell, however, did not properly appraise the spirit of these brave pioneers. His rest upon his laurels was of short duration. With their families safe in Carolina, the men gathered under their leader, Colonel John Dooley, and prepared for resistance. Dooley took a position on the Carolina side of the Savannah River, about thirty miles above Augusta and five miles above the position of Colonel McGirth, a notorious Tory, and his three hundred loyalists on the opposite side of the river. Crossing into Georgia with a hundred men, Dooley was compelled to retreat before Colonel Hamilton, commanding a detachment of McGirth's troops, who pressed him closely and fired upon his rear as he recrossed the Savannah a short distance below the mouth of Broad River. Hamilton encamped at Waters' plantation, about three miles below Petersburg, with one hundred men. Dooley took a position opposite to him in Carolina, where his forces were augmented by two hundred fifty men and under Colonel Andrew Pickens, who was given command.

It was determined to attack Hamilton's detachment with these combined forces. They recrossed the river at the mouth of Broad, on the night of February 10th, with the hope of attacking Hamilton in the early morning, but he, feeling there was no further danger, had marched away to visit the forts and to administer the oath of allegiance to such inhabitants that came under his sway. The Americans surmised that Carr's fort would be the first object of the enemy's attention and set out in pursuit. In this they were not disappointed. They were close upon the enemy's rear as they reached the fort. The enemy, in their haste to escape danger, abandoned their horses and baggage and took refuge in the fort and defended it. A summon to surrender being refused, all avenues of escape were cut off and a siege begun. Sharp firing was kept up by both sides. A request to permit the women and children to leave the fort was refused. The enemy was without food and water, and the Americans settled down to await the fruits of victory which could not be long. Their hopes, however, were to be blasted. About this time Colonel Pickens received a message from his brother that Colonel Boyd was sweeping through South Carolina towards Georgia with eight hundred loyalists, leaving destruction of property and lives, by fire and sword, in his wake. Some of the men proposed setting fire to the fort at different points to force a surrender, but Colonels Pickens and Dooley opposed it on account of the unfortunate families inside. The siege was abandoned, and Colonel Hamilton, stripped of horses and baggage, was left in possession of the fort, from which he retreated to Wrightsborough and later to Augusta. During the siege, Hamilton's loss was nine killed and three wounded, and Pickens and Dooley's five kiled and seven wounded.

Pickens and Dooley recrossed Savannah River and hastened into South Carolina to intercept Boyd. Boyd changed his course in order to avoid them and crossed the Savannah River at Cherokee Ford, where in a spirited skirmish with Captain Robert Anderson, he lost one hundred killed, wounded and missing, including desertions, while the American loss was sixteen killed and wounded, with sixteen taken prisoners. He moved westward to avoid danger, but on the morning of February 13th, he crossed Broad River and turned southward with a view of being joined by McGirth's detachment at an appointed place on Little River. Pickens and Dooley returned to Georgia in swift pursuit and were reinforced by one hundred dragoons under Colonel Clarke. On the night of February 13th, they camped at Clarke's Creek, within a few miles of the enemy. Early on the morning of February 14th, the Americans resumed their march and surprised Boyd at his camp at Kettle Creek, where his men, unapprehensive of danger, had turned out their horses to forage in the swamp, and were preparing breakfast. Colonel Dooley commanded the right wing of one hundred men, Colonel Clarke the left with one hundred men, and Colonel Pickens the center with two hundred men. A bloody battle ensued, lasting nearly two hours, in which Boyd and seventy five of his men were killed, seventy five were taken prisoner, and the remainder of the forces completely routed. The American loss was nine killed and twenty three wounded. With this victory, about six hundred horses and their equipment, a large quantity of arms and much clothing fell into the hands of the Americans.

Decisively beaten and thoroughly disheartened, the remnant of Boyd's army scattered in different directions-- some fled to Florida, some to the Creek nation, some to the Cherokee habitations, some to the post at Augusta, where they were contemptuously received by the British, and some returned to their homes and put themselves at the mercy of the American government. And McGirth, upon learning of their utter rout, hastily retreated to Augusta and united with the troops of Campbell.

Thus, for a time, this section was freed of these scourges. They had more than met their match, and, before the white heat of patriotism, had been driven to inaction or hurled back into their lair.

CHAPTER IV

THE REVOLUTION--CONTINUED

CHAPTER IV
THE REVOLUTION, CONTINUED,
HOPE AND DESPONDENCY

Renewed Courage. The victory at Kettle Creek had a magical effect upon the Georgia patriots --their courage was renewed, and they pursued the conflict with increased vigor. It was now determined to make an immediate attempt to drive the British from their stronghold in Augusta.

Augusta Evacuated. Dragoons, brigades and militiamen, under dauntless leaders, hastened to Augusta to carry out their purpose, some taking a position on the Carolina side, and others on the Georgia side. General Lincoln was at Purysburgh, on the Savannah River, between there and Savannah, with several thousand American troops, and Colonels Pickens, Clarke and Dooly were coming. An outpost of seventy British regulars and militia was surprised and taken. Colonel Campbell became alarmed, and, fearing he would be cut off from the main body of the British army, hurriedly evacuated Augusta, in the latter part of February, and marched towards Savannah, leaving behind him a large quantity of provisions and military stores to fall into the ands of the Americans.

Families Return. With this section cleared of Tories and with Augusta in possession of the patriots, the families, which had fled to South Carolina for safety, returned to Wilkes County with their scanty property. Scarcely had they located in the forts and settlements, however, before they were alarmed by the approach of about eight hundred Creek Indians, under the command of Tate and McGilvery, two Indian agents of the British, to make war upon the whites.

The Indians Scattered. Colonel Clarke remained on the frontier to protect the forts, while Colonel Pickens, with two hundred men from South Carolina, and Colonel Dooly, with one hundred men, joined their forces to proceed against the Indians. They were joined by other forces at Wrightsborough. The Americans marched all night, hoping to surprise and attack the Indians before dawn, but some of the discontented inhabitants warned Tate and McGilvery of their approach. But the Indians were thrown into confusion by being met with an armed force in the open; they had hoped to do their savage work by stealth and surprise. Unwilling to risk a battle, they divided into small bands and fled in various directions. Detachments of the Americans were sent in pursuit, and, in several instances, they were overtaken, some killed and the remainder dispersed--not, however, without suffering a few casualties themselves. With the Indian threat shattered, the inhabitants settled down to a few months of peace. Colonel Pickens returned to South Carolina, where the British were overrunning the State, Colonel Clarke joined the continental army in North Carolina, and Colonel Dooley remained in Wilkes to be on guard against threatened danger while the poverty stricken inhabitants cultivated their crops.

The Enemy Reappears. With the disastrous repulse of the Americans in their attempt to take Savannah from the British, on October 9, 1779, Georgia again was completely under the control of the enemy. They had staked their hopes on this battle and lost. General Lincoln had retreated to Charleston. The inhabitants were mercilessly persecuted and outraged, many seeking refuge in adjoining states. There were only small bands of troops to resist the oppressors. The outlook was indeed gloomy for the patriots of Georgia.

It was not, however, till the fall of Charleston, on May 12th, 1780, that Augusta was again occupied by the British. During that month, Colonels Brown and Grierson, Tory officers, entered it without opposition and established headquarters.

Death Of Colonel Dooley. Brown was a resident of Augusta when the people proclaimed their opposition to English rule, and had been tarred and feathered and drawn through the streets in a cart by a mob for his offensive remarks against the American cause. He made his escape with implacable hatred in his heart for all patriots. He now had an opportunity to give vent to his spleen, nor did he fail to take advantage of it. He confiscated the property of the American sympathizers, and ordered them and their families banished from the State, while he compelled those who remained to take the oath of allegiance to the British crown. Bands of Tory emissaries were sent throughout the country to exact this oath and otherwise to see that his orders were obeyed.

It was at the hands of one of these bands, under Captain Corker, that Colonel John Dooley met his death. Stealing up to his home, near the Savannah River, at the dead of night, they burst in and brutally murdered him in bed in the presence of his wife and children. Revenge had taken its choicest object, for he was a terror to Tories. Thus passed a gallant and indefatigable leader, an irreparable loss to the cause of Freedom, the memory of whose inestimable services Georgia was later to perpetuate in the name of one of her counties.

Tory Pond. After murdering Colonel Dooley, the Tories proceeded to Broad River. A detatchment of several crossed the river and went to the cabin of Nancy Hart where they were captured by her and immediately executed by her husband and a party of patriots. There is a tradition that those who did not cross the river were captured by some patriots and brought back to a pond about three quarters of a mile from Dooley's home and hanged. The place thereafter was called Tory Pond. As late as half a century ago, according to nearby residents at that time, the marks of several graves, near the pond, could be distinctly seen as evidence of this retributive justice.

Augusta Besieged. Brown's acts of cruelty were further enforced by an order from Lord Cornwallis, sent to all of the British outposts in Georgia and South Carolina, requesting that the most rigorous measures be taken to punish the rebels; and it is stated by a reputable historian (McCall) that the next morning after this order reached Augusta, five victims were taken from jail and executed on the gibbet. Conditions were such as to discourage all but the stoutest hearts, but patriotism was still alive.

Colonel Clarke returned to Wilkes County about September 1st. He had stated he would never rest as long as the British flag floated over Augusta, and he began collecting troops to retake it. With three hundred fifty men, he was joined by Colonel McCall, at an appointed place on Soap Creek, with eighty men from South Carolina, and on September 14th they marched to Augusta. They had acted so quickly and so quietly they reached the vicinity of the town unobserved, and found the enemy unprepared for an attack. Near Hawk's Gulley on the west, an attack was made upon an Indian camp. The Indians retreated toward their allies, but returned the fire. This was the first intimation Colonel Brown had of the approach of the patriots. He and Colonel Grierson rushed to the support of the Indians, and a spirited battle ensued in which the Americans were victors. The British retreated leaving a number of killed and wounded on the field and seventy prisoners in the hands of the Americans, and took refuge in a strong building called the White House, which they defended. Several attempts were made to dislodge the enemy, but without avail. Clarke then laid siege to the house with the hope of forcing a surrender.

On the morning of the 16th, the Americans inflicted heavy loss upon a body of Cherokee Indians, who, during the night, had crossed the river in canoes to reinforce Brown. Brown himself was shot through both thighs. On the 17th, Clarke sent Brown a summons to surrender, supposing that the sufferings of the wounded, the lack of food and water and the offensive odor from the decaying bodies of men and horses would induce such a step, but the demand was flatly refused.

Upon Clarke's arrival at Augusta, Brown had sent messengers to Colonel Cruger, at Ninety Six, South Carolina, informing him of his precarious situation, and urging immediate reenforcements. On the night of the 17th, Clarke was informed by his spies that Colonel Cruger was approaching with five hundred regulars and loyalists. On the morning of the 18th, when Brown was on the verge of starvation and surrender, this force appeared on the Carolina bank of the Savannah. Some of Clarke's men had gone to visit their friends and relatives in Burke County, whom they had not seen for some time, and others had decamped to plunder. Weakened and outnumbered, Clarke was forced to raise the siege and retreat, after sustaining a loss of about sixty killed and wounded. About thirty of the wounded were left in the hands of the British.

Brown again had the opportunity to show his cruelty. Thirteen of the wounded prisoners were hanged on the staircase of the White House, near where he was lying, so that he might have the satisfaction of seeing them expire; the others were turned over to the Indians to be put to death with all the horrors of savage brutality.

Clark retreated to Little River, where his men, after appointing a time and place of rendezvous, dispersed to return to their homes to take leave of their friends and relatives and make preparations to quit the country. At the time and place appointed, Clarke found three hundred men and four hundred women and children assembled for the journey. With no chance to cultivate crops and with the country under the absolute control of the enemy, to leave families behind would be to expose them to starvation and the cruelties of a merciless foe.

The Exodus. About the last of September, this company, with Clarke at the head, began an eleven day trying journey to Tennessee, of which McCall, in his HISTORY OF GEORGIA, gives the following description: "With this helpless multitude, like Moses from Egypt of old times, and with not more than five days subsistence, Colonel Clarke commenced a march of near two hundred miles, through a mountainous wilderness, to avoid being cut off by the enemy. On the eleventh day, they reached the Wattauga and Nolachuckie rivers on the north side of the mountains, in a starved and otherwise deplorable condition. Many of the men and women had received no subsistence for several days, except nuts; and the last two, even the children were subsisted on the same kind of food. This is a distressing picture, to which the pen cannot do justice; therefore, it must be filled up by the imagination. Many of the tender sex were obliged to travel on foot, and some of them without shoes; and notwithstanding the difficulties they had to encounter, they yielded without murmuring, and by their smiles cheered the drooping spirits of their husbands. The tenderness of the female heart is always open to the sufferings of the brave and honourable."

These families were hospitably received by the Tennesseeans and were distributed among their homes. Clothing, food and the comforts of life were provided, not temporarily, but as long as the occasion demanded. "In this beautiful region," says Evans in his FIRST LESSONS IN GEORGIA HISTORY, "surrounded by mountains, refreshed with sweet water, and cared for by a generous hospitality, the sad refugees found comfort and cheer until the storms of war passed away, and the coming of peace to a distracted land made it safe for them to return to their homes upon the soil of Georgia."

CHAPTER V

THE REVOLUTION--CONTINUED

CHAPTER V.
THE REVOLUTION, CONTINUED.
VICTORY

Clarke Returns. After disposing of the families among the generous inhabitants of Tennessee, Colonel Clarke gathered the remnant of his regiment, recrossed the mountains, and on about October 20th took a position on the borders of South Carolina. For the next several months he was busily engaged in fighting the British in that State. In an engagement at Long Cane, he was severely wounded in the shoulder, and had to be carried from the field. About the last of March, 1781, he returned to Georgia with his troops. Being seized with small-pox about the 12th of April, and retiring from activity during illness, he entrusted his command to Colonel Micajah Williamson of Wilkes County.

Tory Brutality. As was expected, Brown glutted his vengeance in a most brutal and barbarous way upon the inhabitants of the surrounding country after the attack upon Augusta. "When the Georgians returned into their country," says McCall, previously quoted, "they dispersed into parties of ten and twelve men each, so as to spread themselves over the settlements, and appointed Dennis' mill on Little River, for the place of rendezvous. When these small parties entered the settlements where they had formerly resided, general devastation was presented to their view; their aged fathers and youthful brothers had been hanged and murdered; their decrepit grandfathers were incarcerated in prisons, where most of them had been suffered to perish in filth, famine or disease; and their mothers, wives, sisters, daughters, and young children had been robbed, insulted, and abused, and were found by them in temporary huts, more resembling a savage camp than a civilized habitation. The indignant sigh burst from the war-worn veteran, and the manly tear trickled down his cheek, as he embraced his suffering relatives. There is damning proof of the truth of this unvarnished tale; and the reader may imagine the feelings of the Georgian of that day, and the measure of his resentment. Mercy to a loyalist who had been active in outrage, became inadmissible, and retaliative carnage ensued."

Augusta Again Besieged And Taken. Colonel Williamson's troops assembled on Little River, on April 16th, as appointed, and proceeded to Augusta, where he was joined by other detachments and their leaders. Taking a position three quarters of a mile from the British works, he fortified his camp and kept the town in a state of blockade till the middle of May. At this time, Colonel Clarke, who had recovered from small-pox, arrived, bringing with him a body of one hundred men, and succeeded Colonel Williamson in command. Shortly after his arrival, he sent a detachment against a party of loyalists who were marching towards Augusta to reenforce Brown. The loyalists were surprised at Briar Creek, a number killed and wounded and the rest dispersed, without an American loss.

On May 23rd, Colonel Henry Lee, "Light Horse Harry," the father of Robert E. Lee, and Colonel Pickens, with detachments from the Continental Army, united their forces wit those of Colonel Clarke, and the effort to capture the town was begun with grim determination. Forts Grierson and Cornwallis were the enemy's strongholds. The former was the first objective. Lee took a position south of the fort in order to check Brown should he attempt to come to the rescue from Fort Cornwallis, Pickens and Clarke a position to the north-west and Majors Eaton and Jackson a position to the north-east. The attack was begun from the north-east to the north-west. Brown attempted to come to the fort's relief, but was held at bay by Lee's artillery. Colonel Grierson, finding himself in a hopeless situation, made a daring effort to escape with his men to Fort Cornwallis, but it cost him dearly, thirty of his men were killed and forty-five, included himself, taken prisoners.

Grierson was killed by a Georgia soldier shortly after his capture for his cruelties to the defenseless people. A reward was offered for the arrest of the one who committed the deed, but his identity was never revealed.

With Fort Grierson in their possession, the Americans now centered their attention on Fort Cornwallis, which was much stronger and commanded the ground for several hundred yards around it. Brown improved all his defenses and prepared for a stubborn resistence. With all his ignoble qualities, he was a man of courage. The Americans had but one field piece, and for them to attempt to take the fort, under the deadly fire of the enemy, would mean nothing but a sacrifice of human lives. Colonel Lee conceived the plan of raising a tower, filling it with dirt and brick, and mounting a cannon on it, as a means of reducing the fort. Brown, discovering the work, made three desperate attempts at night to destroy it, but was forced to retreat with loss each time. He was summoned to surrender, but refused. The tower was completed, a six pounder mounted upon it and fire opened upon the fort. The terrific bombardment dismounted the enemy's artillery and put it out of commission. The enemy was in a critical situation. The fire from the American riflemen became more galling. Realizing that further resistance would be vain, on the morning of June 5th, Brown and his forces, under the terms of surrender, marched out of the fort and laid down their arms. Thus Augusta was again in the hands of the Americans.

During the siege the American loss was sixteen killed and thirty five wounded, while the British loss was fifty two killed and three hundred thirty four made prisoner.

Brown and his men were placed under a strong guard of Continental troops and carried to Savannah. Several attempts were made to take Brown's life for his past cruelties to the helpless people, but they were thwarted by the guards.

The Hornet's Nest. All of this territory, including

that surrounding Augusta, was now restored to the Americans, and there were Continental troops enough in the State to hold the British in check. "The Hornet's Nest," as this section was called by the Tories, had lived up to its reputation: The hornets had stung, and stung effectively.

Inhabitants Return. The inhabitants who had fled to other States now returned. They looked upon a scene of desolation--a land that had, indeed, passed through the baptism of blood and fire, whose full suffering could be known only by an avenging God; but--it was home, and its bleedings and sorrows bound them to it with tenderer and more sacred ties. With courage and determination, they joined in the arduous task of building a new civilization upon the ruins of the former.

The War Ends. The surrender of Cornwallis, at Yorktown, Va., on the 19th day of October, 1781, filled the patriots with rejoicing, and the British and Tories with despair. The tide had turned in favor of the Americans, and the British were meeting with reverses throughout the country. In the early part of 1782, England realized she was making a hopeless attempt to conquer America and determined to end the war. On the 21st of July, under order of the King, Savannah was evacuated, and was occupied by the forces of General Wayne. This put the State in complete control of the patriots. On November 30th, a preliminary treaty of peace was signed at Versailles, in which England conceded the independence of the American States, and which was formally ratified at Paris on September 3rd, 1783. Thus the great conflict came to a close, and America had won.

The patriots of Wilkes made a notable contribution to that momentous struggle. Through it all, sustained by an unyielding faith in its ultimate triumph, even in the darkest hours of adversity, they clung with sublime courage and an unconquerable spirit to the American cause, for which all were reduced to poverty, and to which many "gave the last full measure of devotion." In the annals of that conflict, these heroes command an enviable place; and in the galaxy of Georgia's patriot leaders will ever shine the names of Clarke and Dooley.

CHAPTER VI

THE CREATION OF LINCOLN COUNTY

CHAPTER VI
THE CREATION OF LINCOLN COUNTY

Progress. The war left the people of Wilkes County almost destitute, but they faced their condition with the same high courage with which they had faced the enemy. On the ruins of their devastated land they began anew to build another civilization. By rigid economy, self-denial, heroic endurance and patient industry, they braved the first few years of hardships and prepared for a more comfortable existence. And in their work of reconstruction they were joined by many Virginians and Carolinians who settled among them, under Head-Right Land Warrants, following the Land Acts of 1783, referred to in a previous chapter. Progress was rapid, and by 1796 the eastern part of Wilkes was sufficiently developed and populous to be formed into a county.

The Creation Of Lincoln County. Lincoln County was created by an Act of the Georgia Legislature on February 20, 1796, and contains an area of 291 square miles, or 186,240 acres, taken exclusively from Wilkes County. The Act provides, "That one other new county shall be laid out from the county of Wilkes, in the following manner and form, to wit, beginning at Rae's mill on Little River, running a direct line; from thence to _____*Zimmerman's, on the road leading from the town of Washington to Barksdale's ferry on Savannah, from said Zimmerman's a direct line to Drury Cade's mill, on Broad River, from thence down Broad River to its mouth, thence down Savannah River to the mouth of Little River, thence up Little River to the beginning: Which said county shall be called and known by the name of "Lincoln.""

On January 22, 1852, the Legislature enacted, "That the line between the counties of Wilkes and Lincoln be so changed as to include in the county of Wilkes the residence of William M. Jones and the dwelling house on the plantation of Toliver Jones." There is no record as to why this change was made, but Hon. R.O. Barksdale, the present Ordinary of Wilkes County, whose ancestors lived near there in Lincoln County, and who himself was familiar with the section, states that it was because the road to Lincolnton, through the swampy bottoms of Fishing and Morris Creeks, were so bad and boggy and the streams so frequently swollen that it was inconvenient, and often impossible for the residents to get to Lincolnton, while no such handicaps existed on the Washington road. There is also a tradition that the change was made to give one of the residents an opportunity to run for sheriff of Wilkes County. Since then there have been no changes in its boundaries.

Boundaries. Lincoln County is bounded on the North and Northeast by Broad River, separating it from Elbert County; on the East by Savannah River, separating it from South Carolina; on the South by Little River, separating it from Columbia and McDuffie counties; and on the West by Wilkes County.

Militia Districts. Every county, under the law, must be divided into militia districts, and each district, when organized, must contain at least one hundred male inhabitants over twenty years of age liable to military duty. Lincoln County has eight --the 182nd, Shady Hill; the 183rd, Salem; the 184th, Amity; the 185th, Sybert; the 186th, Lincolnton; the 187th, Goshen; the 188th, White Plains; and the 269th, Parks.

Political Location. While it has been in many different senatorial and congressional districts since its organization, Lincoln County is at present, and has been for a number of years, in the 29th Senatorial District and in the 10th Congressional District. From its creation to December 19th, 1818, it was in the Western Judicial Circuit, and from December 19, 1818, to January 1, 1911, it was in the Northern Judicial Circuit. Since January 1, 1911, it has been in Toombs Judicial Circuit.

Name. Lincoln County was named in honor of General Benjamin Lincoln, a distinguished military leader in the American Revolution. While his splendid activities in other sections made him famous throughout the country, yet it was his gallant, though unsuccessful, attempt to wrest Savannah from the British, in the autumn of 1779, which specially endeared him to Georgians and caused his name to be thus fittingly perpetuated.

General Lincoln was born at Hingham, Massachusetts, on January 24, 1733. He did not secure a good education in his youth, but by reading and study he largely remedied this defect and became a man of considerable literary ability. In 1780, Harvard conferred upon him the honorary degree of Master of Arts.**

Prior to the outbreak of the Revolution, Lincoln was chiefly engaged in farming, though during that period he was honored with many civil and military offices. He was an ardent patriot and, with the conflict imminent, determined to devote his energies to the liberties of his country. He entered wholeheartedly into the movement. He was a member of the Second Continental Congress which assumed jurisdiction of the military activities of the Colonies as a central authority and elected George Washington commander-in-chief of the American army. He was made a Brigadier General, and later a Major General of the militia. ·In October, 1776, he joined the regular army in New York, and he was with Washington in his New Jersey campaign. It was during this campaign that Congress, upon the high recommendation of Washington, made him a Major General of the Continental Army. At Bound Brook, through the carelessness of patrols, a surprise attack was made upon him by Cornwallis, but he succeeded in rallying his troops and retreating into the mountains with small loss. In July, 1777, he was ordered by Washington to join the Army on the North, under General Gates, which was opposing the advance of General Burgoyne. This expeditioin contributed largely to the victories of the American forces in the battles of Bemis Heights, N.Y., on Oct. 7, 1777, which resulted in the surrender of Burgoyne on Oct. 17,

1777. He was in command of his forces in the American lines, but he was not personally present during the battle of Oct. 7th. On the following day, while reconnoitering, he came unexpectedly upon a body of enemies and was wounded in the leg by a volley from their muskets. For several months he was confined at Albany from the effect of this wound, and later at his home in Hingham, where he underwent several painful operations.

In August, 1778, he had sufficiently recovered, though lame for life, to join the army, and he was given charge of military operations in the South. He established headquarters at Charleston, S.C., and found conditions in this section discouraging to the American cause. He was forced to organize a new army; the city was threatened by General Provost; and Savannah was held by the British. For several months there were no important engagements between the two armies. At length, General Ashe was dispatched with about two thousand men to take a position on Briar Creek, near Savannah, while he advanced towards that city with a large force. On March 3, 1779, Ashe was surprised and defeated by General Provost, who advanced upon Charleston and demanded its surrender. Colonel Moultrie, its defender, declined to accede to the demand. Lincoln hastened back to the relief of Charleston, and, upon his approach, the siege of the city was abandoned. On June 20, 1779, he made a daring attempt to dislodge a portion of the enemy's forces, under General Maitland, at Stono Ferry, about thirty miles from Charleston, but his attack was repulsed with terrible loss.

Then came that heroic, but ill-starred, effort to capture Savannah. With the French fleet under Count D'Estaing cooperating, the city was besieged for a month. On October 9, 1779, an attempt was made to carry the enemy's works by storm, but it met disastrous defeat. The French and Americans fought bravely, but the British, having been informed of the plan of attack by a deserter, were thoroughly prepared for resistance. The gallant Pulaski fell in action, the brave D'Estaing was twice wounded, and the daring Jasper, of Fort Moultrie fame, fatally shot, was borne dying from the field. After this repulse, D'Estaing sailed away and Lincoln returned to Charleston.

Lincoln now endeavored to put Charleston in a defensive position and he asked Congress for reinforcements of regular troops. On March 10, 1780, Sir Henry Clinton surrounded the city with a large force from New York. A force under General Huger, coming to the relief of the city, was intercepted at Monk's Corner and repulsed by Colonel Tarleton. With no means of communication, with a force too small to risk a battle, and with no hope for relief, Lincoln surrendered on May 12th, after enduring a siege for nearly two months. He was paroled and he returned to his home. In the following November he was exchanged.

In the campaign of 1781, Lincoln commanded a division under General Washington. He took an active part in the siege of Yorktown, Va., the last bloody scene in the drama of the war; and when Cornwallis, who was ill in his tent, sent his sword to General Washington by his deputy, General O'Hara, on Oct. 19, 1781, as a token of surrender, it was

Lincoln who was designated to receive it and to conduct the seven thousand surrendering enemy to the spot where they were to lay down their arms.

While history shows that the campaigns conducted and the attacks made by Lincoln personally, during the Revolution, always proved disastrous, yet his courage, integrity and ability were strikingly conspicious despite his failures. He retained the affection of his troops, the respect of his associate officers and the implicit confidence of General Washington. This certainly attests a creditable military career.

In October, 1781, he was chosen by Congress as Secretary of War, and resigned this position in October, 1783. In 1786-7, he was appointed by the Governor and Council of Massachusetts to command a detachment to put down Shay's Rebellion, which, by his prudent measures, he soon accomplished. In 1787, he was elected Lieutenant Governor of Massachusetts, and he was a member of the convention to ratify the new constitution. In 1789, Washington appointed him Collector of the port of Boston, which office he held until two years before his death. He died May 9, 1810, at Hingham, in the same house in which he was born.

White, in his STATISTICS OF GEORGIA, says: In Lincoln's character, strength and softness, the estimable and amiable qualities, were happily blended. His mind was quick and discriminating. As a military commander he was judicious, brave and indefatigable. From early life he had been a communicant of the church. He was about five feet nine inches in stature; his face round, his eyes blue, and his complexion light. He wrote essays on various subjects. He as a man of true piety. All trusts he performed with incorruptible integrity."

*Evidently Phillip Zimmerman as he lived near the road.
**The author acknowledges the courtesy of Dr. A. Lawrence Lowell, President of Harvard, in giving him the date on which this degree was conferred.

NOTE: The facts stated in the above sketch were gathered from White's STATISTICS OF GEORGIA, Evans' HISTORY OF GEORGIA, Chambers' HISTORY OF THE UNITED STATES and NATIONAL CYCLOPEDIA OF AMERICAN BIOGRAPHY.

CHAPTER VII

ORGANIZATION OF LINCOLN COUNTY

Lincoln who was designated to receive it and to conduct the seven thousand surrendering enemy to the spot where they were to lay down their arms.

While history shows that the campaigns conducted and the attacks made by Lincoln personally, during the Revolution, always proved disastrous, yet his courage, integrity and ability were strikingly conspicious despite his failures. He retained the affection of his troops, the respect of his associate officers and the implicit confidence of General Washington. This certainly attests a creditable military career.

In October, 1781, he was chosen by Congress as Secretary of War, and resigned this position in October, 1783. In 1786-7, he was appointed by the Governor and Council of Massachusetts to command a detachment to put down Shay's Rebellion, which, by his prudent measures, he soon accomplished. In 1787, he was elected Lieutenant Governor of Massachusetts, and he was a member of the convention to ratify the new constitution. In 1789, Washington appointed him Collector of the port of Boston, which office he held until two years before his death. He died May 9, 1810, at Hingham, in the same house in which he was born.

White, in his STATISTICS OF GEORGIA, says: In Lincoln's character, strength and softness, the estimable and amiable qualities, were happily blended. His mind was quick and discriminating. As a military commander he was judicious, brave and indefatigable. From early life he had been a communicant of the church. He was about five feet nine inches in stature; his face round, his eyes blue, and his complexion light. He wrote essays on various subjects. He as a man of true piety. All trusts he performed with incorruptible integrity."

*Evidently Phillip Zimmerman as he lived near the road.
**The author acknowledges the courtesy of Dr. A. Lawrence Lowell, President of Harvard, in giving him the date on which this degree was conferred.

NOTE: The facts stated in the above sketch were gathered from White's STATISTICS OF GEORGIA, Evans' HISTORY OF GEORGIA, Chambers' HISTORY OF THE UNITED STATES and NATIONAL CYCLOPEDIA OF AMERICAN BIOGRAPHY.

CHAPTER VII.
ORGANIZATION OF LINCOLN COUNTY

Inferior Court. Immediately after Lincoln County was created, an Inferior Court, with five Justices, was established as required by law. This Court, besides having authority to try all cases not reserved to the Superior Court, exercised the same jurisdiction over county affairs that is now exercised by the Court of the Ordinary; in fact, in its jurisdiction over estates and purely county matters, it was called the Court of Ordinary. The Justices were appointed by the Legislature for a term equal to their good behavior and during residence in the county; and they could be removed from office only be impeachment, or upon a petition addressed to the Governor by two-thirds of both branches of the General Assembly. With the establishament of this Court and the Superior Court, the county was organized into a local government.

First Justices. The first Justices of the Inferior Court for the County were Thomas C. Russell, William Clements, Peyton Wyatt, William Dawson and John Winn.

Other Justices. A complete list of the Justices of the Inferior Court for the county, with length of service, is given in the chapter entitled, "Miscellany."

Place Of Meeting. The record is silent as to the place at which the early Inferior Court held its sessions, but it may safely be presumed that they were held where the Superior Court held its sessions.

The First Superior Court. The first Superior Court for Lincoln County was held at the home of Josiah Stovall, who resided near the old Tatom place, between Soap and Fishing Creeks, in what is now Sybert District. There was no county seat, and several years were to elapse before Lincolnton could claim that distinction. This place was selected presumably because it was situated in the most populous section of the county and would be convenient for the most people. The records do not show how many sessions of court were held there, but certainly there were several. In "Minutes of the Superior Court, 1796-1805," pages 1-2, in the Office of the Ordinary of Lincoln County, the following record of the first court appears:

"The Honorable Superior Court for the County of Lincoln met agreeable to the Act of the Assembly at the house of Mr. Josiah Stovall on Monday the 16th day of May 1796.

"Present his honor Benjamin Telfair Esq.. Abner Tatom Clerk of the said Court entered into Bond agreeable to Law with John Tatom, William Tatom, Newell Walton & William Smith his securities whereupon he took the oath prescribed by the Law of this State and the oath directed by the Constitution of the United States.

"James Hughes Esq., Sheriff of the said County came

into Court and entered into Bond agreeable to Law with Gibson Woolridge, William Mathews, William Norman, Jessee Hardy, James Hardy & Cuthbert Steal his securities whereupon he took the following oath (to wit) I James Hughes do solemnly swear that I will faithfully Execute all Writs Warrants Receipts and processes directed to me as the Sheriff of the County of Lincoln and true returns make and in all things well and truly and without malice or partiality perform the duties of the office of Sheriff of Lincoln County during my continuance in office and take only my lawful fees. -James Hughes.

LIST OF GRAND JURORS DRAWN

Lott Warren	Shadrack Hogan	Shadrack Turner
Philip Zimmerman	William Lowe	Josiah Stovall
Thomas Crim	Richard Winn	Robert Walton
Benj. Andrews	Duncan Bohanan	Thomas Fullilove
Edward Jones	James Suddith	Moses Tulley
Thomas Bussey	Basille Lamar	Thomas C. Russell
Peyton Wyatt	James Ware	William Walton
John Russell	James Snead	Benjamin Moseley
Wm. Stokes, Jr.	Samuel Farr	Robert Harper, Esq.
Newell Walton	Cuthbert Steel	

LIST OF PETIT JURORS DRAWN FOR NEXT TERM

Thomas Barron	Jacob Sellers	John Seal
John Farrar	Richard Seals	Saml. Thompson
Barret Farrar	Wm. Moore	John Crauson
John Miles	Ezehiel Williams	Elijah Caiter
Hoody Jennings	Thomas Shannon	Wm. Bohanan
Wm. Arrent	Wm. Wallace	Saml. Whitaker
Johnathan Moseley	Wm. Carter	Sterling Combs
Charles Jordan	John Watkins	James Thurmand
John Gilmer	John Taylor	Presley Nail
Thomas Wadsworth	Wm. Bibb	Wm. Quinn
Elijah Moncrief	David Bussey	Thos. Walton Sr.
Cuthbert B. Cantor	Wm. Perdieu	Benj. Samuel
Wm. Stewart	Thos. Wadsworth	Micha Kennon
James Hester	Jacob Bobbit	Richard Graves
Wm. Mays	Wm. Scaggs	Angus Wadsworth
Wm. Overstreet	Abraham Bradley	Arthur Owens
Jessee Hardy	James Smith, Esq.	

"The Court then adjourned till Court in Course.

Benj. Telfair."

The only business transacted by the Court was swearing in the officers and drawing the juries for the next term. The next session convened on the 15th day of November, 1796.

Other Jury Lists. At the June Term, 1797, of the

Superior Court, Judge Telfair, presiding, and Peter Early, acting as Solicitor-General, pro.tem. the following Grand Jury was sworn:

Shadrack Hogan	Britain Lockhart	John Middleton
Stern Simmons	Wm. Covington	Hezekiah Spires
Peyton Wyatt	John Edwards	Jessee Hardy
Richd. Seale	John Seale	Wm. Mathews
Wm. Ratliff	Newell Walton	David Murray
John Cowan	James Smart	Thomas Bussey

There seems to have been no Petit Jury at this term. No cases were tried, though the Grand Jury returned several indictments. IBID, 2-6.

The following jurors were drawn for the December Term, 1797: IBID, 4-5.

GRAND JURY

Henry Goodwin	Cuthbert Steel	Robt. Ware
John Tatom	Stephen Harnesberger	Wm. Stokes, Jr.
John Russell	Thos. Walton	Thos. C. Russell
Thos. Barron	Wm. O'Neal	Geo. Goodwin
Benj. Andrews	Thomas Holliday	Wm. Holliday
Wm. Lowe	Robert Brown	Abel Tatom
Moses Matthews Sr.	Laurence Suddith	Saml. Pharr
Thomas Murray	Leonard Sussett	Edward Smith
Saml. McClenon	Gibson Wooldridge	John Walton
Alexander Johnston	Philip Zimmerman	Wm. Noland
Isaac Avery	Geo. Loflin	Joshua Ballard
John Lockhart		

PETIT JURY

John Par	Henry Kennebrow	Wm. Moseley
Francis Smith	Kimbus Stanford	Benj. Hester
John Marshall	Wm. Carter	Wm. Williams
Absolam Chappell	Mark Golding	Wm. Overstreet
Wm. Wallace	Benj. Bryant	Wm. Luker
Sterling Comb	Wm. Williamson	John Hicks
Wm. Wadsmouth	Rem Remson	Michael Solly
James Swords	John Bradley	Philip Guice
Peter Arrant	Jacob Zellars	Elisha Thomas
Hardy M. Glove	Philip Jones	David Dill
Wm. Wallace	Geo. Simms	John Spinks
John Griffin	Thos. Graves	Augustus Smith
Mathew Golding	Barret Farrar	Chas. Stovall
Wm. Golding	John Florence	David Hunter
Micajah Conner	Anthony Seals	Saml. Weathers
Charles Blanton	John Weathers	Richard Powell
James Harris	Johnathan Moseley	Lunford Gant
John Bailey	Thomas Howard	

The first jury trials were held at the December Term,

1797. Thus the jurors at that term had the honor of serving in the first Superior Court of the county that fully functioned. Minutes, p. 8-9.

By continuing the jury lists for a few years, a fairly accurate roster would be made of the reputable citizens who resided in the county at its creation, but that is not properly within the scope of this work.

Side-Lights On The Early Courts. Some of the members of the Bar, at the April Term, 1802, did not observe the proper decorum, for the Grand Jury, at that term, made the following presentment:

"We present as a grievance that the Special Jury have been treated with contempt and indelicacy by some of the Gentlemen of the Bar and hope their future conduct will atone for the present by observing more delicacy and better order." Minutes, p. 53.

At the April Term, 1804, the Grand Jury makes the following reference, in its presentments, to one of the citizens for his connection with what must have been a fascinating game:

"We present _____ for unlawfully Gaming in an out house in Court Term at Lincolnton at all hours of the night at a Game called Equality." Minutes, p. 82.

The lower courts did not maintain their dignity as they should, for "cussing" was allowed while they were in session. At the April Term, 1804, the Grand Jury took notice of this, and made the following presentment:

"We present as a grievance that so many of the peace officers suffer profane swearing in their presence while they are on the seat of justice." Minutes, p. 82.

This official declaration must not have had the desired effect, for, at the October Term, 1804, the Grand Jury made the following emphatic presentment:

"We present as a great grievance that the Justices of the Inferior Court also the Justices of the Peace of the different districts suffer persons to use profane language before them while acting in their official capacity and do recommend to those Justices to notice those persons and if they should still prove refractory to bind them over to the next Superior Court for their said good Behavior or commit them to the common Gaol of said County and there to remain till taken out by Law." Minutes, p. 91.

At the April Term, 1802, Judge E.W.P. Carnes delivered the following interesting charge to the Grand Jury, which it ordered published:

"Gentlemen. Although we have in this infant country progressed greatly toward a state of civilization, and find that the morals of the people, generally speaking, are rapidly improving, and although we see with pleasure religion and natual liberty disseminating their happy inflence through all classes of men, we find there is yet much to be done to complete the grand work of securing and protecting our lives, liberties, property and reputation. The laws are framed in such a manner as permantly to secure those most desirable objects, but they are ineffectual unless they are rightly executed and implicitly obeyed. We meet in the common walks of life individuals having a propensity, and evidencing their dispositions by their actions, to commit outrage and vices at war with the principles of social order and religion and morality. Men are said to be prone to evil as the sparks fly upwards. Some there are who at an early stage in life, discovering the iniquities and dangers to which this propensity exposes them, control, check and curb this inclination; others who, finding themselves unable from their depraved natures to withstand the temptations of vice, scrupulously shun the places of its abode; others, from sound reason and a determination to do right, put on the mantle of virtue, truth and justice, and by their steady and manly deportment dissipate vice and outrage whenever they meet them; and lastly, unfortunately for poor human nature, there are some who stand forth as champions in the field of iniquity and glory in their evil deeds--by trading their reputation, by; filching from the peaceful and industrious citizen the little pittance he hath earned by the sweat of his brow for the sustenance of his innocent babes, by seducing youths, who want maturity of judgement, into paths of wickedness and licentiousness, and, lastly, by defying and setting at naught all laws both of God and man. This, gentlemen, is a melancholy but too true a picture of our situation. This current must be checked, its force impeded, thrown back to its fountain and sunk, or we are disgraced. These daring and evil disposed characters must be punished, or hunted out of society, otherwise all that the good citizen holds dear is in continual jeopardy." Minutes, p. 52-53.

CHAPTER VIII

HOMES, OCCUPATIONS AND CUSTOMS OF EARLY SETTLERS

CHAPTER VIII.
HOMES, OCCUPATIONS AND CUSTOMS OF THE EARLY SETTLERS

Homes. The homes of the early settlers were one and two room log houses, with mud daubed in the cracks to exclude the wind and rain, with dirt or puncheon floors, and with split boards for covers. The chimney, mostly of rock, was built at the end of the house and contained a large fire-place which furnished not only light and heat for the household, but a place where family cooking was done. Puncheon benches, split board tables and crude homemade beds made up, in the main, the furniture of the home. And on the wall hung the trusted long barreled flintlock rifle which the settler used to supply game for his table, or as a protection from savages. The homes were in keeping with the means and opportunities of the pioneers in their battles with and isolation in the unconquered wilderness, and in no way reflects upon their sterling qualities.

The settlers who came immediately after the Revolution built larger houses of the same type, with wooden floors, but they were not so crudely furnished. The pioneer had softened the severity of the wilderness hardships, and they were enabled to provide more comforts. But for a number of years later the log house was the only kind, as a rule, to be found throughout the length and breadth of the country.

When the people began to erect frame dwellings, many of the log houses were made a part of them and weatherboarded and ceiled, or were left to be used as kitchens and dining rooms. Several comfortable homes of this character are still in use in the county at present, which, in part, are memorials to that early period.

Occupations. The occupation of the early settlers was necessarily farming. Their isolation caused them to devote their attention to the growing and raising of such things as supplied the needs of home life. They grew corn, wheat, potatoes, vegetables and some tobacco, and raised horses, cows, hogs and chickens. They purchased in the towns such things only as could not be produced at home. They grew no cotton for market, for the cotton gin had not been invented, and they had no method of separating the seed and lint except by hand, which was too difficult and tedious for profit.

With the advent of the cotton gin, the cultivation of cotton, as a money crop, became the chief occupation of the people, though they did not cease to cultivate and raise an abundance of the things necessary for living at home. For more than a century after settlement, nearly every farm in the county was self-sustaining.

The people who settled in the county, both before and following the Revolution, were not aristocrats, but democrats--plain substantial people, the kind that forms the backbone of a country and on whom the country must depend for its strength and prosperity. The men did not wear ready-made clothes nor the mothers and daughters imported silks and satins. They manufactured the cloth and made their clothes at home. The cotton or wool was carded into small rolls by the women and placed on the spinning-wheel and spun into thread. After dyeing the thread the desired color, it was woven into cloth on home-made looms, and then was made into garments by the dextrous hands of the women. All the sox and stockings for the family were hand-knitted by the women. For years, and even after the War Between The States, the custom of home manufacture was kept up by many of the people.

Cooking. The cooking was done in the large fire-place common to each of the homes of the early settlers, and which was common to all of the homes for many decades later. Vegetables and meats were boiled over the fire in pots attached to a crane in the fire-place. Bread, meats and potatoes were baked in ovens placed on coals on the hearth with coals in the lids, though potatoes were often cooked in the hot ashes. Hoe-cakes and meats were fried in open skillets set on glowing coals. Turkeys and large game were generally placed on a spit before the fire and roasted. The coffee-pot usually simmered on coals at the side of the fire-place while the other things were cooking. Those who have had the privileges of partaking of a meal thus prepared confess that for preserving a sweet and delicious flavor the old method of cooking surpasses the modern.

Log-Rollings. One of the customs of the settlers following the Revolution, and which persisted for many years, for the county was many years being settled, was the community log-rolling. The people were friendly and sociable and were always ready to assist each other. The farmer desiring to enlarge his acreage would usually fell the trees in the winter months and cut them into logs and let them lie on the ground till the following spring when he would invite the other farmers of the neighborhood to come, on an appointed day, to help him roll them into piles to be burned. This was usually a joyful occasion and was looked forward to with much interest. The farmers, their families and the male slaves, if any, would all gather at his home. The young men would vie with each other at the hand-stick to determine the "best man." The one who could pull down his competitors was the hero of the day. The young ladies attended these feats and each one slyly encouraged her beau, hoping that he would win the honor. Innocent pranks and harmless jokes were played on each other, and usually there was a wit in the crowd who furnished amusement to the workers. The children amused themselves around the premises, and the matrons enjoyed a pleasant day quilting. At the noon hour they all assembled at the house for a bountiful dinner, before partaking of which the older men would take a "toddy" to whet their appetites and sharpen their tongues for the repast. When the day's work was over, they enjoyed a good supper, after which all spent several hours together socially before disbanding, with the young men escorting their sweethearts home.

Corn-Shuckings. Another social custom of special interest to the young people was the corn-shucking, which would take place in the winter evenings after the harvest. The farmer giving it would invite his neighbors, and this was always a great opportunity for the young men to come and go with their sweethearts. The corn was divided into two piles, and sides were chosen among the young men. The side which finished first received a prize. The contest was soon over, and the remainder of the evening was spent in merriment, interspersed with refreshments.

The Square Dance. At frequent intervals, during the winter, the young people of the community would spend the evenings at some neighbor's home enjoying a square dance. This custom, though not common, has not entirely disappeared at the present time. It was a great social occasion for the young men and young ladies. All unnecessary furniture would be taken from the room to make space for the dancers, and comfortable seats would be provided by the fire for the fiddler and the banjo picker. The couples would arrange themselves in a square around the room. The "caller" led the dance and named the figures to be executed. At a signal from him, the musicians would begin to play--usually, "Toddy In The Bowl," "Hop Light Ladies," or "Turkey In The Straw," then he would call, "Honor your partner and the lady on the right! All balance! Turn your partner and promenade all!" --and the dance was on. Many and varied were the movements of the dancers as they kept time to the music with flying feet--each craving the distinction of being a good dancer. A set would last from half to three-quarters of an hour, after which there would be a brief interval for a change of partners and a rest for the musicians. Often the entertainment would continue long past midnight, but what cared these hardy young men and ruddy-cheeked bright-eyed young ladies--they were accustomed to the strenuous life, and this was merely play.

These social gatherings were vital factors in the welfare of the people--they cemented friendships, built up a strong community spirit and added to the happiness of home-life.

CHAPTER IX

OTHER PHASES OF LIFE AMONG THE EARLY RESIDENTS

CHAPTER IX.
OTHER PHASES OF LIFE AMONG THE EARLY RESIDENTS OF LINCOLN

Education. The hardships of frontier life and the Revolution prevented the people from giving much attention to a system of education. It is true the Constitution of 1777 provided that schools should be established in each county at the general expense, but the disturbed condition of the country made the provision ineffective. What learning the boys and girls of this section acquired in those early days was gotten at night, under the guidance of their parents, after the day's work, by the light of pine-knots in the big fire place; for there were no teachers, no lamps and very few books. Under these conditions nearly all learned to read and to write and obtained a fair knowledge of simple arithmetic. This method continued in the sparsely settled communities for many years after the war, while in the more populous sections log school-houses, with puncheon benches, were erected and teachers engaged at a small salary, with free board among the patrons, to conduct the schools. These teachers were usually very much respected by the pupils for their rigid discipline, for the rod was not spared in those days, and were honored by the patrons for their read or apparent knowledge. Yet in such schools as these, with meager facilities, many pupils received the foundation for a liberal education, among whom were Judge John M. Dooley, Judge Richard F. Lyon, and the noted Dr. J. L. M. Curry, whose biographies are given in this volume as an appropriate part of the county's history.

There were no post-offices and mail facilities throughout the country for a number of years after settlement, and, with the exception of those living in the northern part of the country, in the vicinity of Petersburg, the people were without newspapers; but, through contact with those who took papers and travelers in touch with the outside world, news was spread among them, which kept them well informed on current events.

The people were not densely ignorant as represented by Longstreet in his GEORGIA SCENES, but they made the best of their facilities and were keen to learn of progress elsewhere. Even in the section described as the "Dark Corner of Lincoln" were many intelligent and substantial citizens, and there, too, was the birth-place of the luminaries, Lyon and Curry.

Places of Worship. No churches, so far as known, were established in the county until after the Revolution. In fact, prior to and during that time the people were kept so busy fighting Indians and Red-Coats in making it a safe place in which to live that they had little opportunity to provide places of worship. Around the fire-side in the home was the chief sanctuary for worship and bible study, which no magnificent church edifice has ever supplanted, with an occasional assembling, perhaps, at some neighbor's home to engage in religious services. Preachers were scarce in those days, and the frontier settlements were visited by itinerant ministers who sojourned among the people and conducted revivals. On these occasions, the meetings were held under the shade of the trees or in the school-house, if one was convenient. These ministers did not receive much pay, but they loved the work for the Master's sake and were willing to sacrifice to advance the Kingdom. They were usually consecrated men with a burning zeal for the saving of souls, and they had the confidence and respect of the people. They were advised with about differences, misunderstandings, troubles, private affairs, and in their impartial Christian way did more to settle difficulties, restore friendships, promote peace and elevate the lives of the people than any other agency. After the war churches were established, about which more will be said in a later chapter.

Going To Mill. When Lincoln was made a county, there were only two mills in it to grind the corn and wheat of the inhabitants--Cade's water-mill on Broad River, in the northwestern part of the county, and Ray's water-mill on Little River, in the southwestern part. Going to mill became a necessary custom of the people. Usually, a few hours after supper for several nights were spent by the household in shelling the corn by hand to be taken to the mill. It and the wheat were placed in bags and carried by wagons. For those living far in the interior, the trip required several days. The grinding was slow, and each had to await his turn. Often, it was necessary to camp at the mill during the night while waiting, but, as a rule, there were several campers, and they, together, made a congenial party. The boys of the family looked forward with great interest to going to the mill, and they were generally taken by their father. They liked to see the corn and wheat converted into meal and flour, to watch the water fall over the large water-wheel which turned the mill and to play and fish in the river.

As the county developed and became more populous, other water-mills were constructed on streams in other parts of the county for the accommodation of the people. During the last quarter of the past century, these mills began to give place to the steam-mill, and by its close, all had been abandoned, except Lockhart's mill on Little River, in the southeastern part of the county, which continued to operate for the first few years of the present century.

Marketing. Petersburg, at the confluence of Broad and Savannah Rivers, and Augusta were the markets for the people of the county when it was formed, and Augusta at the present is the chief market. Both were mere villages at that time, but there the people could sell their farm products and by goods and merchandise. Petersburg was a great center for the sale of tobacco and Augusta for cotton. With the production of cotton succeeding the production of tobacco and with better and less expensive facilities for handling it in Augusta, the town of Petersburg gradually went down and was finally abandoned.

The two towns were connected by the Petersburg & Augusta public road, which traversed the east-central part of the county, coming within two miles of Lincolnton and crossing Little River at Lockhart's Ferry. This was the main highway through the county, though there was a public road leading from Petersburg, through the northern part of the county, to Washington and one leading from Washington, through the county to Barksdale's Ferry, on Savannah River; the others were settlement roads which led into the main highways.

The only means of transporting cotton to market was by wagon, and for many of the people, if the roads were bad, this required a week's trip. The farmers of a neighborhood would arrange to go at the same time, and would carry cooking utensils, blankets and provisions for themselves and their stock. At night-fall, they would stop near a stream, build a campfire, water and feed their stock and prepare supper. When the meal was finished, they would all gather around the fire for an hour or two, smoke their pipes, and tell interesting stories and funny jokes, after which they would wrap themselves in their blankets and go to sleep. On the return trip with their merchandise, they would follow the same custom. Even as late as a quarter of a century ago, this custom was practiced by many people.

In later years, many of the people living near the Savannah River transported their cotton by boat, while they drove to Augusta in buggies to dispose of it; and their merchandise was conveyed by the returning boat. This custom ceased years ago, and there is now no boating on the Savannah.

Going To Court. The Spring and Fall terms of the Superior Court, from the creation of the county till the advent of good roads and the automobile, were outstanding events in the lives of the citizens. Farming operations were all arranged so that they might have leisure at those times. Friends and relatives from different parts of the county did not see each other often, and those were occasions when they could meet and mingle in congenial intercourse. Large crowds were always present, and much merriment and good fellowship were manifested. The people of Lincolnton made great preparation and kept open house for their entertainment.

The reader will pardon the author for this personal allusion. Around the town spring, about fifty yards below where he was born and reared, was a large grove which the people used for their horses and mules and vehicles, and this was usually jammed during court weeks. There were always some restless animals which resented being hitched, and he recalls vividly how these would break loose and seek refuge in his father's corn-field, imposing on him the exciting task of making the capture. And well does he remember how, from early childhood till years after maturity, the air resounding with the braying of mules, which made so deep an impression that even now he associates Court with that sound, not in the court-house, of course, but in the grove.

CHAPTER X

CHURCHES OF LINCOLN COUNTY

CHAPTER X.
CHURCHES OF LINCOLN COUNTY

Along with the development of the county, the people did not neglect to organize churches and to establish places of worship, believing that real progress and happiness depended upon an abiding, active faith in God. From the early days of settlement to the present, the people have taken an active interest in religion, and have always been known as a church-loving, church-going people.

BAPTIST CHURCHES (WHITE)

GREENWOOD. In 1784 this church, the sixth Baptist church in the state, and then known as Upton's Creek, was constituted in the southern part of Wilkes County. A few years later, it was moved several miles eastward and its name changed to "Greenwood." In 1811 it was incorporated, with John Hammock, George Zoellner, Levin Perkinson, William Montcrief and John H. Walker, as trustees. (Acts, 1811, p. 146-8). About 1820 it was moved two miles further east into Lincoln County, its present location.
Greenwood Church has always been active and progressive, and she holds first place in spreading the Baptist faith throughout this section. According to Baptist history, Salem and Lincolnton Baptist churches are her daughters. Her present membership is 112.
The first Sunday school was organized in 1868. W.H. Dunaway is the present superintendent.
The following ministers, in their order, have served this church: Peter Smith 178_ - 1798; William Green, 1798-1805; Stephen Gafford, supply, 1805-1809; Abram Marshall, 1805-1813; Winder Hillman, 1813-1823; James Armstrong, 1823-1829; J.P. Marshall, 1829; James Armstrong, 1830-1834; J.Q. West, 1834-1853; P.F. Burgess, 1853-1868; E.A. Steed, 1868-1872; T.J. Beck, 187_-1879; H.M. Adams, 1879-1883; T.A. Nash, 1884-1902; J.C. Mays, 1903; R.E.L. Harris, 1904-1906; J.A. Shank, 1907-1911; W.A. Hogan, 1912-1918; W.H. Lord, 1919-1921; W.A. Reid, 1922-1926; and J.R. Kirkland, 1927-present.

GOSHEN. This church was constituted in 1787, about two miles east of Goshen, when Lincoln was a part of Wilkes, and it has the distinction of being the first Baptist church organized in what is now Lincoln County. It was called Soap Creek till 1793, then Rocky Spring till 1817, when its name was changed to Goshen.
The Baptists, Methodists and Presbyterians built a house of worship about 1810, within a half mile of Goshen,

and used it jointly for several years, but in 1835 the Baptists erected their own church about a mile west of Goshen and have used it continually from that time till this as their place of worship.

Goshen has a membership of 110, and conducts a flourishing Sunday school under the superintendency of G.E. Norman.

According to the HISTORY OF THE GEORGIA BAPTIST ASSOCIATION by R.L. Robnson, the following pastors served this church: Rev. Mr. Palmore (evidently Elisha Palmore as he was prominent in the early Baptist history in the county), four years; James Mathews, Sr., thirty-one years; Wychie Jackson, two years; James Armstrong, six years; Jesse Davis, one year; James Mathews, Jr., two years; W.H. Stokes, ten years; I.N. Bolton, five years; M.A. Lane, twelve years; John Hogan, three years; J.H. Foster, twelve years; J.A. Shank, nine y;ears; P.F. Burgess, two years; H.M. Adams, twenty-four years; J.E. LeRoy, two years; V.L. Herndon, one year; W.A. Hogan, nine years; and J.R. Kirkland, the present pastor.

DOUBLE BRANCHES. This church was organized in 1803, in the southeastern part of the county, with fourteen members.

In 1830 Double Branches meeting house was incorporated for all denominations on a spot of one acre, including privileges of spring reserved by James Ware, with Robert Fleming, Jacob Carver, Stephen Stovall, Robert Searles, John Hardy, Jacob Holsenback and Robert Brown, as trustees. (Acts 1830, p.68). On December 27, 1831, Double Branches church was authorized to be built on an acre of land James Ware reserved with spring for religious purposes. Thomas Ayres, David Kinder, Randolph Davy, Robert Searles and Wylie Jeter were made trustees. Other denominations worshipping at said place not precluded from erecting a house of worship on this spot of land. (Acts 1831, p. 64-65). Evidently, the present house of worship was erected following the last named Act.

Double Branches has always shown resplendently in that section, called by Longstreet, "The Dark Corner," and at one time was the wealthiest church in the county. It has a membership of 149, and it maintains a good Sunday Scool, with James K. Reid as superintendent.

The early records of the church are lost, but Robinson, previously quoted, gives the following pastors: Elisha Palmore (or Palmer), 1826-1830; Juriah Harris, 1830-1835; J.Q. West, 1835-1846, 1849; Radford Gunn, 1846-1849; P.F. Burgess, 1849-1879; H.M. Adams, 1879-1889; W.M. Verdery, 1890-1893; T.A. Nash, 1894-1902; J.C. Mays, 1902-1903; and W.A. Hogan, 1904-present.

BEULAH. This church was formed in 1807 in the northwestern part of the county near the line of Wilkes. The early records have been lost, and this is unfortunate, for the church is in a section where many of the early settlers located and would, doubtless, have furnished much rich material. The church was first called Union, but, at the suggestion of its pastor, Rev. T.J. Beck, was changed in

1854 to Beulah.

The present membership of the church is 193. J.M. Rhodes is superintendent of the Sunday School.

Beginning in 1842, the following ministers served this church: I.N. Bolton, M.A. Lane, T.J. Beck, L.W. Stephens, T.B. West, J.H. Stockton, T.J. Pilcher, A.J. Lazenby, J.L. Gillebeau, L.W. Stephens, T.A. Nash, H.M. Adams, J.H. Fortson, E.N. Sanders, J.A. Shank, J.G. Gunter, W.C. Edwards, G.W. Hulme, S.S. Mathis, J.E. LeRoy, Z.M. Leverette, L.P. Class, W.C. Veal. W.R. Taylor is the present pastor.

LINCOLNTON. This church was organized January 29, 1825, and from Baptist records, is an offshot of Greenwood church. The presbytery constituting it were Wychie Jackson, Enoch Callaway, Elisha Palmore, John W. Walker and B.M. Sanders. From then till 1876, its pastors were Wychie Jackson, James Armstrong, Jonathan Toole, W.H. Stokes, M.A. Lane, J.B. Butler, B.M. Callaway, P.F. Burgess and J.S. Callaway.

Till 1876, the Baptists used old Union church as a place of worship, which was common to all denominations. During that year there was a rift in the church and a large number withdrew and formed Siloam church and erected a house of worship, the place now known as the Green or Powell Hotel. The presbytery constituting this church were J.J.S. Callaway and T.J. Beck. The pastors of Siloam church were J.J.S. Callaway, T.J. Beck and T.A. Nash. (See Chapter XI concerning schools).

In 1880 the old Lincolnton church dissolved, and in 1883 Siloam changed its name to Lincolnton Baptist Church. Rev. T.A. Nash continued as pastor till 1893. Other pastors served the church in the following order: J.M. Sale, 1894; R.E.L. Harris, 1895-1898; W.H. Green, 1899; J.C. Mays, 1900-1903; D.W. Swindler, 1904-1906; and W.A. Hogan till the present. Up to 1925, services were conducted only once a month, but since that time they have been held twice a month--the second and fourth Sundays.

In 1920 the old church building was sold, and an elegant up-to-date commodious two-story brick building, with modern facilities for preaching services and for the work of the various other religious organizations, was erected at an approximate cost of $50,000. The building is very attractive and would be a credit to a much larger town. It has not been fully paid for, due to the financial depression, and the seats are not as elegant as planned, but progress is being ;made toward these objectives.

The progress of the church during the first seventy five years was slow, the membership in 1900 being only 103, but in later years the enrollment has been rapid. In 1910 the enrollment was 131, in 1920 it was 260, and in 1931 it was 395.

The church has a live and flourishing Sunday school, with an enrollment of 267, conducted by T.L. Perryman, as superintendent.

SALEM. This church was constituted in July, 1827, in

the southern part of the county, and is a daughter of Greenwood church. It was located on a site where Rock Hill Methodist Church once stood. The presbytery organizing this church was composed of Elisha Palmore, Wychie Jackson, B.M. Sanders, James Blanchard, F.L. Taylor and J.P. Marshall. On December 22, 1835, it was incorporated with John Bentley, Benjamin Graves, Eli Garnett, John McCord and John Wright as trustees. (Acts 1835, p. 13). The original building was destroyed by fire and a new one built on the same site.

In 1856 Rev. John Hogan, an outstanding minister of the county and father of Dr. W.A. Hogan, was ordained to the ministry by this church.

Rev. J.P. Marshall ws the first pastor of this church, and he served till his death in 1832. The succeeding pastors are as follows: A.L. Kennedy, 1832-1836; John Wilson, 1837-1838; A.L. Kennedy, 1838-1841; M.A. Lane, 1841-1844; Radford Gunn, 1844-1846; J.C. West, 1846-1850; P.F. Burgess, 1851-1878; H.M. Adams, 1879-1886; T.A. Nash, 1887-1902; M.D. Entzminger, 1903-1905; H.M. Adams, 1906-1910; Z.M. Leverette, 1911-1915; R.E. Lee, 1915-1916; W.F. West, 1917; J.E. LeRoy, 1918; W.H. Lord, 1919-1922; Paul V. Berry, 1923; I.R. Walker, 1924-1925; and J.R. Kirkland from 1926 to the present.

The church has a present enrollment of 242, and it maintains an excellent Sunday school, with John C. Bentley as superintendent.

NEW HOPE. This church, located about seven miles southeast of Lincolnton, was constituted November 5, 1830, by a presbytery composed of J.P. Marshall, D. Kinder, John McCord, James Blanchard, J.H. Walker, Juriah Harris, Francis Taylor and R. Davie. It was incorporated in 1849, with Thomas Tillery, John H. Little, Wiley Montcrief, William Brown and Lewis Howell as trustees. (Acts 1849, p. 72). The present building was erected in 1910 and dedicated September 8, 1911.

New Hope has always been an outstanding church in the county, and might properly be called the mother of ministers. During its history it has produced seven-- Zebulon Howard, William Borum, William LaFayette Hawes, John Lucius Gillebeau, William Ambrose Hogan, Luther Rice Hogan and John Jacob Gillebeau.

It is doubtful if any church in Georgia could claim the distinction of having as few changes in pastors as New Hope. During its 101 years, only four pastors have served this church. Its first pastor, Francis E. Taylor, served four years; its second pastor, J.A. Carter, served twenty-four years; its third pastor, John Hogan, was called in 1858 and served till 1896, or thirty-eight years; and its fourth and present pastor, W.A. Hogan, succeeded his father and has served thirty-five years. Dr. W.A. Hogan, the last named pastor, was born and reared near this church, united with it at the age of eleven, and was ordained to the ministry by it during his twenty-sixth year; and it was a beautiful expression of its love and devotion in calling him to take the light of the Gospel from the failing hands of his faithful father and to carry on for the glory of God and the advancement of His Kingdom. How well he has wrought is attested by his long and fruitful ministry to this loyal and appreciative church.

New Hope has a membership of 277, and it maintains a splendid Sunday school, with Boyce Hogan as superintendent.

HEPHZIBAH. This church, located six miles southwest of Lincolnton, near Graves Mountain, was organized September 6, 1831, by a presbytery composed of J.H. Walker, Wychie Jackson, Francis Taylor and J.P. Marshall. The present church building is an attractive wooden structure, situated a short distance south of the Lincolnton and Washington highway, and is kept nicely painted and in good repair.

Rev. J.M. Hudson was ordained to the ministry by this church.

Hepzibah has grown to be one of the strongest churches of the county, with a present membership of 267. It has an excellent Sunday school, under the superintendency of E.E. Hill, with an enrollment of 231.

The following pastors have served this church: J.A. Carter, 1831-1856; P.F. Burgess, 1856-1867; J.A. Carter, 1867-1876; J.A. Shank, 1876-1880; John Hogan, 1880-1904; T.A. Nash, 1904-1913; V.L. Herndon, 1914-1915; C.H. Dickey, 1916; R.E. Lee, 1917; W.A. Hogan, 1918-1925; and J.R. Kirkland, 1926 to the present.

WELL'S CREEK. This church was organized in 1886 about eight miles east of Lincolnton, and it dissolved about 1905 or 1906. Rev. William H. Green was its first and only pastor.

LOCO. This church was constituted September 29, 1895, by a presbytery composed of W.H. Green, J.E. LeRoy, William Woods and J.V.M. Paradise. It is located five miles south of Lincolnton, on the site once known as Wheat's Campground. In April, 1894, Rev. J.E. LeRoy began preaching at this campground and the organization of this church is an outgrowth of those services. The first deacons were William Woods, E.C. Jones and W.L. Wellmaker.

The Sunday school has an enrollment of 62, and it has the unique distinction of having a lady superintendent, Miss Minnie Holsenback.

The following pastors have served this church: J.E. LeRoy, J.C. Mays, W.D. Entzminger, P.A. Motes, and W.A. Reid, who has served since 1920.

(Much of this history ws taken from the HISTORY OF THE GEORGIA BAPTIST ASSOCIATION, by R.L. Robinson, which the author has used freely, and from the 1931 Minutes of the same Association).

METHODIST EPISCOPAL CHURCHES OF LINCOLN COUNTY

PINE GROVE. The early records of this church were destroyed by fire when the home of James A. Hardy, Secretary of the Quarterly Conference, was burned some years ago, but it was organized before 1800 and is the oldest existing Methodist church in the county. It is located about seven miles east of Lincolnton and about two miles from the Savannah River. From its organization till 1806, services were held under a brush arbor where the cemetery is now located. During that year, a church building was erected, facing the west, the dimensions of which are unknown. This building was used till 1846, when the present building, a neat one-story wooden structure, about 40 feet by 60 feet in dimensions, and facing the north, was erected. After the M.E. Church at Lincolnton was established, it became a part of the Lincolnton charge.

With the erection of the first church building, a Sunday school was organized with Louis Parks, Sr., as superintendent. As no Sunday school literature could be conveniently obtained in those early days, and as there were no public schools, the small children were taught, according to tradition, their A B C's and how to read from Webster's Blue Back Speller. Mr. Parks served the school for several years and was succeeded by Aaron Hardy, who served it for half a century. Others serving as superintendents were Charles R. Hollenshead, Elisha Gresham, Thomas Albea, William P. Tatum, J.A. Hardy, B.C. Clary, Ollie Weeks, J.A. Hardy, V.M. Walker, R.F. West, William F. Hardy and F.A. Hardy, the present incumbent. The school has had a continuous existence from its organization to the present, and it now has an enrollment of 72. George G. Smith, D.D., in THE STORY OF GEORGIA AND THE GEORGIA PEOPLE, 1732-1860, published in 1900, states, on page 227, in speaking of the Methodists of the county, that "it is perhaps somewhat remarkable that the oldest Sunday-school which has had a continuous life in Georgia is in a country church in Lincoln; where for over eighty years a Sunday school has been held every Sunday." He could not possibly have been referring to any other church than Pine Grove.

From extant records, the Albea, Bivens, Clary, David, Fortson, Hardy, Hollenshead, Leverett, Lyon, Martin, Parks, Samuels, Spires, Sturkey, Tatum, Thurmond and Ulm families were prominently identified with this church.

The earliest existing records of this church show that W.C. Norman was pastor in 1846, John Dunn in 1855, and Goodman Hughes in 1860-61. Beginning with 1875, the following pastors have served it: C.C. Cary, D. Kelsey, W.H. Trammell, M.H. Dillard, W.H. Speer, W.D. Turner, J.W.G. Watkins, S.D. Evans, G.E. Bonner, F.B. Reese, W.W. Oslin, F.P. Langford, A. Lester, N.Z. Glenn, J.W.G. Watkins, Sanford Leake, N.E. McBrayer, H.F. Branham, E.G. Dunnegan, W.S. Gaines, A.J. Sears, J.G. Davis, supply, J.F. Yarbrough, E.F. Dempsey, H.C. Emory, B.P. Searcy, A.D. Echols, Arthur Maness, W.L. Singleton, G.A. Teaseley, Z. Speer, A.M. Smith, J.L. Franklin, R.F. Elrod, H.O. Green, G.H. Bailey, A.M. Sprayberry, T.L. Rutland, W.H. Boring, and B.W. Hancock, the present pastor.

The membership of Pine Grove has been greatly reduced in the last twenty five years, due to the deaths and removals from the community, but the church is in a flourishing condition, and has an enrollment of 109.

LINCOLNTON. Unfortunately the early records of this church are not in existence, but it was organized during the first quarter of the last century. Services were held in the Union Church until the year 1915, when a new church building was erected. One of the earliest families connected with this church, and whose descendants are still prominently identified with it, is the Willingham family. There is no record showing when the first Sunday school was organized, but for years before moving into the new church, Sunday school was held in the afternoon.

Following the abandonment of camp-meetings at Wheat's Camp Ground, it was sought to establish, as nearly as possible, these meetings at Union Church, with entertainment in the private homes and dinner on the grounds each day, but the setting was lacking, the usual thrill and interest were wanting and the church was too small; so, after two annual meetings, the idea was given up.

In 1913, while Rev. John L. Franklin was pastor, the Methodists began the construction of the present church building. The building was not completed under his pastorate, but Mr. Franklin was the orginator of the movement. During 1915 the building was completed and services were transferred from the Union Church. Rev. Roscoe Davis, a ministerial student of Emory University, was the first pastor to serve in the new church. Since then, Sunday school has been held in the morning.

The new building is an attractive wooden structure, with stained glass windows, plastered walls, elevated floor and comfortable seats. To the rear of the pulpit are two Sunday school rooms, and on the right corner of the building rests the bell tower. It is a credit to the town.

The church has a membership of 198, with Mrs. T.S. Hardy as Recording Secretary. Its organizations are an active Epworth League, a strong Woman's Missionary Society and a live Sunday school, with an enrollment of 119, under the superintendency of W.L. Candler.

From information furnished by Rev. George W. Barrett, Secretary of North Georgia Conference, as far back as his records show, Rev. Miller D. White, M.D., was pastor of this church in 1836, and Rev. W.T. Norman, in 1853-4. Other pastors who served it were W.P. Arnold, 1857-8; D.W. Coleman, 1859; Goodman Hughes, 1860-1; R.J. Harwell, 1867; Britton Sanders, 1868-9; W.F. Quillian, 1870-1; G.R. Park, 1872; L.P. Neese, 1873; and J.L. Lupo, 1874. From 1875 on, the list is the same as for Pine Grove, and it is very likely that the above list would apply to Pine Grove.

From 1887 to 1931, Lincolnton charge was in the Elberton District, but in the latter year it was placed in the Augusta District, in which Rev. W.H. LaPrade, Jr., is Presiding Elder.

ANTHONY'S CHAPEL. Anthony's Chapel is located about

six miles west of Lincolnton, near the village of Lovelace. In May, 1925, a short history of this church by Mrs. Bessie Strickland, nee Candler, of Metasville, Ga., was published in one of the Atlanta papers, which is quoted in full:

"Before the year 1848 there was a brush arbor built on to a school room so local preachers could preach the gospel to the neighbors' wives and children who had no way to go seven miles to the nearest church house.

"Then in 1848 a building committee composed of N.C. Ware, Joseph Ware and Alexander Frazier (a deacon of the Baptist Church) took their carpenters and built Anthony's Chapel church. Every piece of timber was hewn with an ax except the floor and weather-boarding. The benches were substantially made and are still used in chapel church. The pulpit, a kind of box at one end of the church, had four steps to get up on it. You could not see the preacher when he knelt to pray. Preaching was held any day of the week except Monday, as the few preachers went from place to place preaching. In those days we had a love feast on Sunday morning. This exercise is a sad loss to the church now.

"The land on which this church stands was donated by Mrs. Rachel Sims, a Baptist lady. The trustees accepted this gift but never had a deed until twenty five years after her death, when her son, Leonard Sims, voluntarily gave the deed. The old church was torn down in 1897 and the present church built. There is a very interesting Sunday school, ladies' Missionary society and Epworth league.

"This data was furnished by a young man, R.A. Ware, who united with this church seventy-six years ago, when a lad of 10. He is still an honored member of this church and is against unification. We are not satisfied with our work, but striving to do better."

The Ware family had been connected with Anthony's Chapel from its organization. Robert A. Ware, to whom reference was made by Mrs. Strickland, died in November, 1929, at the ripe old age of ninety, leaving descendants and relatives prominently identified with this church.

Death and removals from the community have reduced the numerical strength of this church in late years, but it still has a membership of 40. An active Sunday school, with an enrollment of 25, is conducted by Mrs. Marshall Brown, as Superintendent.

Data is not available for a list of the ministers who served this church prior to 1908. During that year it was placed in the South Lincoln Circuit, and, since then, the following pastors have served it: George A. Teaseley, 1908; T.L. Rutland, 1909-10; T.B. Middlebrooks, 1911; T.H. Maxwell, 1912-14; C.S. Martin, 1915-17; S.A. Bales, 1918; supplied 1919-20; H.G. Garrett, 1921; M.C. Allen, 1922-23; J.E. Statham, 1924-25; S.A. Dailey, 1926-27; I.J. Lovern, 1928; H.D. Pace, 1929-30; Carl Stanley, 1931; and A.A. Phillips, supply, 1932.

Mrs. Lewis, in her comment upon Mrs. Strickland's article, published at the same time, says: "This wonderful old church echoes the joyful shouts of many noble men and women for almost a century, and some of the present day members count the shades of their ancestors for generations past. Hallowed memories linger here."

BETHANY. This church is located about six miles northeast of Lincolnton and about two miles south of "The White House," the old home of Judge Dooley. In 1898 Rev. J.G. Davis, who was a supply in the Lincolnton charge, was impressed that this section in the eastern part of the county was "white unto the harvest," and he began holding monthly services under a brush arbor, near the community school house in which Sunday school had been held for a year or two. Much interest was manifested by the people and immediate steps were taken to establish a church. In 1899 a neat wooden building 28 by; 40 was erected and called Bethany Church. At its organization the church named T.T. Albea as steward and J.D. Brown, T.T. Albea and H.E. White as trustees. G.E. Albea succeeded T.T. Albea as steward, and later J.M. Ivey and W.C. Ivey were added to this office. The present trustees are Benjamin Fortson, Geo. L. Sims, G.E. Albea, J.A. Teasley and J.M. Ivey.

Rev. A.J. Sears was the first regular pastor of Bethany, and, following him, the church has been served by the ministers of the Lincolnton Charge, Rev. B.W. Hancock being the present pastor. The church now has 85 members.

After the establishment of this church, J.D. Brown, who was superintendent of the community Sunday school, continued in that capacity in the Methodist Sunday school. Others who followed him were J.M. Ivey, G.E. Albea, L.P. Teasley and G.E. Albea, the present superintendent. The school is live and active and has an enrollment of 51 pupils.

ST. PAUL. This church was constituted in 1898 with eighteen members, and it is really a re-organization of Camp Ground Church which disbanded about 1894. At first services were held under a brush arbor, but in 1899 the present building, located six miles south of Lincolnton just beyond the Loco post office, was erected from the proceeds of the sale of the Camp Ground property to A.H. Tyler and from contributions. At its completion the membership had doubled. A.H. Tyler was the first steward and W.T. Cartledge and Benjamin Fortson the first trustees. Rev. W.S. Gaines, supply, was pastor while services were held under the arbor. Other pastors, in their order, were A.J. Sears and B.C. Prickett, 1899; A.J. Sears, 1900; A.J. Sears and J.F. Yarbrough, 1901; J.F. Yarbrough and H.C. Emory, 1902-03; B.P. Search and H.J. Strother, 1904; A.D. Echols and Arthur Maness, 1905-06; W.L. Singleton and G.A. Teasley, 1907. In 1908 this church was made a part of the South Lincoln Circuit, and the pastors from then on were the same as those at Anthony's Chapel. During that year, a comfortable parsonage was built near St. Paul for the minister who served the Circuit. The present membership of the church is 72.

A Sunday school, with W.L. Candler as superintendent, was organized with the establishment of the church, and for a time it alternated Sundays with the Loco Baptist Sunday school; then , by mutual agreement of the two, the Methodist Sunday school met each Sunday morning and the

Baptist each Sunday afternoon. Under this arrangement the attendance of each was greatly increased. This plan, with temporary changes to suit the convenience of each, still exists. Other superintendents of the school were A.H. Tyler, J.W. Edmunds, C.H. Tyler, J.H. Reviere, J.A. Ferguson, J.H. Reviere, J.L. White and W.M. Smalley, the present incumbent. The Sunday school is progressive and has an enrollment of 36.

MIDWAY. This church, located about seven miles north-west of Lincolnton, was organized in the summer of 1906. This section had not been served by a Methodist church since the abandonment of Goshen church many years before. In the meantime several Methodist families had moved into the community, and these, with those who were already attached to this faith, made the field inviting. Dr. A.W. Burch, E.H. Albea, W.R. Barrett, M.E. Smith, Mrs. T.C. Ward and others invited Rev. A.D. Echols, of Lincolnton Charge, to hold services in the community with a view of establishing a church. At first these services were held in homes, but the interest was so great and the attendance so large they were transferred to a brush arbor, which had been built for that purpose. A church was established and called Midway. In the fall, the present building was erected, though it was not completed till the following year. The Baptists and those who were not affiliated with any church co-operated in the work. A.W. Burch was made steward and W.R. Barrett, M.E. Smith and A.W. Burch trustees. Till 1908 the ministers of the Lincolnton Charge served this church, but during that year it was incorporated in the South Lincoln Circuit and has since been served by the ministers of that Circuit. The church is in a thriving condition and has a membership of 79.

When the church was established a Sunday school was organized with A.N. Glaze, a Baptist, as superintendent. In the following year, T.C. Ward, who had recently been converted and united with this church, succeeded A.N. Glaze. W.T. Norman is the present superintendent, and the school has an enrollment of 53 pupils who take a lively interest in the work.

ARAMATHEA. This church, located about eight miles southeast of Lincolnton, is one among the old churches of the county, but no records are extant showing the exact date of its organization. ON December 25, 1832, John Willingham made a deed to the proper authorities of the Methodist Church, conveying the tract of land on which the building is situated. (Deed Book K, p. 703-4). According to tradition the church was established years before then, but the deed to the land was not made to the proper grantees, and that this last deed was executed to perfect the title. On January 20, 1852, it was incorporated with Joseph Jacobs, John Peed, William Spires and John Landers, as trustees. (Acts 1851-2, p. 360). Among the first members of this church were the Peeds, Landers, Bohlers, Busseys, Ayres, Spires, Wares, Jacobs and Willinghams, some of whose descendants are still affliated with it; and other families prominently connected with it later were the McCords, Gunbys, Bennetts, McCorkles, Smalleys and Colvins. The ministers of Lincolnton Charge served this church till it was placed in the South Lincoln Circuit in 1908, after which it was served by the ministers of that Circuit. The present stewards and trustees are B.N. Smalley, W.N. Spires and R.L. Covin.

In the past Aramathea was a large and flourishing church, occupying an outstanding place in Methodism in the county, from whose membership J.L. Ware, Cleo B. Ware, and, possibly, William Bussey and Hezekiah Bussey went forth to preach the Gospel, but death and removals have reduced the enrollment to 30. No Sunday school is maintained at present.

In connection with this church it is appropriate to mention L. Pearl McCord, now of Jacksonville, FL., who has succeeded in the business world and who stands high in Methodism. He was born and reared near Aramathea and united with it at an early age. His education was secured in the common schools of this county and at Young Harris College. After his graduation he took up banking and became cashier of the Bank of Crawfordville, which position he later resigned to become cashier of a bank in Miami, FL. He served this bank for several years, and then became cashier of the Peoples Bank of Jacksonville, FL., and later became vice president of that institution. He is prominent in his determination, and has served as a delegate to the General Methodist Conference, and he is now a trustee of Wesleyan Female College and of Emory University.

OTHER CHURCHES

Other Methodist churches which once existed in the county, but about which there is very little record, were Cherokee, located in the eastern part of the county below Double Branches, the only mark of which is an old abandoned cemetery; Rock Hill, located where Salem Baptist Church now stands; New Hope, located in the northern part of the county, incorporated in 1840, with J.F. Matthews, Joel B. Sutton, H.T. Bussey, William Norman and Pressley N. Seal, as trustees (Acts 1840, p. 83); Goshen, located six miles north of Lincolnton, which had a membership of 20 in 1884; Antioch, located nine miles south of Lincolnton, abandoned and sold to the Negroes, and which had a membership of 41 in 1884; Camp Ground, located six miles south of Lincolnton, and which had a membership of 40 in 1884; and Watkins Chapel, organized in the late 80's or early 90's and abandoned in 1924.

WHEAT'S CAMPGROUND. No history of Methodist activities in the county would be complete witout special mention of this camp ground, which was located six miles south of Lincolnton. On May 11, 1820, John Zellenor conveyed to certain commissioners four acres of land to be used for a Methodist meeting house and camp ground. On a survey it was found that the tract contained six acres, and on July 29, 1845, Harvey Wheat, Francis McKinney and William Paschal, as commissioners, and Francis Tyler, as adjoining land owner, passed deeds to perfect the title. (Deed Book M, p. 356-7). Camp Ground Church was soon established there and existed till 1894. A spring of pure cool water, the smooth land and the spreading oaks furnished an ideal setting for camp meetings. It is not known just when the Methodists began to use this tract for that purpose, but Wheat's Camp Ground was incorporated by an Act of the legislature in 1842, and these meetings continued till 1892.

Camp meeting was a notable occasion in the county, and it was looked forward to with great interest not only for its religious purpose, but for its social features a well. Others of different creeds, and many witout a creed, were as enthusiastic as the Methodists in anticipating pleasant experiences at this annual gathering. It was always held in August, after laying-by time, when the people were free to put aside business cares and to enjoy a season of refreshment. Elaborate preparations were made to attend it. By common consent it was a time of new wearing apparel for men and women, boys and girls. Whatever may have been the indifference to attire at other times, this was a time for which plans were made and energy spent for the best personal appearance. Only the well-to-do Methodists, with servants to do the menial labor, owned or rented tents, and for days before the meeting their homes were astir making ready for two or three weeks of camp life with friends and relatives as guests.

Besides the owned and rented tents, there was a special tent for the ministers and a public tent to care for the visitors. With the weeds and undergrowth cleared away and the tents put in order, the camp ground looked like a miniature village set in a lovely grove over which hung the sweet benedictions of Peace.

From far and near the people came. In the vast assembly could be seen the old and the young, the rich and the poor, the high and the low--all mingling together in a beautiful spirit of Christian fellowship.

Four services were held daily; the sun-rise prayer-meeting and preaching at eleven, four and eight o'clock, each preceded by the blast of a bugle calling the people to worship. Between the services, the people mixed and mingled in pleasant social intercourse, communing with friends, meeting relatives, renewing old acquaintances and forming new friendships, and, with it all, the campers dispensed a lavish hospitality.

And romance was there. Strolling over the grounds or sitting beneath the shade of the trees could be seen gallant young men and beautiful young women advancing a romance already in flower or ministering to one just in the bud. Many a couple, happily united, could look back with glowing memories to the halcyon days at Wheat's Camp Ground.

The meeting was under the leadership of the Bishop, the Presiding Elder and devout laymen. There was no professional evangelists, no professional singers, no professional pianists, no professional soul-winners to work up a revival and cumber the church with unregenerate members, but consecrated men and women came together "with one accord in one place," and, moved by the power of the Holy Spirit, by their supplications brought down a heaven-born revival to the saving of souls and the upbuiilding of the Kingdom. The hymns were lined by the ministers and sung in one grand chorus by the congregation; the prayers of ministers and laymen came from the heart and men and women were moved by their fervent appeals; the Gospel was preached in power as it is found in the Word, unadulterated by scientific theories and uncolored by questionable doctrines, and the people were stirred to the depths by its mighty sweep. No spurious methods were used to stir the emotions or to create excitement. The Spirit was at work. As the saintly old fathers and mothers thought of the goodness and mercy and love of God to the children of men, their hearts were filled to overflowing and they shouted praises of exultation to His Name. And scores of sinners, touched by the Holy Fire in answer to prayer, were born unto the Kingdom amid glad hallelujahs of the children of God. Pentecost was a reality and the Gospel a saving force.

Christian people went forth from these meetings with their convictions deepened and their faith strengthened "to do justly and to love mercy and to walk humbly with ...God," to practice the Golden Rule, and, by their example, to lead others to nobler lives.

Gone now are those soul-refreshing days. Gone is the last vestige that marked the old camp ground. And gone, too, are the old saints who experienced in those annual love-feasts a foretaste of Glory. Only a few remain who remember those happy times. Yes, years ago, Finis was written to those spiritual gatherings, but who will say that the church was not the loser.

PRESBYTERIAN AND OTHER CHURCHES

LINCOLNTON. The early records of this church suffered the same fate as those of many of the other old churches of the county, being lost or destroyed. The church was established about the year 1823, for during that year, Col. Peter Lamar, a Presbyterian, donating the three acre tract of land in Lincolnton for school and religious purposes, to which reference has previously been made; and immediately following this gift Union Church was built and used by the Methodists, the Baptists and the Presbyterians. For the past twenty years it has been used exclusively by the Presbyterians, who keep it painted and in good repair, and who have improved its interior appearance. It is the only church of this denomination in the county. Its growth has not kept pace with the other denominations; in fact, it has never had a large membership and has never been self-sustaining. It is a mission church, and for a number of years it has been under the jurisdiction of the Home Mission Committee of the Augusta Presbytery, though it pays a part of the pastor's salary and contributes to benevolent causes. The present membership is 40.

In 1918, a Sunday school was organized with A.L. McMahan, as superintendent, and which has since functioned without a break. It has played an important part in keeping the church organized when it was without a pastor. In 1930, A.L. McMahan, due to failing health, resigned and was succeeded by C.J. Perryman, the present superintendent. The school has an enrollment of 32 pupils.

Other agencies of the church are a Woman's Auxiliary, organized April 18, 1921, by Mrs. C.P. Crawford, President of the Woman's Missionary Work of the Augusta Presbytery, and a Christian Endeavor Society, organized in 1930.

In 1927 the church received a legacy of $750 under the will of James L. Fleming, a Presbyterian, late of Augusta, GA, the income of which is to be used to care for the graves of his parents in Lincolnton cemetery and to help support the Sunday school.

Beginning in 1877, as far back as the local church has any authentic record, the following ministers have served this church in the order named: Wm. H. Davis, F.T. Simpson, Thomas Cartledge, F.T. Simpson, A.L. Whitfield, J.B. Hillhouse, G.M. Howerton, T.P. Burgess, F.G. Hartman, M.W. Doggett, C.S. Evans, W.B. Clemmons, W.H. Porter, J.C. Plexico and I.T. Hawk, the present pastor. At intervals, in late years, it was without a pastor, and, at times, it weas served by ministrerial students of Columbia Seminary.

HOLINESS CHURCHES

CONGREGATIONAL HOLINESS. This church is located about seven miles southeast of Lincolnton, at Martin's Cross Roads, and was organized, December 16, 1920, with W.L. Myer, of Cannon, Ga., as its first pastor. It has an enrollment of 36 members. The church is live and active, and its protracted services are largely attended. Other pastors in their order are Hugh Bowling, W.J.A. Russell, H.A. Smith and Hugh Bowling, the present pastor.

One of the outstanding organizations of this church is its flourishing Sunday school in which some of the members of other denominations in the community take part. It has an enrollment of 90 pupils and is under the superintendency of Richard Ashmore.

OTHER HOLINESS CHURCHES. Prior to the organization of the above named church, a Pentecostal Holiness Church was established at Leverett, about six miles east of Lincolnton, and one about four miles south of Lincolnton, but both of them have been abandoned.

COLORED CHURCHES

During slavery the Negroes belonged to the church of their masters, and in some instances they remained members for a number of years after the War Between The States. On the post-war minutes of several of the white churches of the county reference is made to the withdrawal of the colored membership to establish churches of their own. Of course, the Negro members never had the same privileges of the white, but membership was permitted for their spiritual enlightment. While the whites worshipped, the Negroes occupied a place in the church specially set apart for them and listened, and, at the conclusion of the services, the building was turned over to them for their services. They now have churches in every section of the county.

BAPTIST CHURCHES. Thankful, New Tabernacle, Goshen, St. Luke, Lovelace Chapel, Harmony, Mount Zion, White Rock, Tabernacle, Newberry, Price's Grove and Lincolnton.

METHODIST CHURCHES. Mulberry, Pleasant Grove, Antioch, Smith's Chapel and Pharr's Chapel.

HOLINESS CHURCH. This church is located between Leverett and Chamberlain's Ferry.

CHAPTER XI

LINCOLNTON

CHAPTER XI.

LINCOLNTON

Founded. Lincolnton was founded near the close of the last century when it was selected for the location of the public buildings of the county, the exact date of which is unknown. One may wonder why it is founded in a valley rather than on some of the surrounding level lands. As in the days of the patriarchs, water was quite in inducement for settlement. Wells were uncommon and the people located near springs. Here in a large grove of sweet-gum, elm and oak trees was an over-flowing spring of good water, sufficient to meet the needs of the founders, and near it the people settled. It was specially reserved for public use. For years and years the inhabitants used it for drinking water, as a place to do the family washing, and for all other household purposes. It is still kept in good condition, and even now is used by several families.

First Court-House and Jail. The first court-house and jail for the county were not built till about the year 1800; for at the June Term, 1797, of the Superior Court, the Grand Jury presented as a grievance "that the Commission of the Public Buildings have neglected to use means to forward the same," and recommended "that they immediately proceed to the duties of their appointment." Minutes Superior Court 1796 to 1805, p. 6. And again at the June Term, 1798, the Grand Jury takes notice of the failure to complete the public buildings. (IBID, 21). The Commissioners, appointed in the Act creating Lincoln County to select a location for the court-house and jail, either did not function or failed to agree on a site, so the Legislature, on February 2, 1798, passed an Act repealing their appointment and appointed Isaac Avery, John Winne, Duncan Bohannon, John Moss and John Lockhart in their stead. These last named Commissioners were the ones who made the selection. The failure of the Commission to act was alikely due to differences as to the place of location. According to tradition, there were two factions, one of which, known as the Murray faction, wanted the court-house and jail located on what is now the Otis Wright place; and the other, known as the Lamar faction, wanted them located on or near the lands of Peter Lamar. Doubtless, the convenience of the spring, for the people attending court, decided the issue in favor of the Lamar faction. The exact location of the court-house is unknown, but the conclusion is warranted that it stood on the lot about where the Confederate monument now stands, as this spot has always been considered, and now is, the center of town. A description of these two buildings cannot be given, but there is a tradition that the court-house was a square structure built on rock, and that the jail was built of hewn logs. The county jail before the present one was built of logs, and there is no reason to assume that any previous ones were built of different material. With the erection of the court-house and jail, Lincolnton became the county seat.

Incorporated. Lincolnton was incorporated by an Act of the Legislature, on the 19th day of December, 1817, with Peter Lamar, Rem Remson and Lewis Stovall as Commissioners. Its limits extended half a mile in each direction from the courthouse as a center, making it a circle. Exclusive of the courthouse and jail, it was no more than a cross-roads community, with its one or two small stores, six or seven dwellings and a few Negro cabins. A public road from the Petersburg-Augusta road on the north led by the jail to the courthouse square, where it connected with a public road from Washington by what is now Metasville, then turned to the east and followed what is now the Augusta road back into the Petersburg-Augusta road. The other roads of the village were merely private ways. Other than the public roads mentioned, the streets and side-walks as they are today were, then, parts of cultivated fields. There was nothing to mark the village as an industrial center. In common with the other people of the county, its inhabitants were chiefly engaged in farming. Its main distinction was that it was the county seat. So slow was its progress and so small its increase in population that for seventy-five years, after its incorporation, the people of the county generally would not speak of going to town, or to Lincolnton, but to the "Court House." For at least sixty years it appeared to be a village born almost fully grown.

Other Charters. On the 24th day of October, 1887, a new charter was granted to the town by the Legislature, enlarging its powers but not extending its limits; on the 4th day of August, 1917, this charter was repealed and a new charter granted extending the limits of the town three-quarters of a mile in each direction from the old courthouse square, and conferring upon it all the rights, powers and privileges of a modern municipality. On the 14th day of December, 1929, by a vote of the people, the incorporate limits were extended to a mile from the old court-house site as a center.

Lincolnton began to grow some in the 80's, but it was very gradual; its real growth began with the coming of the Washington & Lincolnton Railroad in 1917. A later chapter will cover the progress of the town during those periods and up to the present time.

Schools Prior To The War Between The States. For several years after its incorporation, there was no established school at Lincolnton, though, of course, parents arranged to give their children instruction, even if meager. On May 8, 1821, the House of Representatives, in extra session, passed the following resolution: "A Public Academy for the County of Lincoln, in the Village of Lincolnton, declared, with Rem Remson, Peter Lamar, Lewis Stovall and William C. Stokes as Commissioners." On March 3, 1823, Peter Lamar conveyed to Rem Remson and John M. Dooley, Commissioners of Lincolnton Academy, a tract of land containing by estimation three acres "for the use of public or private schools, houses of public worship, or any other public use the commissioners, or successors in office, may apply it to, so as not to interfere with the free use of house or houses of worship and academy which may be built thereon," as shown by Deed Book K, p. 170-71, in the office of the Clerk of the Superior Court of Lincoln County. This is the tract of land now used as a public cemetery, and on which Old Union Church is located. Following this conveyance, a commodious two room wooden structure, one room above the other, was built, with a chimney at each end, and was located south of the church in what is now the cemetery. The school became popular and was attended by many boarding pupils not only from Lincoln, but from the surrounding counties. It flourished till the outbreak of the War Between The States. The building was destroyed by fire during or a few years after the war and was not replaced.

By an Act of the Legislature, passed on December 30, 1836, Lincolnton Female Academy was incorporated, with Shadrack Turner, Harvey Wheat, William B. Cantelou, Nicholas Fox, Thomas Dallas, Sr., and Alexander Johnson as trustees. This Act was passed just twenty days after the passage of the Act incorporating Georgia Female College, later Wesleyan, the oldest chartered female college in the world. It must not be inferred, however, that Lincolnton missed first honor, for other female academies had been chartered prior to that time. No records are in existence to furnish a description of this building, or what became of it, or how long the school continued to operate. It was evidently a modest wooden building, but sufficiently commodious to meet the needs of that day. There is a tradition that the building was located on the tract of land conveyed by Peter Lamar, to which reference has already been made, and that the school flourished for a number of years and was recognized as one of the best institutions of its kind in the state.

First Church Building. One of the landmarks of Lincolnton is Old Union Church, erected about the year 1823, on the three acre tract, previously referred to, conveyed by Peter Lamar. It was the first and only church in the town till years after the war, and was used by the Methodists, the Baptists and the Presbyterians. Hence its name. It is a wooden structure, and, when originally built, was 30 feet by 50 feet in dimensions, but later was made 10 feet longer. It is now used by the Presbyterians, who keep it painted and in good repair, and on account of its nearness to the cemetery is frequently used by other denominations for funeral services.

CHAPTER XII

THE COUNTY TO THE WAR BETWEEN THE STATES

CHAPTER XII.

THE COUNTY TO THE WAR BETWEEN THE STATES

Nothing of unusual historic interest happened in the county from its organization to the War Between The States. The people devoted their energies chiefly to the development of the county from an agricultural standpoint. All of the lands subject to disposition by the Land Grant Courts were disposed of to grantees, and every section became inhabited. Some of the early settlers and many of their descendants scattered to different parts of the state and were succeeded, in turn, by many new comers from other states, largely from South Carolina. The farmers were prosperous and their farms self-sustaining. More comfortable homes were built and living conditions generally were improved. Some of the farmers became large slave owners and ceased to do manual labor, though they did not practice the gaieties and leisure of the Virginia and the South Carolina gentlemen, but, as a general rule, all were an industrious hard-working people.

County Jail. By a special act of the legislature (Acts, 1815, p. 84), the Justices of the Inferior Court were authorized to levy an extra tax for two years, not exceeding one fourth part of the general tax for that period, for the purpose of defraying the expense of building a common jail for the county. This jail was built by Peter Ashmore, the grand-father of Hon. Otis Ashmore, of Savannah, and was located about where the present one stands. It was a one story structure, about twenty feet by thirty feed in dimensions, constructed of hewed pine logs, and divided into four cells. Its small barred windows did not furnish sufficient light to scatter its gloom and darkness, the ventilation was bad, and the facilities for sanitation were scant. At the present time, it would more accurately be called a dungeon. It was used by the county for more than eighty years.

A plat of the prison bounds of the county appears in Deed Book L., p. 54, in the office of the Clerk of the Superior Court, and on which are indicated several residences. Date of record, February 6, 1839.

Education. The people took an interest in providing educational facilities for their children. Besides a few scattered community schools, academies were established in different parts of the county. On November 24, 1824, Goshen Academy was incorporated, with John McDowell, William M. Lampkin, Richard Prather, Noah Welton and James E. Todd, as Trustees. (Acts 1824, p. 25). On December 23, 1825, Double Branches Academy was incorporated, with Thomas Lyon, Stephen Stovall, Jacob Carver, John A. Burke and Robert Runnells, as Trustees. (Acts 1825, p. 16). On December 22, 1835, Salem Academy was incorporated, with John Bentley, Benjamin Graves, Eli Garnett, John McCord and John Wright, was incorporated, with Benjamin Samuels, John H. Little, Greenville Jones, John Reid and James Cartledge as Trustees. (Acts, 1849-50, p. 72). In addition to these, academies were established at Lincolnton, to which reference has been made in the preceding chapter.

These schools and academies were supported almost entirely by private subscriptions of the patrons. It is true the legislature in 1830 (Acts 1830, p. 14-15) directed the clerk of the superior court to pay over to the commissioners of the academies of Lincoln County equal shares of the funds arising from fines and forfeited bonds, but only a small amount could have been raised from that source. Teachers were paid by the Ordinary out of the poor school fund for teaching the children whose parents were too poor to contribute to the schools, and, while only a little sum was realized from this source, it had the virtue of giving the poor child an equal opportunity with the fortunate. At times, however, there was delay and uncertainty in getting this compensation, as shown by an Act of the Legislature in 1855, by which authority was given the "Ordinary to pay all accounts he deems just and right to teachers, teaching poor children in Lincoln for 1854, provided sufficient surplus poor school funds remain after paying teachers for 1855."

In 1858, a Board of Education for Lincoln County was created with LaFayette Lamar, Henry J. Lang, Benjamin O'Neal, Henry Freeman and Jeremiah Ashmore as members. The officers of the Board consisted of a superintendent and a secretary, to be elected on the first Monday in January of each year. The Board had power to fill vacancies and to examine all teachers who presented themselves as to their competency. The Superintendent and the Secretary of the Board were authorized to issue certificates to the teachers found to be competent. Teachers were directd to exhibit their certificates to the Ordinary in order to receive from the poor school fund the amount of their accounts for teaching poor children. (Acts 1858, p. 112). Henry J. Lang was elected Superintendent of the Board, but there is no record as to who was Secretary. It is quite possible that Mr. Lang filled both offices.

Mail Facilities. Prior to the War and for many years thereafter, the U.S. Mail was brought to Lincolnton once a week from Augusta on horse-back, and, according to pre-war tradition, connection was made here with a weekly carrier from Elberton.

The subscribers to papers were always represented at the post-office, either in person or by another, so there would be no delay in getting the latest news. And, in addition to these, a number of the curious were attracted to learn of current events. Mail day was looked forward to with great interest.

Tannery. Sometimes in the early days of settlement, the exact date of which is unknown, a tannery was established in the southern part of the county and the place called Leathersville, a name which it still retains, and was the first one in Georgia, if not in the south. According to tradition, it was established by Balaam Bentley, the progenitor of the Bentley family in the

Bentley, the progenitor of the Bentley family in the county, and was operated by him for a number of years. It was later owned and operated by his son, Dr. John Bentley. It was patronized not only by this county, but by all of the surrounding counties, for in the early days, and for many years later, shoes and harness were made locally by hand. During the latter years of its existence, most of the leather was shipped to northern markets.

Masonic Lodge. In 1851, Lincoln Lodge No. 78 of Free and Accepted Masons was incorporated, with Henry J. Lang, W.M., Mosely Hawes, S.W., and Austin J. Davis, J.W. (Acts, 1851-2, p. 384).

The Masons added a brick story to the rock court house and used it for their lodge room; and it is said the organization was strong and flourishing at the outbreak of the War.

Churches. Churches were organized and established in different sections of the county, whose histories have been given in preceding chapters.

Sale Of Whiskey Regulated. The age-old whiskey question was of concern to the people of the county during the pre-war period. In 1858, Justices of the Inferior Courts were given athority to grant or to refuse, at discretion, applications for license to retail whiskey, or to keep a tippling house. And where license was granted to demand whatever sum they pleased and to impose whatever terms and conditions they pleased. (Acts, 1856, p. 16). The legal traffic in whiskey was thus placed exclusively in the hands of the court, which, according to the sentiment of the times, exercised its discretion in favor of temperance, though there were evasions of the law by trafficers as at the present time.

Politics. During this period, the people were not without their political differences. Apart from local politics, their first division came in 1806. In that year, General John Clarke, the prominent son of General Elijah Clarke, brought charges against Judge Charles Tait before the legislature, and the distinguished William H. Crawford, who was a member of that body, voted to acquit him. This was resented by Clarke and he and Crawford became bitter and lasting enemies. In a duel fought between them, Crawford was wounded in the wrist. Their enmity became an issue in Georgia politics and resulted in forming the Clarke and Crawford parties. Though Crawford had a strong following in the county, Clarke was more popular, chiefly because a large portion of the people were from North Carolina, the state from which he came, and there was little congeniality betweeen the people of that state and the Virginians, on account of different social customs, because his parents lived here during the last years of their lives, and because, as a lad, he had fought beside his father in the battle of Kettle Creek. This issue lasted for years, and even grew more intense after Crawford retired from political activity and George M. Troup became his successor. Their followers were then known as Clarkites and Troupers. Each faction was rewarded with victory. In the first race for governor, Clarke was defeated by William Rabun, of the Crawford party, and he, in turn, twice defeated Troup for the office.

The people of the county were next divided, in state and national politics, into Whigs and Democrats. The Democratic party in the state was composed laregly of the old Clark party and the Whigs, or State-Rights party, of the old Crawford party and the Troupers. Both parties were headed by illustrious and eloquent leaders, and brilliant campaigns were waged throughout the state until secession overshadowed all other issues. Though the people of this county, in common with the other people of the state, were divided in their views on that question, yet, when Georgia seceded from the Union, on January 19, 1861, old party lines were erased and all united in upholding the action of the state and in their devotion to the Confederacy.

Note: During this period the United States and Mexico engaged in war, but I have not been successful in getting the names of the veterans who went from this county. CJP.

CHAPTER XIII

THE COUNTY IN THE WAR BETWEEN THE STATES

CHAPTER XIII.

THE COUNTY IN THE WAR BETWEEN THE STATES

Loyalty Of The People. Upon the formation of the Confederate States of America, by the convention of the seceding States, in Montgomery, AL., in February, 1861, the people of the county gave the new government their loyal and enthusiastic support. Excitement was intense throughout the nation, and it was soon evident that war was inevitable. Immediately after the fall of Fort Sumter, in April, 1861, President Lincoln issued a call for seventy-five thousand volunteers to subdue the seceding States. The die was cast and the bloody conflict was on.
Lincoln Does Her Part. The Confederate capital was moved from Montgomery to Richmond, Va., in May, 1861, and the Union forces raised the battle-cry. "On to Richmond." President Davis called for volunteers to protect the State from invasion. The call was promptly answered in Georgia. In this county, Captain LaFayette Lamar organized a company, which became Company G. of the 15th Georgia Regiment, and in June, 1861, it left for Virginia. A short while after reaching Warrenton, Va., Captain Lamar became ill and died in a hospital and was succeeded by Lieutenant Stephen Harnesberger. Another company was formed by Captain John Gibson, proprietor of the Lincolnton Hotel, which became Company F of the 22nd Georgia Regiment, and in August, 1861, it set out for the Virginia battle-fields. After two years of service, Captain Gibson resigned and returned to Lincolnton, but, after a short stay, re-joined his company, resigning again before the close of the war. Still another company was soon organized from Wilkes and Lincoln counties which became Company H of the 37th Georgia Regiment. And many others enlisted in various Georgia companies. As the war progressed, recruits were fu;rnished to these companies by the counties. During the 1st years of the war many were called into the State Militia, a number of whom were not in actual service.
Soldiers from Lincoln, then whom there were none braver, were in most of the important battles of the war. They were at Bull Run, in the first bloody encounter, where the Union forces were put to flight and taught they were not fighting "rebels" but brave defenders of a new nation; they were at Shiloh, where the gallant Sidney Johnston, in his victorious sweep, lost his life; they were at Seven Pines, where the result was doubtful and the brave Joe Johnston was severely wounded; they were in the Valley Campaign, where Stonewall Jackson, by his rapid strategies, out-witted, bewildered and defeated four superior armies; they were in the Seven Days' Battle, where McClellan was hammered and driven from point to point and finally to the shelter of his gun-boats; they were in the second battle of

field; they were at Antietam, where the carnage was terrible and the battle indecisive; they were at Fredericksburg, where the army of the North was decisively beaten; they were at Chancellorsville, where the enemy was routed and the dauntless Jackson met a tragic death; they were in the fatal battle of Gettysburg, where southern bravery reached its zenith and furnished an unsurpassed example of heroism in Pickett's Charge; they were at Murfreesboro, where seeming victory was turned into defeat; they were at Chickamauga, where the fearless Longstreet shattered the Union lines and won the day; they were in the battle of the Wilderness, where for three days the Confederates fought and won against overwhelming odds; they were in the bloody battle of Spottsylvania, where the beloved Gordon triumphantly breasted the storm and Lee was forced to the rear by the urgent appeals of his own men; they were with Johnston in Georgia, where every effort was made to check Sherman's victorious march to the sea; they were at Cold Harbor, where the enemy met with terrible repulse; they were in the battles around Richmond, where the last stands were made to save the tottering Confederacy; and they were at Appomattox, where the last solemn scene was enacted and the peerless Lee made an honorable surrender. Many came home bearing the scars of battle and some with loss of limbs, while others, as the full measure of their devotion, lie buried in the battle-fields.

The women of the county, in common with the other women of the South, were no less patriotic, in their sphere, than the men. While their tender emotions often found expression in silent tears and prayers for the husband, or son, or brother, or sweetheart, who might never return, yet, with sublime endurance, they toiled, sacrificed and suffered privations to keep the home fires burning and to furnish what necessities they could to the soldiers at the front. The cares, the anxieties, the heart-aches, the sorrows they experienced through those trying years, with their unfailing devotion to the Confederacy, give them an honored place by the soldiers of the line.

The following roster of the Confederate soldiers, who went from Lincoln County, is as complete as the author has been able to make it:

COMPANY F, 22ND GEORGIA REGIMENT

OFFICERS

John Gibson, Captain; John L. Wilkes, 1st Lieut., Surgeon; W.R. Cunningham, 2nd Lieut.; J.N. Mercier, 3rd Lieut.

NON-COMMISSIONED AND PRIVATES

Allen, Curtis (Died in service); Allen, G.P.; Ashley, A.J.

Bentley, J.B.; Bussey, James R.; Bussey, John R. (Killed at Battle of Manassas); Burgess, Alvin (Killed at Battle of

Battle of Manassas); Burgess, Alvin (Killed at Battle of Gettysburg); Bouchillon, L.D.

Cox, John W. (Drowned in service); Crook, Noah; Crook, Henry; Crook, William (Killed at Battle of Manassas); Carrol, J.W.; Crozier, Silas; Cliatt, Peter; Conner, E.J.; Connor, James; Cox, P.A.

Eubanks, William.

Faulkner, William; Faulkner, Ambrose; Freeman, H.N.; Freeman, Robert L.

Goldman, Marion (Died in service); Goldman, Jasper; Goldman, M.L.; Goldman, Thomas F.; Goldman, Newton (Killed at Battle of Gettysburg); Glaze, Alford; Gross, Dudley; Griffin, William (Killed at Battle of Manassas); Griffin, J.L. (Killed at Battle of Petersburg).

Henderson, W.H. (Killed at Battle of Petersburg); Henley, John; Henley, Matthew (Died in service); Hawes, James L. (Died in service); Hopkins, William (Died in service); Hopkins, John (Killed at Battle of Seven Pines); Humphreys, Thomas S.; Hambrick, A.P. (Killed at Battle of Gettysburg).

Jennings, Charles; Jennings, Robert; Jennings, Sim; Johnson, Henry (Killed at Malvern Hill); Johnson, Thomas (Died in service).

Kennedy, Arthur (Died in service); Kennedy, H.C.; Knox, John.

Leverett, A.J.; Leverette Robert C.; Leverette, W.A. (Killed in action); Lockhart, Joel.

Mallet, James (Died in service); Martin, L.C. (Died in service); Martin, W.E.; Moseley, L.E. (Died in service); Mercier, W.N.; Moseley, B.J.; Murphrey, Thomas; McCorkle, Matthew.

Novell, T.B.

Paradise, J.C.; Paradise, A.G.

Revier, John (Died in service); Roberts, T.H. (Died in service); Roberts, A.Q. (Killed in service); Reid, A.J.; Reid, Griffin; Reid, R.R. (Killed at Battle of Seven Pines); Reid William.

Spires, Carter (Died in service); Spires, W.J.; Samuels, E.L.

Trammell, J.W.; Tunnage, James (Killed at Battle of Seven Pines); Tyler, Edwin (Killed at Battle of Petersburg).

Wallace, Dave (Died in service); Wallace, T.A. (Killed at Battle of Petersburg); Wallace, Jerry (Died in service); Woods, William.

COMPANY G, 15TH GEORGIA REGIMENT

Albea, W.H.; Albea, Thomas.

Bivins, John; Bohler, John T.; Brown, Marshall.

Clary, S.J. (Wounded in leg); Clary, James; Clary, William, Clary, Thomas; Clary, Henry; Clary, Harrison; Crawford, Thomas; Cullars, R.T.; Cartledge, James T.; Cartledge, Walton; Cartledge, Jesse M.; Cartledge, William H.

Dunaway, John L.

Flanigan, W.A.; Fouche, Jered.

Gresham, J.H.; Glaze, Houston; Glaze, Thomas R.

Hawes, T.D. (Captain); Harnesberger, J.T.; Harnersberger, Adam (Lost left arm at Battle of Gettysburg); Harnesberger, Henry; Harnesberger, Stephen (1st Lieut.).

Jones, Moses; Jones, Seaborn; Jones, Joshua (Killed at Gettysburg).

Lamar, LaFayette (Captain, died at Warrenton, Va.); Lane, John A.

Mumford, R.D.; Martin, William G.

Norman, Peyton; Norman, George W.

Rumbley, Rad W.; Remson, Rem; Remson, James; Reid, Jabe M.; Remson, T.H.

Stevenson, N.W.; Stone, J.D.; Sale, Thomas (Killed at Warrenton, Va.); Sale, H.M.

Tatum, William P.; Thurmond, Felix; Tatum, Wiley G.; Tebow, John.

Wheatley, Leonard; Wright, B.S.

COMPANY H, 37TH GEORGIA REGIMENT

Ashmore, George P.; Ashley, J.R.

Bennett, William (2nd Lieut.); Bivins, J.B.; Bussey, N.D.; Bentley, J.W.

Crook, Jamison; Crook, Isaih; Conner, W.G.; Conner, Shadrack.

Graves, R.N.; Glaze, A.N.; Glaze, T.R.

Hollenshead, C.R.; Hollenshead, T.S. (Sergeant); Henderson,

James H.; Hogan, James.

Jennings, Thomas A.

Moseley, Henry (Wounded in foot); Moncrief, Joseph; McCorkle, Hezekiah (Sergeant); McCorkle, Arch; McCorkle, John.

Nash, J.H.

Roberts, Jesse

Spires, W.B.; Spires, J.N.; Spires, James; Smalley, James; Searles, T.C.

Trammell, David

Wright, W.M. (Sergeant); Wright, F.M. (3rd Lieut.).

MEMBERS OF MISCELLANEOUS UNITS

Arnett, J.A. (Co. A, 1st Ga.); Andrews, M.L. (Co. A., 15th Ga.); Ashley, Charles (no data); Ashmore, Peyton (no data).

Bohley, W.H. (Co. K, 48th Ga.); Blakey, P.A. (Co. H, 1st Ga.); Bentley, W.P. (Co. K, 1st Ga.); Broom, Solomon (Co. E, 10th Ga.); Bullard, J.W. (Co. C, 7th Ga.); Blakey, C.S. (Co. H, 30th Ga.); Bentley, A.J. (Co. K, 1st Ga.); Bentley, D.B. (Jackson's Battalion); Bentley, B.F. (no data); Bentley, Charles M. (no data, Killed at Gettysburg); Bentley, H.N. (no data); Bentley, J.T. (no data); Bonner, J.W. (Co. F, 10th Ga.); Blakey, J.F. (Co. C, Caper's Battalion); Banks, Wyatt (no data); Bird, Adolphus (no data); Bussey, W.W. (no data).

Cliatt, John (no data); Cliatt, Isaac (no data); Cliatt, Lee (no data); Cliatt, Thomas (no data); Cliatt D.W. (no data); Conner, Jerry (no data); Caver, Henry (no data); Caver, James (no data); Campbell, C.A. (Co. C, Cutts Battalion); Cox, John E. (1st Ga. Militia); Cartledge, W.T. (Brooks Battalion); Crawford, N.A. (Starr-Cobb's Legion).

Dallas, Z.B. (Co. K, 1st Ga.); Dill, P.H. (Cutts Battalion); Dill, Joseph (Co. I, Toombs' Battalion); DuBose, B.J. (Co. D, 27th Ga.); Dozier, W.Z. (Co. B, 48th Ga.); Davie, William (no data); Davie, Robert (no data).

Edmunds, J.A. (Co. C, 20th Ga.); Elam, J.P. (Co. B, 27th Ga.); Elam, William F. (Co. B, 27th Ga.).

Freeman, W.F. (Co. I, Ga. State Troops); Florence, W.K. (Co. A, 1st Ga.); Fleming, Hill (Co. A, 12th Ga.).
Goldman, T.J. (Co. D, 44th Ga.); Gill, I.M. (Co. A, 15th

Ga.); Gillebeau, J.J. (State Militia); Graves, George W. (no data).

Hardy, Harrison (no data); Harper, V.E. (Co. C, 7th Cavalary); Hawes, J.N. (Co. K, 1st Ga.); Harper, J.C. (Co. C, 1st Ga.); Harmon, Anthony (Co. G, 1st Ga.); Hardy, J.A. (Co. F, 1st Ga.); Hogan, William (Co. K, 1st Ga.); Hogan, W.G. (no data); Hardy, John (no data); Henderson, Ezekiel (no data).

Ivey, Marion (Co. K, 2nd Ga.).

Jones, W.J. (Irvin's Brigade, 9th Ga.); Jones, G.W. (Co. E, 27th Ga.).

Kennedy, George (Co. I, Toombs' Battalion; Kennedy, James (no data).

Leverett, C.R. (Co. K, 1st Ga.); Lang, H.J. (no data); Lang, Miller (no data); Loflin, W.P. (no data); Loflin, James (no data); Leverette, Ollie (no data); Lockhart, Asa (no data); Leverett, John (no data).

Moncrief, John (no data); Morgan, William (no data); Martin, R.A. (Co. G, 38th Ga.); Mu;rphry, A.J. (3rd Ga.); Moseley, S.T. (Co. C, Barnes' Battalion); Matthews, Joseph (Co. C, 20th Ga. Cav.); Moseley, P.N. (no data); Moseley, James (no data); Moseley, William (no data); Matthews, John W. (no data, Machinist); Mumford, J.J. (no data); Martin, W.Q. (no data); Murray, James H. (no data); Murray, W.T. (no data); McCord, R.W. (Co. H, 2nd Ga.).

Parks, Jabe (no data); Powell, B.F. (Co. K, 55th Ga.); Parks, E.H. (Co. K, 1st Ga.); Poss, M.C. (Co. G., 7th Ga.); Parker, James R. (Co. G, 12th Ga.); Parks, W.E. (no data); Parks, Louis (no data); Prather, A.M. (no data); Paschal, William (no data); Pearl, Towns (no data); Parks, John (no data, killed in service).

Ross, M.C. (Co. G, 61st Ga.); Ramsey, I.N. (Co. E, 9th Ga.); Ray, Jonathan (Co. H, 1st Ga.); Roberts, R.E. (Co. A, Cobbs' Legion); Revier, J.G. (Co. E, 9th Ga.); Reese, J.J. (Cobbs' Battalion); Reid, W.M. (Co. C, Maxwell's Battalion); Robertson, Frank (no data); Robertson, Augustus (no data).

Scott, Noah (Co. A, 15th Ga.).; Strother, A.E. (Co. A, Cutts' Battalion); Strother, J.E. (Co. A, 9th Ga., lost left leg at Gettysburg); Strother, C.A. (Co. A, Cutts' Battalion); Spires, Sim (no data); Searles, John (no data); Sims, G.S. (Co. K, 10th Ga.).

Tatum, J.W. (Co. B, 27th Ga.); Tatum, J.H. (Co. G, 30th Ga.); Tutt, William D. (Clinch Rifles); Tutt, Henry (no data); Tutt, George (no data); Thompson, Furman (no data).

Ulm, Asbury (no data)

Wallace, Ollie (no data); Walker, Augustus (no data); Willingham, Z.S. (no data); Willingham, John (no data).

Zellars, I.N. (Co. H, 30th Ga.); Zellars, John (Co. G, 1st Ga. Militia).

CHAPTER XIV

A HISTORIC RAID AND RECONSTRUCTION

CHAPTER XIV

A HISTORIC RAID AND RECONSTRUCTION

The Raid On The Treasure Wagons. A few weeks after the close of the War Between The States, a train of Confederate wagons, laden with gold and silver coin and bullion, and under guard, was drawn up, at evening, for the night's encampment, near what was then the Moss home, now known as the Quinn Dallas home, in the northern part of the county, about twelve miles from Lincolnton. Whether these wagons were coming from Abbeville, S.C., to Washington, Ga., or going from Washington to Abbeville, is a fact about which statements conflict. The tradition in this county is that they were coming from Abbeville and crossed the Savannah River on a pontoon bridge just below Lisbon and bore Confederate treasure, while some of the residents of Washington, past and present, are positive they were going from there and contained treasure belonging to banks in Virginia. Mrs. T.M. Green, late of Washington, in her description of this event, as found in, GEORGIA'S LANDMARKS, MEMORIALS AND LEGENDS, V1, p. 214-17, by L.L. Knight, states that there were five of these wagons, and that they left Washington about ten o'clock, A.M., the latter part of April, 1865, for Abbeville. She says, "These wagons contained gold and silver coin and bullion, belonging to certain Virginia banks. Suffice it to say that the treasure had been concealed in Washington for weeks. The guardians of it had obtained from General Upton, at Augusta, an order for its safe conduct back to Richmond and, armed with this passport, they hoped to make their way quietly without arousing suspicion, across the gap, over to Abbeville, where they hoped to land it safely on board freight cars bound for Richmond." And Hon. R.O. Barksdale, the present Ordinary of Wilkes County, who was five years old at the time and lived in Lincoln County, within two miles of the place of encampment, agrees with her. He says this treasure was shipped into Washington by train, from Augusta, for safe keeping, a short while before the close of the war, and it was being transported back to Virginia, and that the Confederate treasure reached Washington while President Davis was there, during the first days of May, 1865. Evans, in his HISTORY OF GEORGIA, p. 302, states: "While President Davis and his cabinet were in Washington, Ga., a train of wagons arrived, carrying a large amount of gold and silver belonging to the Confederate government. This was known as the "Specie Train," and was guarded with great care by an armed force. Rolls of troops were made out, and twenty-six dollars and twenty-five cents each were paid to as many as could be reached. Forty thousand dollars worth were set aside to pay for rations for other soldiers returning from the war. The orders about this specie and its distribution were the last orders of the Confederate reader. Mrs. Green places the encampment in a horse-lot at the old Chenault home, but to this Mr. Barksdale does not agree. He places it near the old Moss home, about two miles further towards the river, which is the commonly accepted spot.

After the travelers had retired and were peacefully sleeping, they were suddenly aroused by the shouts and yells of an armed body of horsemen, who surrounded the camp. The surprised guards and drivers were captured without resistance, and the wagons were raided. Boxes and bags of the treasure were torn apart, and it is a tradition that the wagon bodies were ankle deep with the precious metal. The raiders loaded their pockets, their haversacks and bags, and some even tied the bottoms of their undergarments and filled the legs with gold. With their purpose accomplished, the guards and drivers were released. It is said their horses were so heavily laden, as they went away, they staggered under the weight and that much of the silver had to be thrown aside. A few of the men deposited the treasure in creeks and some others buried it to await a favorable opportunity to carry it away.

"When the report of the outrage," says Mrs. Green, "reached Washington next day General E.P. Alexander raised a company of men and went to the rescue. But it was too late to do anything except to gather up the fragments. Many Confederate soldiers who were camped in the neighborhood, hearing the noise and believing the stories circulated by the raiders that it was Confederate treasury money, helped themselves liberally, but, when told that it was private property, much of it belonging to widows and orphans of Virginia soldiers, they at once turned it all over to General Alexander. The money was kept under guard for several days, and it was hoped that the bankers might be able to take it back to Richmond. But, alas, the town was soon put under Federal control and one General Wilde was made commander. He no sooner heard of the existence of the treasure than he took possession of it, and not one dollar was ever returned to the rightful owners." She further states that the wagon started with $250,000 or $300,000, that about $75,000 was recovered by General Alexander, that $10,000 or more was found secreted among the Negroes, and that the raiders are supposed to have carried off an equal amount.

The event created great excitement, and, with the Freedman's Bureau set up in Washington, the Negroes had an opportunity to circulate wild stories of the raid. Many of the whites were arrested and brought before General Wilde's court for investigation. The most notable was the arrest and treatment of the men and women of the Chenault family, one of the most prominent and influential in that section of Lincoln. Their home was noted for its lavish hospitality and as a retreat for travelers between Abbeville and Washington over the old stage-coach road. Mrs. Jefferson Davis, who preceded her husband several days before his flight from Richmond, upon the fall of the Confederacy, was entertained in this home while on her way to Washington to await the President's arrival. Acting on reports that the Chenault had thousands of dollars of this money, General

Wilde sent a band of soldiers to search the home. A touching incident happened when they arrived. The elder Chenault owned a dog to which he was greatly attached, and one of the soldiers started to shoot him; whereupon, Mr. Chenault pleaded for his life, explaining that he was harmless and was so faithful to him. "What is his name?" asked the soldier. "Jeff Davis," was the reply. "Well, I'll be d... sure to shoot him," the soldier gruffly remarked, and then killed the poor animal in the presence of his defenseless master.

The soldiers roughly entered the house, broke locks on bureaus and ward-robes, scattering their contents over the floors, and searched the house from top to bottom like a band of ruffians. Failing to find an evidence of the money, they, without any sense of decency or honor, stripped the helpless young women, who had to endure their vulgar gaze and indecent remarks. Mrs. Chenault had a three or four months old baby, but no consideration was shown her on that account. The entire family, except the young children, were taken to Washington and placed in prison. A kind neighbor cared for the children. The elder Chenault, his brother and son were hung up by the thumbs with the hope of extorting a confession that they possessed this treasure. With their hands tied behind them, they were swung up by the arms, causing excruciating pain. It is said that this torture took place in the hearing of their wives, mothers, and sisters,· and that it was so great the elder Chenault fainted under the ordeal and had to be cut down to save his life. After a week or ten days they were all released.

For years after the raid, reports were frequent that some of the treasure had been found. Creeks were dredged, rocks overturned, hollow stumps were dug into, and all places where there was a possibility of concealment were carefully examined. Some small amounts may have been found, but the great bulk of the treasure, if not all of it, concealed on the night of the raid was removed as quickly as the raiders could make arrangements to take it away. Even at this late day there are occasional reports of finding some of this gold, but they do not create any excitement.

Reconstruction. While it was humiliating to the people for the county to be under Federal control during theyear of reconstruction, to have their conduct under constant scrutiny, the witness the disfranchisement of many of her best citizens, while the Negroes went to the polls under the protection of Yankee bayonets, yet, though they often expressed themselves in no uncertain terms, there were no serious clashes with the authorities in power. Platt Madison was in charge of the Radical regime in the county, and in 1867 he was elected by that element as a member of the House of Representatives of Georgia and served from 1868-70. At the time he was elected, Tom Barksdale, a Negro boatman on the Savannah River, was elected Ordinary of the county to succeed Hon. B.F. Tatum, incumbent. On the day for him to take office, Tom came to town and went in to see Mr. Tatum. He walled his eyes over the big shelves of big leather-bound records and the immense files of legal papers, and he was over-awed by the immense files of legal papers, and he was over-awed by the greatness of his duties, for which he knew he was incompetent. Turning to Mr. Tatum, he said, "Marse Frank, you keep this office and run it, and I'll go back and run my boat." That was the nearest the county came to having a Negro officer.

Ku Klux Klan. There was a strong Ku Klux Klan in the county during the days of Reconstruction, but there was little regulator work for it to do here. The knowledge of its existence and the little work it did, no doubt, had a salutary effect in keeping the new order in proper bounds. However, the Klan was not idle. South Carolina was under the yoke and needed aid, and it co-operated freely with the Klans in the counties across the river and helped, in many exciting ways, to rid that State of oppression and undesirable conditions. At times, too, it was called by Klans of the surrounding counties to help put through certain disciplinary measures. There is no instance in which it was used to work private vengeance, but its activities were employed solely for the public good.

CHAPTER XV

PROGRESS OF THE COUNTY SINCE THE WAR

CHAPTER XV.

PROGRESS OF THE COUNTY SINCE THE WAR

Period of Readjustment. The progress of the county was halted for several years following the war. The people were impoverished, they were in a state of unrest while the Federal government had charge of affairs, and it took them time to readjust themselves to the changed conditions and the new order, but, with these obstacles removed, they again turned their attention to the county's advancement.

County Schools. A deep interest was taken in education. Free common schools, as provided by the State Constitution, were established, as needed, in various sections of the county and loyally supported; and, at times, in some of them, the salaries of the teachers were supplemented and their terms extended. Though the buildings were crude and poorly equipped, they were the expression of a stricken people for the welfare of their children. But this interest never waned with the passing years. As the educational system developed, improved facilities were provided, great care, as a rule, was exercised to select conscientious and efficient teachers, and what was best for the elevation of the schools met with a hearty approval. At the present, each of the fourteen rural school buildings for whites is neat, attractive and well equipped, and excellent work is being done in them under the guidance of trained teachers. 1191 pupils were enrolled in 1931.

The people of the county have also shown a remarkable interest in advanced training for their children. Scores of boys and girls have gone from the elementary schools to seek a finished education. For a number of years, even before there was an accredited high school in the county, Lincoln held the distinction of having more students in the higher institutions of learning than any other county in the State according to population.

Progress has also been made by the negro schools since their crude beginnings. While they have not reached a high degree of efficiency, they have attained to a fair standard of work and are gradually improving. There are twenty-one of these schools in the county, each of which is largely attended, and in which a few of the teachers have had some college training. The buildings are of rough material and are poorly equipped, but they are fairly comfortable. In 1931 the enrollment of these schools was 1236.

In 1924 six school districts - Double Branches, Kenna, Maxim, New Hope, Pine Grove and Union Hill - consolidated and formed Four Points Consolidated School District. Jas. P. Sturkey, Walter T. Moss and John L. Gassaway were elected trustees. $8,000 in bonds was voted and issued by the district for the erection and equipment of a school building. This building was erected near Martin's Cross-Roads about six miles southeast of Lincolnton and named

CHAPTER XV.

PROGRESS OF THE COUNTY SINCE THE WAR

Period of Readjustment. The progress of the county was halted for several years following the war. The people were impoverished, they were in a state of unrest while the Federal government had charge of affairs, and it took them time to readjust themselves to the changed conditions and the new order, but, with these obstacles removed, they again turned their attention to the county's advancement.

County Schools. A deep interest was taken in education. Free common schools, as provided by the State Constitution, were established, as needed, in various sections of the county and loyally supported; and, at times, in some of them, the salaries of the teachers were supplemented and their terms extended. Though the buildings were crude and poorly equipped, they were the expression of a stricken people for the welfare of their children. But this interest never waned with the passing years. As the educational system developed, improved facilities were provided, great care, as a rule, was exercised to select conscientious and efficient teachers, and what was best for the elevation of the schools met with a hearty approval. At the present, each of the fourteen rural school buildings for whites is neat, attractive and well equipped, and excellent work is being done in them under the guidance of trained teachers. 1191 pupils were enrolled in 1931.

The people of the county have also shown a remarkable interest in advanced training for their children. Scores of boys and girls have gone from the elementary schools to seek a finished education. For a number of years, even before there was an accredited high school in the county, Lincoln held the distinction of having more students in the higher institutions of learning than any other county in the State according to population.

Progress has also been made by the negro schools since their crude beginnings. While they have not reached a high degree of efficiency, they have attained to a fair standard of work and are gradually improving. There are twenty-one of these schools in the county, each of which is largely attended, and in which a few of the teachers have had some college training. The buildings are of rough material and are poorly equipped, but they are fairly comfortable. In 1931 the enrollment of these schools was 1236.

In 1924 six school districts - Double Branches, Kenna, Maxim, New Hope, Pine Grove and Union Hill - consolidated and formed Four Points Consolidated School District. Jas. P. Sturkey, Walter T. Moss and John L. Gassaway were elected trustees. $8,000 in bonds was voted and issued by the district for the erection and equipment of a school building. This building was erected near Martin's Cross-Roads about six miles southeast of Lincolnton and named through the efforts of the Woman's Club and the P.T.A., all of its eleven rooms and auditorium have been well equipped.

In 1921 Wright's Academy, Cherokee, and Powell's Academy were consolidated with the Lincolnton school, and during the same year it was placed on the accredited list of high schools by the State. The High School department is largely attended by pupils throughout the county, who are admitted on the same terms as those of the town. The annual enrollment of the school, including the high school and the grammar grades, ranges from 350 to 400.

In 1928, due to crowded conditions, the town erected a comfortable three room wooden building, about fifty yards south of the other school building, to care for the first three lower grades.

The superintendents who have served this school are J. E. Guillebeau, 1920-21, 1921-22, Jordan Sanford, 1922-23, C. V. Parham, 1923-24, 1924-25, J. W. Hogan, 1925-26, G. H. Markey, 1926-27, and J. T. Garner, 1927 to the present.

In 1920 an Act was passed by the legislature providing for an independent school system for the Town of Lincolnton (Acts 1920, p. 1093), but the authorities thought it to the best interest of the school not to put this provision into effect.

By an Act of the legislature in 1924, the Board of Education was increased from three to five members to be elected in April of each year, whose terms were to run from June 1st to June 1st, and who were to elect the teachers for the school (Acts 1924, pp. 651-55). Thus provision was made for the old Board to serve through the school term with the faculty it had elected, and for the new Board to serve throughout with the faculty it elected.

Court-Houses. In March, 1874, the legislature passed an Act authorizing the Ordinary of the county to raise money to build a suitable court-house, by issuing $12,000 in bonds payable in such sums, at such interest and on such terms as he might select and determine, and authorizing him to raise such sums by taxation as he might deem necessary to pay iterest and annual installments of such bonds. (Acts 1874, p. 326). B.F. Tatum was Ordinary at the time, and in pursuance of the enactment, he issued the bonds and had the court-house erected. The building was an oblong two-story hipped roof structure, about 42 feet by 50 feet in dimension, with four office rooms on the lower floor, separatead by ten foot hall-ways--one running east and west through the building, and another running from the south entrance back to the stairway leading to the upper story, and with two jury rooms on the south side of the court-room on the second floor. It was located on the public square, covering the spot where the Confederate monument now stands, facing the south, and it was used as a court-house till 1916.

In 1915, while Samuel L. Wilkes was Ordinary, the present court-house was built and equipped from the proceeds of a $30,000 bond issue which the people of the county had voted for that purpose. G. Loyd Preacher, of Augusta, GA., was the architect, the Little-Cleckler Construction Company, of Anniston, AL., were the contractors, and Willis Irvin, of Augusta, GA., was the contractors, and Willis Irvin, of Augusta, GA., was the superintendent.

The building (60 feet wide by 96 feet long) is constructed of re-enforced concrete and tiling, with an outer facing of pressed brick, and its artistic finish, both inside and out, makes it a structure of striking beauty. It is crowned by a shapely tower, which emphasizes its distinction, and in which a hugh clock from its four dials, reveals the hour of the day and the march of Time; and its magnificent portico, with its stately Corinthian columns, gives it an imposing appearance and marks it as a Temple of Justice. The tile-floored corridors, leading from the four entrances, are wide and attractive and furnish easy access to the various county offices, while the double stair-ways at the east and the west end of the building provide ready and ample ingress and egress to and from the second floor. The splendidly equipped court-room is commodious, with a seating capacity of three hundred seventy-five, including the gallery, and the two jury rooms flanking the ends of the spacious Bar add a unique convenience. All of the rooms are neat and comfortable, and, besides accomodations for the public, the ladies' rest room, the judge's room and the traverse jury rooms are each equipped with a lavatory and other sanitary conveniences, supplied with water from a local system owned by the county. The landscaped lawn, the cement walks, the three entrances to the grounds, guarded on each side by heavy brick columns, the shade trees and the luxuriant shrubbery give a lovely setting to the building and increase its beauty. For setting, beauty of design, convenience of arrangement and excellent equipment, the building is not surpassed by any other country-county court-house in the State, and it is one of which the people are justly proud.

The old court-house was unsafe and dangerous, and, in 1916, after it had been abandoned, Judge Wilkes advertised the property for sale under sealed bids. The Town of Lincolnton offered $100 for it for the purpose of tearing the building down, and, being the highest bidder, it was accepted. An amusing incident then happened. A rumor reached the ears of the town authorities that a citizen of the town who had thought of buying it to use the building, was dissatisfied and was threatening to try to set aside the sale in the courts. This was communicated to Judge Wilkes, who directed to county Warden to start the convicts on the building early next morning and by noon of that day it had been razed beyond judicial interference. With no expense for tearing it down, the town sold the usable material for a little more than enough to re-imburse itself for the purchase price.

Newspapers. In 1882 John D. Colley, late of Washington, Ga., and Thomas B. Hollenshead, since deceased, established The Lincolnton News, the first newspaper published in the county, with Mr. Colley as editor. This paper continued under him and succeeding editors, George W. Patterson and R. G. McGowan, for about fifteen years before its publication ceased. It fought the Peoples' Party, and as that party was in the overwhelming majority in the county, its patronage and business dwindled to such an the year 1893, the leading Populists founded The Lincoln Home Journal, with Thomas H. Remsen, Sr., as editor. This paper was published under that name till it was purchased, in 1898, by James H. Boykin, who changed it to The Lincoln Journal. Mr. Boykin built a nice brick home for the paper and equipped it with a modern printing plant, operated by motor power, and under his able management and editorship the publication grew to be state-wide in circulation and in influence. On December 1st, 1924, he sold the paper to John P. Drinkard, whose efficiency as manager and editor kept it up to a high standard of popularity. In 1929 Mr. Drinkard sold it to T. C. Burton' who retained him as editor. In February, 1931, Mr. Burton sold it to Mrs. Boyce Ficklen, Jr., who operated it till January, 1932, when she gave it up to assume her duties as Secretary of the State Board of Control. Mr. Burton again retained Mr. Drinkard as editor, under whose able direction the paper is live and flourishing.

Mail Facilities. During the 80's the mail route between Augusta and Lincolnton, via Double Branches, was abandoned and a daily Star route established between Lincolnton and Plum Branch, S.C., with an intervening post-office at Leverett. In the early 90's it was changed to McCormick, S.C. The old route from Elberton to Lincolnton, by Lisbon, Honora and Goshen, continued for a number of years later. For the convenience of the people in the southeastern part of the county, a Star route was established, the date of which is unknown, between Modoc, S.C., and Double Branches, which continued until 1916, when it was changed to run from Plum Branch, S.C., with Bussey as an intervening post-office. Another Star route went from Lincolnton to Metasville, in Wilkes County, by Sybert post office. From time to time county Star routes were established to contact some of these main routes, and in that way the entire county had fairly good mail facilities. In March, 1903, the county was given its first Rural Free Delivery route, with R.W. Humphries as carrier. The Lincolnton-Metasville Star route was discontinued in the early part of this century. In 1917 a daily Star route was established between Lincolnton and Thomson, GA., by way of Loco and Amity, with W.A. McKinney as carrier, and in 1918 additional mail facilities were provided by the Washington & Lincolnton Railroad. In 1922 the Plum Branch-Double Branches route was discontinued, and on March 31, 1923, the Lincolnton-McCormick was abandoned. In the meantime, five other rural routes were established, one going from Amity and the others from Lincolnton, which eliminated all of the local Star routes, except the one going from Agnes, by way of Leathersville and Clay Hill, to Amity, giving every section the benefit of a daily route. The only post-offices in the county at present are Agnes, Amity, Clay Hill, Leathersville, Loco, Lincolnton and Lisbon, the last named being served by a Star route from Mt. Carmel, SC.

Telephone System. The first telephone line in the county was built from Washington to Lincolnton, in 1891, to the store of P.J. Holliday, where the only phone was located. In 1900 J.M. Price built a line from Modoc, SC, to Double Branches, which was later extended to R.C. Nash's store in Lincolnton. A number of people in the town and out in the county subscribed for phones and Mr. Nash put in a telephone exchange, connecting with Washington and later with McCormick, SC. The system has expanded till it requires both day and night service. It has changed hands at various times, but it is now owned by Georgia Continental Telephone Company. About ten or fifteen years ago, the people around Loco organized a community telephone exchange, which connects with the exchange at Lincolnton, thus giving them good facilities.

County Jail. In 1899, while Thomas H. Remson, Sr., was Ordinary, the presnt brick jail was built with the proceeds of an $3000 bond issue. The old jail, a hewed log structure, which has been previously described, was destroyed by fire, supposedly of incendiary origin. The only inmate was a Negro man, and his piercing cries of distress aroused the jailer, William M. Cartledge, living about a hundred yards distant, who hastened to the rescue. The steps and platform, leading to the entrance, were ablaze, but by quick action Mr. Cartledge was enabled to open the door and both escaped uninjured.

Highways. Very little progress was made in road building till 1906, when the county established a chain-gang; in fact, the county had a reputation for bad roads. From then on there was a marked advance. The old roads were greatly improved and several new ones built. In 1917 a first class road, leading by Graves Mountain to the Wilkes county line, was constructed, and later it was taken over by the State Highway Department. In 1929-30 a State Aid Road was built by the county from Lincolnton to Little River toward Augusta, and in conjunction with Columbia County a beautiful bridge was erected over the stream. In 1931 the road from Lincolnton to Lisbon to connect with a highway from Elberton was placed in the State Highway System, and, while it had not as yet been rebuilt, it is kept up by the highway department. A State Aid Road is now in the course of construction by the county from Savannah River, near Fortson's Ferry, to Lincolnton, which will form a part of a highway leading from Columbia, SC, to Atlanta. Though none of the roads are paved, yet, as a whole, the county has good highways.

Banks. In 1905 The Bank Of Lincolnton, capitalized at $25000, was organized with C.L. Groves as president and Peter Zellars as cashier, and, with changes in the personel of some of its officers at different times, it continued to operate till 1928, when it was taken over by The Farmers State Bank to save it from liquidation by the State Banking Department. Under this arrangement, its stockholders were saved from assessments on their worthless stock and its depositors were paid in full.

In 1911 The Farmers State Bank, with a capital stock of $25000, was organized, with James H. Boykin as president and H.B. Pitt as cashier, and it is now the only bank in the county. It is noted for its successful operation and its efficient management. Mr. Boykin is still its president, and Mr. Pitt, with the exception of the years 1925-29, when he was connected with the State Banking Department, has continued as its cashier.

The Coming Of The Railroad. In 1916 the Washington & Lincolnton Railroad was completed from Washington to Lovelace, near the western boundary of the county. The money for its construction was raised by the sale of its stock to the people along the route, but largely to the citizens of Washington. The people of this county then raised $75000 in stock subscriptions, and in 1917 the road was extended to Lincolnton. Under the subscription notes, the road was to be within the incorporate limits by Tuesday, November 1, 1917. On Saturday, October 29th, the track had been laid nearly to the limits. It was stated that the construction company had to leave on the following Monday for another section of the State to begin a contract on November 1, so the work was continued on Sunday. A large crowd lined the highway to witness this notable event. About 3:00 p.m., the required distance had been reached, the locomotive steamed in, and Lincolnton, one hundred years after she was founded, had her first and, possibly, her last railroad.

With the coming of the railroad a new business and industrial era began in the county. Dr. T.B. Lovelace, a lumberman from North Carolina, anticipating its coming and contributing for that purpose, purchased large areas of timber throughout the county for a low sum, for the sellers thought it an excellent opportunity to clear the land as the then prevailing opinion was that land was more valuable without timber than with it. When the road was completed to Lovelace, a place named for him, he organized the Lovelace Lumber Company, which began to convert the timber into lumber and to convey it to a large planing plant it established there. Upon completion of the road, it established another large plant at Lincolnton. Following the entry of the United States into the World War, lumber soared to unprecedented prices, which held for several years after the war, and these planers were operated both day and night to meet the demand. The large number of employees engaged at the saw-mills, in transporting lumber, and at the planers made a heavy pay-roll, while the finished product brought enormous profits to the company.

In 1922 W.A. Bunch and J.J. Harnesberger, local citizens, organized the firm of Bunch & Harnesberger and went into the lumber business, and in 1923, T.C. Burton, H.B. Pitt and J.H. Boykin, other local citizens, formed the Burton-Pitt Lumber Company and entered that field, both of which established large plants at Lincolnton, and still later the T.B. Lovelace Lumber Company set up another plant there. For a few years the whole county was alive with the lumber industry.

The large pay-rolls of these companies were of speical benefit to the merchants at Lincolnton, for most of the employees traded there and goods were kept moving. Following the advent of the boll-weevil, in 1920, many farmers, whose cotton crops were ruined, obtained temporary relief by using their teams to haul lumber.

In 1928 the T.B. Lovelace Lumber Company wound up its business and moved its plants away; in the summer of 1932, Bunch & Harnesberger shut down its plant; and in July, 1932, the plant of Burton-Pitt Lumber Company was destroyed by fire. The great bulk of the timber suitable for saw-mill purposes has been cut and removed, and at present the lumber industry has ceased.

The greatest boom from the coming of the railroad was in Lincolnton. In the fall of 1917 two separate fires destroyed the block of wooden stores on Enterprise Street east of the Guillebeau Hotel and the Clary block of wooden buildings west of the old court-house square, and on their ruins attractive brick stores, the present post-office and a movie theater were erected. A block of modern businesws houses, adjoining the Farmers State Bank, was built on a lot which was then a peach orchard, and other up-to-date stores were erected in different sections. A number of local enterprises sprang up. New streets were opened, and what was then farm lands became residentialsections. The business activity commanded the favorable comment of all visitors. In a few years, Lincolnton had grown from a quiet little village, with five stores and three hundred fifty inhabitants, to an enterprising town of seventeen stores and a population of nearly a thousand. The financial depression of the past several years checked her growth, and, during that time, she has lost some of her enterprises. Just what effect the loss of the railroad will have on her future is yet to be seen, but at present she is wide awake and does a large volume of business.

The Going Of The Railroad. In December, 1930, upon the hearing of the petition there for its bond holders and the objections thereto by its directors, the Washington & Lincolnton Railroad was placed in the hands of a Receiver by the United States District Court, at Augusta, with the provision, however, that it was to be operated for a year by the Receiver to ascertain whether its income warranted its continuance. At the expiration of that time, the report showed that its income was far below its operating expenses, and on December 5, 1931, the Court gave authority to the Receiver to sell it under the bond foreclosures upon his obtaining permission from the Interstate Commerce Commission to discontinue it. Application was made by the Receiver for that purpose, and a petition by a number of citizens and business men of the county was filed with the Commission protesting the discontinuance of the road. On April 8th, 1932, a hearing on the application and protest was held in Washington, Ga., by a special Examiner from that body, who recommended that the Receiver's application be granted. It was learned that the road could be bought for a sum far below the bonded indebtedness, but the financial depression was so great that what little effort was made to that end was futile. On July 30, 1932, the last train was run to Lincolnton, and on August 11, following the road was sold at public out-cry, at Washington, and was bought as junk by the bondholders for $15000. The work of removing the rails and cross-ties began at once. On October 9th, the depot at Lincolnton, which was being used as a cotton warehouse, was destroyed by fire. And so the road bed is all that remains to remind one that this wonderful developing agency once existed in the county.

CHAPTER XVI

LINCOLN SOLDIERS IN THE WAR WITH SPAIN AND IN THE WORLD WAR

CHAPTER XVI

LINCOLN SOLDIERS IN THE WAR WITH SPAIN
AND IN THE WORLD WAR

The Spanish-American War. At the outbreak of the war with Spain, in 1898, the United States government called for volunteers. Those who answered the call from this county were N.P. Remson, Rem Remson, Henry H. Freeman and Clarence E. Freeland. All of these were given training at the encampments preparatory for service, but the war ended without their being sent to the battle lines. It will be remembered that the war was won on the sea by the disastrous defeat of the Spanish fleets at Santiago and at Manilla Bay. All of these volunteers returned to civil life, except Mr. Freeland, who remained with the army and, as a member of Co. M, 41st U.S. Infantry, was in service in the Philippine Islands while it was in revolt under the leadership of Aguinaldo. He was still in the army during the World War, having risen to the office of 2nd Lieut., and while he was not sent over seas, he was active in military duties in the United States, and later he was promoted to the rank of Captain.

The World War. Immediately following the declaration of war against Germany and her Allies, in 1917, plans for the registration and the selection of eligible men, between the ages of 18 and 30, to serve in the army, were put in operation in this county in common with every other county in the Union. The Board for the Selective Draft consisted of William M. Cartledge, Clerk of the Superior Court, James W. Kelley, Sheriff, and William B. Crawford, M.D., with Fred A. McWhorter, as Clerk, till he entered training, then E.N. Gunby, and Clinton J. Perryman, as Government Appeal Agent. Several patriotic citizens volunteered their services in assisting those within the age limits to fill out their questionnaires to be turned over to the Board, and the work progressed rapidly. There was very little friction with the Board, either over registration or in the selection of men for service, and what little there was passed off satisfactorily in the end and to all concerned. A number of young men voluntarily entered the service without waiting to be selected by the Board. Of the three hundred twenty-six who went from this county, the War Department reports only one deserter, Eddie Bothwell, a Negro.

Death entered the training camps and took the lives of a number in service from this county, both white and colored. Those of the whites who died were Jesse H. Blackburn, Titus B. Booker, Richard Esley Lewis and Edward Smalley; those of the colored were Willie Blackwell, Doyle Harmon, Ausby Jones, L.B. Leverett, John Mahoney, Dan

73

Marigay, Jesse Norman, Tom Partlow, George Pullen, Charlie Scott, William H. Tucker and Roy Williams.

A majority of the men from this county were sent over seas but the Armistice was signed before a large number entered the battle lines. Private Edgar H. Freeland was wounded in the Battle of Argonne Forest by an enemy shell.

Captain Ralph W. Humphreys, of Lincolnton, who volunteered before the entry of the United States into the war, while serving as an intern at Charity Hospital in New Orleans, and who went across in August 1917 and was detailed for service in the English Medical units, was gassed in France, in the line of duty with the 16th Field Ambulance Corpsd, on October 18, 1918, from the effect of which he died, on November 1, 1918, at Le Havre, France. He was buried by the American soldiers with military honors in the cemetery at St. Marie, at Le Havre, in the section set apart for the Allied soldiers.*

Private E.D. Mims, of Lincolnton, had the distinction of being one of the Presidential and Peace Conference Guard Company while President Wilson was in Paris, following the close of the war, formulating plans for World Peace, and he returned to the United States with the President on board the S.S. George Washington.

Below is a complete roster of Lincoln veterans in the World War, as taken from the list furnished by the War Department on file in the office of the Ordinary of the county.

WHITE

Ashmore, Evans	Lincolnton
Banks, Johnnie O.	Lincolnton
Banks, Willie W.	Lincolnton
Beard, Edwin	Lincolnton
Bentley, Fred	Amity
Blackburn, Jim	Lincolnton
Bonner, James W.	Lincolnton
Booker, Cloves M.	Lincolnton
Boyd, Robert E.	Lincolnton
Brown, Leonard M.	Lincolnton
Burton, Thomas C.	Lincolnton
Callahan, Arthur	Lincolnton
Cartledge, Cleveland L.	Lincolnton
Cartledge, Jesse M.	Lincolnton
Chafin, Fred H.	Lincolnton
Chafin, Jesse M.	Lincolnton
Cliatt, Am H.	Lincolnton
Cliatt, Edward J.	Lincolnton
Cox, Clifton Mailon	Honora
Cox, John T.	Lincolnton
Crawford, Hicks M.	Lincolnton
Cromer, John O.	Lincolnton
Crook, Florence M.	Amity
Cullars, Robert W.	Lincolnton
Dallas, Albert H.	Lincolnton
Deason, Manley	Double Branches
Deason, Harry	Lincolnton
Dill, William P.	Leathersville

Dye, William H.	Lincolnton
Edmunds, Fred L.	Lincolnton
Edmunds, John C.	Lincolnton
Edmunds, Samuel Robert	Lincolnton
Ellenburg, Henry G.	Loco
Ferguson, Walter L.	Loco
Florence, Thomas S.	Lincolnton
Freeland, Edgar	Lincolnton
Gassaway, Patrick H.	Lincolnton
Goldman, Welcome J.	Loco
Groves, John W.	Lincolnton
Guillebeau, William W.	Maxim
Gunter, George I.	Honora
Hardaway, William G.	Amity
Harper, William H.	Amity
Harris, Bert Lee	Lincolnton
Harris, John C.	Lincolnton
Hill, Robert G.	Lincolnton
Hogan, Wayne A.	Agnes
Holloway, Bonnie S.	Double Branches
Ingram, Albert E.	Loco
Jones, Samuel A.	Amity
Justice, Jim C.	Amity
Lane, Henry G.	Bussey
Leverett, John P.	Lincolnton
Leverett, Lum	Lincolnton
Linenkohl, Lewis E.	Clay Hill
Long, George R.	Amity
Lovelace, Ralph A.	Lincolnton
McGee, James E.	Honora
McKinney, William G.	Lincolnton
McWhorter, Fred A.	Lincolnton
Maloof, Joe	Lincolnton
Martin, Bonnie W.	Lincolnton
Martin, Clifford E.	Lincolnton
Martin, John C.	Lincolnton
Mathews, Thomas A.	Lincolnton
Mathews, Wesley W.	No Address
Mercier, Frank	Lincolnton
Mims, Eunice D.	Lincolnton
Moore, James R.	Double Branches
Morgan, John M.	Amity
Moss, Roy L.	Lincolnton
Murray, Harry M.	Lincolnton
Nanney, Spurgeon	Lincolnton
Newberry, James	Lincolnton
Norman, Robert T.	Lincolnton
Norman, Toombs A.	Lincolnton
Paradise, Albert W.	Amity
Paradise, Howard H.	Amity
Paradise, Pink	Amity
Paradise, Marshall	Lincolnton
Penland, Buster L.	Leverett
Penland, Carl	Lincolnton
Price, Julius J.	Lincolnton
Quarles, Robert	Lincolnton
Reed, Fletcher L.	Lincolnton
Reese, Albert G.	Double Branches

Reid, Grover C.	Amity
Reid, Mell J.	Double Branches
Scott, George W.	Honora
Smith, Reuben C.	Lincolnton
Spires, Luther B.	Lincolnton
Spratlin, Clark T.	Lincolnton
Stovall, Wade	Lisbon
Strother, Jerrimiah	Amity
Thurmond, Roy C.	Leverett
Trammell, Sam W.	Lincolnton
Tullis, Miller C.	Lincolnton
Ware, Henry B.	Lincolnton
Wells, Clarence W.	Lincolnton
West, James E.	Lincolnton
White, Edgar Henry	Amity
Wilkes, Nathan C.	Lincolnton
Wilkes, Samuel Dorsey	Lincolnton
Williams, George E.	Loco
Williams, Simmie	Lincolnton
Willingham, Frank Z.	Lincolnton
Wood, Johnnie R.	Lincolnton
Wright, Guy H.	Lincolnton
Wright, Thomas B.	Lincolnton

DECEASED

Blackburn, Jesse H.	Amity
Booker, Titus B.	Amity
Humphreys, Ralph Wilbur	Lincolnton
Lewis, Rishard Esley	Lincolnton
Smalley, Edward W.	Leathersville

OFFICERS

Freeland, Clarence Earl	Lincolnton
Sturkey, Edgar Lafayette	Lincolnton

Miss Rob T. Tarver, of Lincolnton, now Mrs. Harold Bocock of Atlanta, GA, served in France as a Red Cross Nurse.

NAVY

Crook, Horace A.	Amity
Dedge, Guss	Agnes
Edmunds, Willie Timmons	Amity
Elam, Lincoln Patrick	Lincolnton
Gaskin, James Lafayette	Lincolnton
Hardaway, Olin Forest	Amity
Hogan, John Walker	Agnes
Hogan, John Walker	Lincolnton
Howard, James Henry	Lincolnton
Leverett, Thomas H.	Lincolnton
Moss, William Caesar	Lincolnton
Paradise, John Alvin	Lincolnton
Powell, Joe Grimsley	Lincolnton
Smalley, Benjamin	Leathersville
Walker, Lawrence Jehu	Amity

COLORED

Allen, Robert	Lincolnton
Andrews, Roy W.	Lincolnton
Andrews, Wyatt	Lincolnton
Banks, George W.	Lincolnton
Banks, Lewis	Lincolnton
Barksdale, Mose	Lincolnton
Beard, Dewey	Lincolnton
Beard, Guss	Lincolnton
Bentley, Cary N.	Leathersville
Blackwell, Box	Lisbon
Blackwell, James	Lisbon
Bohler, Addie	Double Branches
Bond, James	Lincolnton
**Bothwell, Eddie	Lincolnton
Boyd, Willie	Amity
Brown, Cleve	Lincolnton
Brown, Henry	Lincolnton
Bussey, Joseph	Bussey
Bussey, Will	Lincolnton
Cade, Matthew	Lincolnton
Calhoun, Solomon	Lisbon
Chenault, Joe	Lincolnton
Cade, Winslow	Lisbon
Colquitt, Charlie	Lisbon
Crite, Shermon	Honora
Cullars, Joe	Honora
Curry, Abe	Lincolnton
Curry, Dooley	Lincolnton
Curry, Ephriam S.	Lincolnton
Curry, Luther	Amity
Dallas, Fate	Lincolnton
Davis, Alex	Clay Hill
Davis, Alexander	Lincolnton
Douglas, Doss	Leverett
Drayton, Henry	Lincolnton
Dunn, Willie R.	Agnes
Edwards, Hogan	Lincolnton
Edwards, M.D.	Lincolnton
Elam, Floyd	Lincolnton
Elam, John B.	Double Branches
Elam, Paul	Leverett
Ferguson, F.M.	Lincolnton
Fields, Claud	Clay Hill
Fleming, John W.	Bussey
Florney, Harrison	Lincolnton
Ford, Willie	Lisbon
Fouche, Eddie Y.	Clay Hill
Freeman, Samuel	Lincolnton
Garnett, John M.	Lincolnton
Garnett, Nathan	Lincolnton
Glaze, Peyton	Lincolnton
Glaze, Watson	Lincolnton
Glaze, Will	Lincolnton
Glaze, Willie	Lincolnton
Grier, Euclid	Lincolnton
Grier, Nathaniel	Lincolnton

Hamp, Robert	Lincolnton
Harper, Philmore	Lincolnton
Harris, Buster	Lincolnton
Harris, Henry	Lincolnton
Harris, Will	Lisbon
Hawes, Albert W.	Lincolnton
Hawes, Burl	Lincolnton
Hawes, Fred	Honora
Hawes, Percy	Honora
Hawes, Ulysses	Lincolnton
Henderson, Alex	Lincolnton
Henderson, Pete	Lincolnton
Henderson, Frank	Leverett
Henderson, Rufus	Lincolnton
Henry, Charley	Lisbon
Hill, Ben	Lisbon
Hill, Dolphus	Lincolnton
Hogan, Blanchard	Lincolnton
Hogan, Sim	Lincolnton
Hogan, William	Lincolnton
House, Frank	Lincolnton
Jenkins, Amy	Lincolnton
Jennings, Robert W.	Lincolnton
Johnson, Frank E.	Clay Hill
Johnson, George D.	Lincolnton
Johnson, Tommie	Lincolnton
Jones, Erwin	Double Branches
Jones, Tom	Double Branches
Kelley, George W.	Lincolnton
Kelley, Henry	Lincolnton
Kendricks, Nathaniel	Maxim
Kennedy, Doyl	Double Branches
Kennedy, Frank	Lincolnton
Lee, Sam	Amity
Lee, Will	Amity
Leverett, Ed	Lisbon
Leverett, George W.	Lincolnton
Leverett, Lonnie	Pansy
Leverett, Pat	Lincolnton
Leverett, Remus	Pansy
Leverett, Sam J.	Lincolnton
Leverett, T.B.	Lincolnton
Leverett, Thomass	Lincolnton
Leverett, Zederick	Pansy
Levitt, Sol	Double Branches
Lewis, John H.	Lincolnton
Lewis, James	Double Branches
McCurry, Andrew	Honora
McCord, Harvey E.	Amity
McCord, Lloyd	Amity
McMurray, Will	Lincolnton
Marshall, Grant	Honora
Martin, Jim	Leverett
Mason, Nathan	Lincolnton
Mason, William T.	Lincolnton
Matthews, Dan	Lisbon
Mercier, Jim	Lincolnton
Murray, Aggie	Lincolnton

Murray, Aaron	Lincolnton
Murray, Britt	Lincolnton
Murray, Cleophus	Amity
Murray, Dan	Leverett
Murray, Dandy	Lincolnton
Murray, Harrison	Lincolnton
Murray, Isiah	Leverett
Murray, Jim J.	Lincolnton
Murray, John	Lincolnton
Murray, Morris	Lincolnton
Murray, Nathaniel	Lincolnton
Murray, Thomas	Lincolnton
Murray, Will	Lincolnton
Murray, William T.	Lincolnton
Murray, Willie	Leverett
Murray, Willie	Lincolnton
Nash, George	Lisbon
Norman, Cliff	Honora
Norman, George	Lisbon
Norman, Jake	Lisbon
Norman, Jim	Honora
Norman, Johnnie	Honora
Norman, P.C.	Lincolnton
Nunally, John E.	Lisbon
Partelow, Robert	Honora
Parks, Ben	Double Branches
Parks, Collie	Bussey
Randall, Joe Henry	Lincolnton
Reed, Alexander	Double Branches
Scott, Jack	Lincolnton
Searles, Arges	Lincolnton
Searles, Will	Double Branches
Simmons, Fess	Lincolnton
Sloan, Fred	Double Branches
Soffold, Andrew	Lincolnton
Statom, Willie	Honora
Stokes, Henry	Lincolnton
Stokes, Willie H.	Lisbon
Story, Sam	Pansey
Tate, Pearl	Lincolnton
Taylor, Milledge	Bussey
Taylor, Thomas	Bussey
Thomas, Charlie	Lincolnton
Thomas, Jake	Lisbon
Thomas, Johnnie	Lisbon
Tutt, George	Honora
Tutt, Jackson	Lincolnton
Tutt, Willie	Honora
Turman, George	Lisbon
Turman, Roy	Lincolnton
Wakefield, Ben	Lincolnton
Walton, Edward	Lincolnton
Walton, Lewis	Lisbon
Ware, Leonard	Lincolnton
Warren, Bennie	Leverett
Warren, Collie	Leverett
Watson, Bob	Amity
Weems, George	Lincolnton

Williams, Calvin	Leverett
Williams, Eddie	Lincolnton
Williams, Jake	Lincolnton
Williams, Lee	Lisbon
Williams, Tom	Lincolnton
Wynn, Steve	Honora
Wynn, Willie	Honora
Zellers, John	Lincolnton
Zellers, Robert L.	Lincolnton

DECEASED

Blackwell, Willie	Honora
Harmon, Doyle	Amity
Jones, Ausby	Bussey
Leverett, L.B.	Lincolnton
Mahoney, John	Lincolnton
Marigay, Dan	Lisbon
Norman, Jesse	Lincolnton
Partlow, Tom	Honora
Pullen, George	Lisbon
Scott, Charlie	Leverett
Tucker, William H.	Double Branches
Williams, Roy	Lincolnton

*See Biographical Sketch
**Deserter

CHAPTER XVII

MISCELLANY

CHAPTER XVII

MISCELLANY

Population And Taxable Wealth. In 1800 the population of the county was 4,766. In 1810 the population was 4,555, of which 2,212 were negroes, and the amount of tax collected was $1250.18. In 1820 the population was 6,458, and the amount of tax collected was $1535.09. In 1830 the population was 6,145, of which 3,276 were negroes, and the amount of tax collected was $1630.82. In 1840 the population was 5,895, and the amount of tax collected was $994.48. In 1850 the population was 5,998, of which 1,109 were white males, 1078 white females, 15 free colored males, 16 free colored females, and 3,780 slaves. Value of real estate $611,312, and of personal property $1,735,722 (this does not mean property returned for taxation, as only $2,243.58 was collected for taxes). Population of Lincolnton 166. In 1860 the population was 5,443, of which 1,675 were whites and 3,768 colored. Property value, $3,842,938. In 1870 the population was 5,413 of which 1,797 were whites and 3,616 were colored. Property returned for taxation, $577,728. In 1880 the population was 6,412, of which 2,254 were whites and 4,158 were colored. Property returned for taxation, $671,733. In 1890 the population was 6,146 of which 2,473 were whites and 3,673 were colored. Property returned for taxation, $634,745. Population of Lincolnton, 220. In 1900 the population was 6,556, of which 2,883 were whites and 3,673 were colored. Property returned for taxation, $639,285. Population of Lincolnton, 221. In 1910 the population was 8,714, of which 3,539 were whites and 5,175 were colored. Property returned for taxation, $970.538. Population of Lincolnton, 375. In 1920 the population was 9,759, of which 4,584 were whites and 5,175 were colored. Property returned for taxation, $1,421,817. Population of Lincolnton, 657. In 1930 the population was 7,847, of which 1,897 were white males, 1,855 white females, 1,991 colored males, 2,101 colored females, 2 of foreign birth, 2 of foreign parentage, and 3 mixed. Property returned for taxation, $1,376,224. Population of Lincolnton, 952.

The slump in the population following 1920 was due largely to the advent of the boll-weevil, which worked havoc with the cotton crops, causing numbers of people to move to other localities for employment.

Surface of the County, Soil and Products. The surface of the county is generally hilly, with stretches of level lands in the various sections, but not too hilly to prevent easy cultivation. The lands on Savannah and Little Rivers and on the larger creeks have, for the most part, a dark mulatto soil, which is specially adapted to corn; the other lands have a gray or a red soil, mostly gray, with a red clay subsoil, adapted to cotton, though other kind of crops produce well on them. Most of the county is under cultivation. Cotton is the leading crop. Under favorable conditions the county produces around 8,000 bales, but since the advent of the boll-weevil in 1920, the production has been curtailed, on an average, nearly half. Corn, oats, wheat, peas, potatoes and hay yield abundantly, but these crops are grown only for home and farm consumption. Nearly every farm has a nice orchard for home use. Some of the lands are admirable adapted to cattle raising, but little progress has been made in this line.

Minerals. "Geologically," says Mr. McCallie, State Geologist, "Lincoln County is divided into two unequal parts by a line drawn in a northeast direction through Goshen, north of Soap Creek. North of this line the rocks are coarse chists and gneisses mixed with a good deal of granite. There occurs one large area of porphyritic granite extending from near Honora north to near Lisbon and west nearly to Tignall, Wilkes County. In this area the common minerals are quartz, fieldspar, light and dark mica. There are no deposits of certain commercial value in this area. Pegnatite dikes (coarse granite veins) are abundant in places but none are known to be of large enough size or of good enough quality to warrant mining."

"The southern part of the county, south of Goshen, the following rocks occur: conglomerate, quartzite, sericite, slate, mica, chist and volcanic rocks. These rocks are a direct continuation of the McDuffie gold belt. In them the gold occurs in quartz veins and partly disseminated through the surrounding chists. The precious metal is associated with sulphides, particularly that of iron, pyrite."

"The commonest minerals found in Lincoln County are: quartz, fieldspar, muscovite, biotite, hornblende, chlorite, zicon, rutile, lazulite, anthrophyllite, pyanite, hematite, galena, pyrite, native gold, chalcopyrite."

A few years ago manganese was mined on the Charles Hardy place, about three miles east of Lincolnton. Sale's Gold Mines were operated in the northwestern part of the county, forty-five or fifty years ago, with a fair yield. Gold has been found on the old Paschal place in the southern part of the county, but little effort has been made toward mining it. In the western part of the county, the McGruder Gold Mines were successfully worked for a number of years. This property changed hands several times, the last mining being done by the Georgia Copper Company about 1926.

Graves' Mountain. This mountain, six miles southwest of Lincolnton, is one of the distinctive marks of the county. From the topography of this section, it seems out of place and foreign to its surroundings. It rises abruptly to a height of three hundred feet and extends nearly half a mile. The State Geologist, Hon. S. W. McCallie, says: "The mountain owes its prominence to the hard and resistant quartzite of which it is composed. It is not volcanic, as is locally supposed. On the crest of Graves Mountain rutile, lazulite and pyrophillites crystals are common. The crystals of rutile at this locality are amongst the finest in the world and are to be found in mineral collections all over the country. Some of the crystals are as much as 5 inches long. The late Dr. Kunk reports finding single crystals weighing 4 pounds. Pyanite and hematite also occur in this locality." He further states, "I have been pretty much all over Graves Mountain more than once and have never seen anything whatever that even suggested the idea that the mountain was of meteroic origin."

Up to half a century ago, one could gather an abundance of chestnuts and chinkapins upon the mountain, but these trees are all gone, and in their stead have come the small oaks and the scrub pines. It has its Wolf Den and a Lovers' Leap with its legend. From its summit a fine view is given of the surrounding country. Several springs of clear cold water issue from its base and make it an inviting place for the young people of this and adjoining counties to have picnics during the summer.

Lisbon. The first town authorized by the legislature to be laid out in what is now Lincoln County was Lisbon, in 1786. Marbury & Crawford's Digest of the Laws of the State of Georgia, page 554, where the Act is found, erroneously refers to it as "Lincoln". The Act provides, "That Zachariah Lamar, of the aforesaid county (Wilkes), be and he is hereby authorized and empowered to lay out a town on his own lands, situate on the south side of the mouth of Broad River, into any and number of half acre lots as he may think proper, and to dispose of and make titles to the same according to the usual manner of conveyance; which said town shall be called and known by the name of Lincoln (Lisbon). And the said Zachariah Lamar is hereby further authorized and empowered to erect a public warehouse for the reception and inspection of tobacco in the said town of Lincoln (Lisbon), subject always to the laws that have been or may hereafter be provided for the inspection of tobacco." There is neither evidence nor tradition that a town was established, though the name of the place is still retained.

Goshen. Goshen is located six miles north of Lincolnton. It was evidently named by the early settlers for the country wherein Jacob and his brethren dwelt, for it is surrounded by fertile lands. At one time it was one of the outstanding business centers of the county. "White's Statistics of the State of Georgia," page 382, published in 1849, refers to it as having a church, hotel, school and several mechanics' shops. A post-office was located there till the establishment of rural routes in the county.

Earth Tremors. At intervals, in the past, in Lincolnton, strange sounds have been heard, like a heavy blast or the roar of distant thunder. The last occurrence was on a Sunday evening in 1912. A full moon shone and not a cloud was in the sky. The author, his father and one of his sisters were at supper. Suddenly a deep roaring noise was heard. The house shook and the dishes rattled. Thinking that the top of a chimney had fallen on the house, we rushed out to investigate, when we discovered the neighbors in great excitement had vacated their houses. Believing that an explosion of some kind had occurred, careful inquiry was made of the people in and near the town, but no one could give any information; in fact, those living near Lincolnton did not hear the noise or feel its effect. Some of the oldest residents stated that similar sounds had been common years ago. White, in his "Georgia Statistics," (1849), pages 383-4, states: "At Lincolnton, at various times for the past five years, curious sounds, resembling those of distant thunder, have been heard. The noise has been so great as to produce a shaking of the glasses, fences, etc." The reasonable explanation is that these sounds were caused by earth tremors.

Sterne Simmons. In the family burial ground, about nine miles north of Lincolnton, near what was formerly Honora post-office, rests the remains of a prodigy in weight. On the slab which marks his grave, the following epitah appears: "Sterne Simmons. Born August 22, 1824. Died August 25, 1853. Aged 29 years and 3 days. The deceased weighed at the time of his death 650 pounds."

It is said he had a ravenous appetite, causing many exaggerated stories of the quantity of food he ate at a meal. No doubt much more than an ordinary meal was required to satisfy his immense organism. The buggy in which he traveled was twice the size of an ordinary vehicle, and it was made specially for his use. Many people, out of curiosity, came from a distance to see him, but he was sensitive about his size, and, if he knew their purpose, he would not be seen. He was unmarried and lived with his parents, who were prominent people. On the day of his funeral, the door-facings had to be removed for his body to be taken from the house. The old Simmons home, since remodeled, is now owned by T. Watson Cullars, one of the largest landowners and planters of the county.

Two Sad Tragedies. On the morning of February 28, 1929, between one and two o'clock, while returning by automobile from the Tenth District Athletic Meet, at Warrenton, GA, by way of Harlem and Appling, to Lincolnton, Mr. Fred A. McWhorter and three of his children, John Price, Nina and Fred A., Jr., aged eleven, nine and eight years respectively, were drowned at Cherokee Creek, in Lincoln County, about two miles south of Double Branches. It had been raining for several days, and on the night of the tragedy the rain had fallen in torrents. The force of the swollen stream had washed out the ten or fifteen foot fill at the north end of the bridge, without disturbing the concrete pier, leaving the bridge intact and giving the appearance to one on the opposite side of the water having risen several inches above the fill. This was the condition when Mr. McWhorter attempted to cross the bridge. The children were supposedly asleep. As the front wheels rolled off on the bridge, the car plunged downward and out of sight. Prof. J.T. Garner, Superintendent of the Lincolnton High School, who was traveling in another car about fifty yards behind, saw the occurrence and speeded forward to be of assistance, but neither Mr. McWhorter nor any of the children came to the top. He left his car, with the lights burning as a warning to others, and hastened back several miles to the nearest telephone to report the sad news. Numbers of men from in and near Lincolnton, as well as from that community, gathered at the scene, but, due to the darkness and the high water, little could be done till daybreak. The car was located about thirty feet below its place of entrance, with one door open and the bodies gone, indicating that Mr. McWhorter perished with his children in a heroic effort to save them. Between eight and nine o'clock, A.M., the bodies were found some distance down the stream from fifty to one hundred yards apart in the order of their ages.

When the news of the tragedy reached Lincolnton, it was stated that two white men had left there about midnight in a car for Augusta over the same road, and that, perhaps, they had suffered the same fate. While the work of rescue was in progress, a Pontiac tire cover was found down the stream and later a letter. The creek was dragged, and, a short distance below where the other car was located, a Pontiac coupe was found, with doors closed, containing the bodies of the two men, who were identified as Mr. B.F. Foreman of Allendale, SC, and Mr. Ed Barrett, of Grovetown, GA. Relatives were immediately notified and their bodies were taken to their respective homes for burial.

The bodies of Mr. McWhorter and his chiildren were taken to the home of Mr. J.M. Price, of Double Branches, Mr. McWhorter's father-in-law, and prepared for burial; and all were buried side by side in one large grave, in the cemetery at Double Branches Baptist Church, in the presence of the largest crowd, perhaps, that ever assembled at that sacred spot.

Mr. McWhorter was born in Greensboro, GA, on May 9, 1896, and he located in Lincolnton to practice law in 1916. On May 15th, 1917, he married Miss Loudell Price, of Double Branches. He had built up a lucrative practice, had served as a member of the local schoolboard, as a member of the council and as mayor of the town, and, at his death, was Representative-elect of the county. He left surviving him his widow and his two youngest children, Billie and Sarah.

JUSTICES OF THE INFERIOR COURT*

(This Court consisted of five justices, and it was abolished in 1868).

Thomas C. Russell	3-26-1796 - 8-24-1796
William Clements	3-26-1796 - 8-24-1796
Peyton Wyatt	3-26-1796 - 8-24-1796
John Winn	3-26-1796 - 8-24-1796
William Dawson	3-26-1796 - 8-24-1796
Henry Ware	8-24-1796 - 2-14-1799
Robert Walton	8-24-1796 - 2-14-1799
Newell Walton, Jr.	8-24-1796 - 2-14-1799
Basil Lamar	8-24-1796 - 2-14-1799
Sirth Barksdale	8-24-1796 - 2-14-1799
Robert Walton	2-14-1799 - 1811
Sith Barksdale	2-14-1799-1800 resigned
Newell Walton, Jr.	2-14-1799-1802 resigned

Name	Dates
Robert Ware	2-14-1799-1807 resigned
John Lockhart	2-14-1799-1811 resigned
Philip Zimmerman	11-25-1800-1807 resigned
William Evans	6-16-1802 - 1807
James Ware	1-13-1807 - declined
Newel Walton	9- 8-1807 -
	12- 9-1807-1811 resigned
John H. Walker	1-13-1807 -
	12- 9-1807-1812 resigned
Isaac Brakefield	12- 9-1807 - 11-9-1813
Thomas Murray	3-14-1811 - 12-5-1811 - 11- 9-1813
John Parks	3-14-1811 - 12-5-1811 - 11- 9-1813
Henry Jones	3-14-1811 - 12-5-1811 - 11- 9-1813
Robert Ware	2-28-1812 - 11-30-1812 - 11- 9-1813
Robert Ware	11- 9-1813 - 11-1-1817
Arthur Frazer	11- 9-1813 - 11-1-1817
Henry Jones	11- 9-1813 - 11-1-1817
Thomas Murray	11- 9-1813 - 11-1-1817
Samuel Davis	11- 9-1813 - 11-1-1817
Thomas Murray	11- 1-1817 - 10-26-1821
Samuel Davis	11- 1-1817 - 1819
William Dowsing, Jr.	11- 1-1817 -1820 resigned
James E. Todd	11- 1-1817 - 10-26-1821
Rem Remson, Jr.	11- 1-1817 - 10-26-1821
David Glaze	6- 5-1819 - 1821 died
William Parks	12-28-1820 - 10-26-1821
Arthur Frazer	2-26-1821 - 10-26-1821
Rem Remson	10-26-1821 - 1-11-1825
James E. Todd	10-26-1821 - 1-11-1825
Arthur Frazer	10-26-1821 - 1-11-1825
Thomas Murray	10-26-1821-1823 resigned
James Wadsworth	10-26-1821-1824 resigned
Leonard Sims	6- 4-1823 - 1-11-1825
Thomas Curry	1-13-1824 - 1-11-1825
Rem Remson	1-11-1825 - 1-16-1829
James E. Todd	1-11-1825 - 1-16-1829
Leonard Sims	1-11-1825 - 1827 died
Thomas Curry	1-11-1825 - 1827
Arthur Frazer	1-11-1825 - 1-16-1829
William Jones	1-23-1827 - 1-16-1829
Robert Fleming	6-11-1827 - 1-16-1829
Peyton Hawes	1-16-1829 - 1830
Rem Remson	1-16-1829 - 1-15-1833
Thomas Walton Murray	1-16-1829 - 1832 died
William Jones	1-16-1829 - 1-15-1833
Robert Fleming	1-16-1829 - 1-15-1833
Thomas Curry	4-14-1830 - 1-15-1833
John Frazer	10-17-1832 - 1-15-1833
Rem Remson	1-15-1833 - 1-13-1837
John Frazer	1-15-1833 - 1833
Wiley G. Tatom	1-15-1833 - 1-13-1837
Thomas Curry	1-13-1833 - 1-13-1837
John Wright	1-15-1833 -4-6-1836 died
John McDowell	12-16-1833 - 1-13-1837

Peter Lamar	1-13-1837 -	1-14-1841
William B. Cantelow	1-13-1837 -	1839
Stephen Stovall	1-13-1837 -	1-14-1841
Lewis Parks	1-13-1837 -	1-14-1841
John Moss	1-13-1837 -	1838
Harrison W. Hagerman	5-28-1838 -	1-14-1841
Aaron Hardy	4-29-1839 -	1-14-1841
James Jennings	1-14-1841 -	1-15-1845
Aaron Hardy	1-14-1841 -	1-15-1845
Harrison W. Hagerman	1-14-1841 -	1844
Peter Lamar	1-14-1841 -	1844
Jared E. Groce	1-14-1841 -	1842
Alexander Johnston	2-5-1842 -	1-15-1845
Nicholas Giles Barksdale	1-18-1844 -	1-15-1845
John Quinn	4-22-1844 -	1-15-1845
Aaron Hardy	1-15-1845 -	1-12-1849
James Jennings	1-15-1845 -	1-12-1849
Nicholas Giles Barksdale	1-15-1845 -	1-12-1849
Hardy Leverett	1-15-1845 -	1-12-1849
Alexander Johnston	1-13-1845 -	1846
Benjamin Bentley	1-13-1846 -	1-12-1849
Aaron Hardy	1-12-1849 -	1850
Benjamin Bentley	1-12-1849 -	1852
Hardy Leverett	1-12-1849 -	1-8-1853
James Briscoe Neal	1-12-1849 -	1-8-1853
Henry Freeman	1-12-1849 -	1-8-1853
Alexander Frazer	1-15-1850 -	1-8-1853
Wilkes R. Wellborn	3-10-1852 -	1-8-1853
Hardy Leverett	1-8-1853 -	1-12-1857
Henry Freeman	1-8-1853 -	1-12-1857
Aaron Hardy	1-8-1853 -	1-12-1857
Alexander Frazer	1-8-1853 -	1855
Wilkes R. Wellborn	1-8-1853 -	1856
Mosley Hawes	1-9-1853 -	1-12-1857
Benjamin P. Oneal	1-12-1856 -	1-12-1857
Aaron Hardy	1-12-1857 -	1-10-1861
Mosley Hawes	1-12-1857 -	1-10-1861
Benjamin P. Oneal	1-12-1857 -	1860
John L. Wilkes	1-12-1857 -	1-10-1861
Virgilius Maro Barnes	1-12-1857 -	1860
LaFayette Lamar	2-15-1860 -	1-10-1861
Joseph M. Dill	2-15-1860 -	1-10-1861
Aaron Hardy	1-10-1861 - 1-21-1865	3-30-1861 -
Mosley Hawes	1-10-1861 - 1-21-1865	3-30-1861 -
LaFayette Lamar	1-10-1861 - 1862	3-30-1861 -
John L. Wilkes	1-10-1861 - 1862	3-30-1861 -
Joseph M. Dill	1-10-1861 - 1-21-1865	3-30-1861 -
James W. Murray	1-25-1862 -	1-21-1865
William Dallis	1-25-1862 -	1-21-1865
Aaron Hardy	1-21-1865 -	1868
Mosley Hawes	1-21-1865 -	1868
Joseph M. Dill	1-21-1865 -	1868
William Dallis	1-21-1865 -	1868

John L. Wilkes   1-21-1865 - 1868

*The author acknowledges with thanks the kindness of Miss Ruth Blair, State Historian, in furnishing him this list.

ORDINARIES.

B. Franklin Tatum	March 1852 to May 1884
Thomas H. Remson	May 1884-1900
W. Homer Bennett	1901-1904
Samuel L. Wilkes	1905-1916
Ben Hill Dunaway	1917-1920
Samuel L. Wilkes	1921-1924
Homer Legg	1925 to date.

CLERKS OF THE SUPERIOR COURT.

Abner Tatum	1796-1808
J. Walker	1909-1811
James E. Todd	1812-1814
Thomas Stovall	1814-1815
Peter Lamar	1816-1834
Eliel Lockhart	1834-1837
Joshua Daniel	1837-1839
Henry Murray	1840-1844
Micajah Henley	1844-1848
Alexander Johnston	1848-1880
Thomas B. Hollenshead	1889-1892
Jesse M. Cartledge	1893-1908
William M. Cartledge	1909 to Oct. 1922
Mrs. Lula M. Cartledge	10-1922 - 12-31-1922
W. Tutt Dunaway	1923 to date

SHERIFFS.

James Hughes	1796-1797
Robert Hughes	1798-1799
Henry Jones	1800-1801
Robert Hughes	1802-1803
George Norman	1804-1805
Charles Stovall	1806-1807
John Stovall	1808-1809
William H. Norman	1810-1811
John McDowell	1812-1819
Stephen Stovall	1820-1821
Nathan Bussey	1822-1823
Stephen Stovall	1824-1825
Charles Jennings	1826-1827
Stephen Stovall	1828-1831
John McDowell	1832-1833
Thomas Lyon	1834
Hardy Leverett	1835-1836
Francis F. Fleming	1837-1838
Anthony Samuels	1839-1840
B. F. Tatum	1840-1842
Isaac Willingham	1842-1843
Felix Crosson	1844-1845
William H. McConly	1846-1848
John W. Hamrick	1849-1853
Zack S. Willingham	1854-1855
Thomas D. Cullars	1856-1857

Zack S. Willingham	1858-1871
Michael B. Smalley	1872-1873
Lucius C. Coleman	1873-1874
Zack S. Willingham	1875-1876
R. Toombs Cullars	1877-1878
R. Bruce Lang	1879-1880
George P. Murphy	1881-1882
R. Bruce Lang	1883-1886
R. Toombs Cullars	1877-1888
R. Bruce Lang	1889-1890
R. Toombs Cullars	1891-1900
John C. Moncrief	1901-1902
Robert F. Guillebeau	1903-1906
Gustavus T. Wright	1907-1914
James W. Kelley	1815-1920
Wiley S. Harrison	1921-1924
William J. Hammond	1925 to date

COUNTY SCHOOL COMMISSIONERS.

Thomas T. Wilheit	July 1876 to June 1880
Henry J. Lang	June 1880 to Feb. 1894
Nathan A. Crawford	Feb. 1894 to March 1908
William B. Crawford	Mar. 1908 to 1-1-1916*
T. Leland Perryman	Jan. 1, 1917 to date

*In 1911 the name of officer was changed to County Superintendent of Education.

SENATORS.*

Thomas Murray	1797-1802
Robert Walton	1802-1808
Rem Remsen	1809-1810
John Mitchell Dooly	1811
John Parks	1812
John Mitchell Dooly	1813-1815
Micajah Henley	1816-1818
John Fleming	1819
Micajah Henley	1820-1821
Rem Remsen	1822
William Harper	1823
Rem Remsen	1824-1825
John Frazer	1825-1826
Rem Remsen	1827-1828
Asa Beall	1829
Micajah Henley	1830-1832
William Parks	1833
Peter Lamar	1834-1838
Micajah Henley	1839
Benning B. Moore	1847-1848
Benning B. Moore	1851-1856
Eliel Lockhart	1857-1860
James W. Barksdale	1880-1881
Joseph E. Strother	1888-1889
Adolphus E. Strother	1896-1897
James R. Hogan	1905-1906
Nicholas B. Chenault	1913-1914
James H. Boykin	1921-1922
James H. Boykin	1927-1928
James H. Boykin	1933...

*This list was compiled largely from the Georgia Official & Statistical Register, 1927, prepared by Miss Ruth Blair, State Historian.

REPRESENTATIVES.*

Sith Barksdale	1797-1798
John M. Dooly	1799
Sith Barksdale	1799
Edward Smith	1800
John M. Dooly	1800
James Espey	1801-1802
Phillip Zimmerman	1801-1802
Elijah Clarke, Jr.	1803-1804-Ex.
Elijah Clarke, Jr.	1804
Phillip Zimmerman	1804
Samuel Fleming	1805-1806
John H. Walker	1805-1806
Wheeler Gresham	1807-1809
Samuel Fleming	1807-1809
Samuel Fleming	1810
Gibson Clark	1810
Gibson Clark	1811
Peter Lamar	1811
Robert Ware	1812
Peter Lamar	1812
Micajah Henley	1813
Thomas Lamar	1813
Micajah Henley	1814
Samuel Fleming	1814
Micajah Henley	1815
William Jones	1815
John Fleming	1816
Burwell York	1816
John Fleming	1817
John Lampkin	1817
Thomas W. Murray	1818
William Dowsing, Jr.	1818
Thomas W. Murray	1822
John Fleming	1822
John Fleming	1823
William Jones	1823
Thomas W. Murray	1824-1825
John Fleming	1824-1825
Thomas W. Murray	1826
John McDowell	1826
William Curry	1827
John McDowell	1827
William Curry	1828-1829
Nicholas G. Barksdale	1828-1829
William Curry	1830-1831
Thomas W. Murray	1830-1831
Vincent Lockhart	1832
William Curry	1832
Vincent Lockhart	1833-1835
John Wright	1833-1835
Vincent Lockhart	1836
Charles Jennings	1836

Elial Lockhart	1837-1838
Charles Statham	1837-1838
H. W. Hagerman	1839
Jefferson Winn	1839
H. W. Hagerman	1840-1842
Aaron Hardy	1840-1842
James Jennings	1843
Shadrach Turner	1843
James Jennings	1845
James B. Neil	1847-1850
Micajah Henley	1851-1852
C. R. Strother	1853-1854
J. H. Tatum	1855-1856
John L. Wilkes	1857-1858
James W. Barksdale	1859-1860
J. M. Dill	1861-1862-1863
James W. Barksdale	1863-1864-1865
T. S. Humphries	1865-1866
Platt Madison	1868-1869-1870
Henry J. Lang	1871-1872
William D. Tutt	1873-1874
N. A. Crawford	1875-1876
John L. Wilkes	1877
Josephus E. Strother	1878-1879
Adolphus E. Strother	1880-1881
James W. Barksdale	1882-1883
John Sims	1884-1889
James R. Hogan	1890-1897
George Hays David	1898-1899
James R. Hogan	1900-1901
James H. Boykin	1902-1906
W. C. Powell	1907-1908
H. L. Culberson	1909-1910
T. P. Mitchell	1911-1912
W. H. Estes	1913-1917
John B. Cullars	1917-1918
John B. Cullars	1919-(Died May, 1919)
John M. Bussey	1919-1920
John M. Price	1921-1924
Robert F. Guillebeau	1925-1928
Fred A. McWhorter	1929-(Died Feb.,1929)
James H. Boykin	1929-1930
William F. Sims	1931-1932
Lucius C. Groves	1933-

*This list was compiled largely from the Georgial Official & Statistical Register, 1925, by Miss Ruth Blair, State Historian.

ATTORNEYS-AT-LAW.

*Thomas W. Murray
*John M. Dooly
 Micajah Henley. Died before the War Between the States.
 Hiram Hemphill. Admitted to the Bar in 1829.
 William Harper. Moved to Appalachicola, Fla., before 1851.
*Richard F. Lyon
 Henry J. Land. Born 8-14-1821, died 9-14-1894.
 Chapley R. Strother. Born 2-24-1822, died 9-11-1892.
 Joseph E. Strother. Born 1840, died 6-8-1901.

Benning B. Moore. Moved to Columbia County before the war.
*William D. Tutt
Thomas H. Remsen, Jr., Died 11-19-1915. Aged 38 years.
Wyatt A. Harnesberger. Born 7-15-1871, died 10-11-1916.
Clinton J. Perryman. Judge Superior Court.
Fred A. McWhorter. Born 5-9-1896, died 2-28-1929.
Present Members of the Bar:
Homer Legg. Native of Fannin County, Ga. Ordinary.
David H. Pope. Native of Worth County, Ga., Offical Court Reporter.
Lucius C. Groves. Native of Lincoln County. Member Georgia House of Representatives.
Lincoln Attorneys in other places:
Len B. Guillebeau, Atlanta, Ga.
Walker H. Hogan, Orlando, Fla.
Hatcher H. Hogan, Orlando, Fla.
Fred A. Paradise, Miami, Fla.
Robert W. Ware, Sanford, Fla. Judge Municipal Court.
Garland Watkins, Judge Juvenile Court, Atlanta, Ga.
Moody Paradise, Atlanta, Ga.
*See Biographical Sketches.

MINISTERS OF THE GOSPEL WHO WERE BORN OR RESIDED IN LINCOLN.
John Dunn, Methodist. Deceased.
William Borum, Baptist. Deceased.
Zebulon Howard, Baptist. Deceased.
William L. Hawes, Baptist. Deceased.
P. B. Burgess, Baptist. Deceased.
W. A. Florence, Methodist. Deceased.
J. Lane Ware, Methodist. Deceased.
John Hogan, Baptist. Deceased.
T. A. Nash, Baptist. Deceased.
William H. Green, Baptist. Deceased.
John L. Guillebeau, Baptist. Deceased.
*W. Ambrose Hogan, Baptist. Resident.
Joseph E. LeRoy, Baptist. Resident.
William A. Reid, Baptist. Resident.
Luther R. Hogan, Baptist. Professor at Oglethorpe University.
J. Jacob Guillebeau, Baptist. Resident.
Julius R. Kirkland, Baptist. Resident.
Samuel P. Wright, Methodist. Houston, Texas.
Mark B. Prince, Presbyterian. Charlotte, N.C.
B. Paul Holloway, Congregational Holiness. Resident.
Pat M. Myers, Congregational Holiness. Resident.
*See Biographical Sketches.

PHYSICIANS

John Bentley, b. Lincoln Co., 2-1-1797; d.age 70.
Ezekiel Lamer, b. Lincoln Co., d. 5-24-1846, age 46.
John L. Wilkes, (7-20-1819 - 2-23-1882), b. Anderson Co.SC.
S.G.N. Ferguson (10-10-1821 - 10-19-1887), b. Lincoln Co.
J. Simeon Lane, (3-11-1825 - 10-8-1893), b. Wilkes Co.
Thomas S. Humphries (12-9-1827 - 4-18-1907), b. Anderson Co., SC.
Benjamin F. Bentley (2-1-1828 - 1-5-1892), b. Lincoln Co.

John Sims, b. Lincoln Co.; d. 3-4-1901, age 67.
G. Mitchell Lane (3-2-1838 - 4-12-1911), b. Wilkes Co.
Henry L. Culbertson, b. Laurens Co., SC; d. 11-1-1913, age 63 years.
William H. Groves (12-17-1853 - 11-30-1894), b. Madison Co.
James J. Burch (8-31-1862 - 7-22-1913) b. Elbert Co.
Ben Sheats Bentley (7-12-1864 - 5-3-1899), b. Lincoln Co.
*William B. Crawford (8-22-1866 - 7-10-1927) b. Lincoln Co.
J. Coleman Groves (2-16-1880 - 11-27-1911), b. Lincoln Co.

Those residing in the county at present:

Thomas P. Mitchell, b. Edgefield Co., SC.
Alexander W. Burch, b. Elbert Co.
William H. Estes, b. Lincoln Co.
Ellis R. May, b. Lincoln Co.
Racy H. Smith, b. Washington Co.

Those who were born in but went from Lincoln:

Pelham C. Ward, located in Atlanta.
John B. Hawes (12-18-1867 - 11-13-1904), McBean, GA.
Albert S. Hawes, located in Elberton.
Fritz L. Ware, located in Warrenton.
B. Harvey H. Ward, located in Atlanta.
Delon L. Murray, located in Dexter.
W. Hammond Groves, located in Clearwater, FL.
F. Gilderoy Colvin, located in Ocilla.
Joseph W. Williams, located in Augusta.
*Miss Loree Florence.

*See Biographical Section.

PHARMACISTS

Homer D. Breazeale, b. Anderson Co., SC. Resident
Eunice D. Mims, b. Lincoln Co. Resident
Clark T. Spratlin, b. Wilkes Co. Resident

Those who went from Lincoln:
B. Frank Murray, b. Lincoln Co.; located Rome, Ga. Dead.
James W. Murray, b. Lincoln Co.; located Atlanta, Ga.
R. Elam Guillebeau, b. Lincoln Co.; located Atlanta, Ga.
Robert T. Lewis, Jr., b. Pickens Co., SC; located in Jacksonville, FL.

DENTISTS

Samuel L. Wilkes, b. Lincoln Co. Resident. Retired.
George H. Murray, b. Lincoln Co. Resident.
William H. McLendon, b. Richmond Co. Resident.
Edward E. Parson (12-10-1848 - 12-6-1924) b. Northhampton, Mass.; d. Lincolnton. Itinerant, practicing in Wilkes, Warren, Jefferson, Glascock, & Lincoln counties.

Non-Resident:

C. Julian May. b. Lincoln Co. Located in Washington, Ga.
John A. Sims. b. Lincoln Co. Located in Richland, Ga. Has retired from practice & resides in Augusta
John M. Wilkes, (9-16-1866 - 2-7-1932) b. Lincoln Co. Located in Tampa, FL.

TEACHERS

Lincoln County has a notable record for the number of efficient teachers she has produced. Those who attained special distinction, some who are holding positions of prominence, and others of long experience who are making and who have made teaching their life work are given below:

J.L.M. Curry   Otis Ashmore
James T. Hudson   Peter Zellers
Luther Hogan   Welcome T. Smalley
Miss Minnie T. Perryman   Miss Nannie Ware
Miss Lavilla A. Ward   (*Above in Biog. Section)

Tell H. Wilkinson, son of Thomas P. & Georgia Murray Wilkinson. Elementary education received in schools of Lincoln County. Has a B.S. degree from Mercer University and an A.B. degree from Peabody College. Studied one summer at University of Chicago. Taught one year at Metasville, Ga., one year at Bowman, Ga., two years at Cuthbert, Ga., 21 years at Pelham, Ga., atwo years as principal and 19 years as superintendent of the high school, one year at Prattville, AL, three years in the mathematical department of Miami High School, FL, and for the past three years has been the superintendent of the Cuthbert City Schools.

T. Leland Perryman, son of Edwin R. & Martha (Bouchillon) Perryman. Received his elementary education in Lincolnton High School. Did not attend a literary college, but by hard home study, he obtained a well-rounded education. Graduated with the degree of L.L.B. at the Southern Normal University, Huntingdon, TN. Is gifted in mathematics. Taught in the common schools of Lincoln County, two years at Red Hill, SC, three years at Metasville, GA, six years as principal of Lincolnton High School, and three years as principal of Leah High School, Leah, GA. For the past 16 years he has been County Superintendent of Education of Lincoln County.

Joseph E. Guillebeau, son of Robert F. and Nora (Elam) Guillebeau. Elementary education was received in Lincolnton High School. Was president of the senior class at Mercer University, from which he graduated in 1917 with the degree of A.B. Taught one year in Locust Grove Institute, two years in Gordon Institute, and three years as principal of the Lincolnton High School, during which time it was placed on the class 1 accredited list. In 1923 he was made Vice-President of Gordon Institute, retaining that position till

1929, when he was made President of the institution, which position he now holds.

B. Clark Kinney, son of George B. and Emma (Hudson) Kinney. Received his elementary education in the common schools of Wilkes and Lincoln counties. Graduated at the State Normal School, now the Georgia State Teachers College, with an A.B. degree. Later he received the M.A. degree at the University of Georgia. Paid all of his expenses through college and the University by working at the institutions. He is in his thirtieth year. Taught three years in the G.S.T.C., as Assistant Professor of History and English. During the present year he is Assistant Business Manager of the Dormitories and Dining Halls at the University.

Miss Jennie Hogan, daughter of Simeon W. and Emmie (Hawes) Hogan. Elementary education was received in the common schools of Lincoln County and in Lincolnton High School. Graduated at Bessie Tift College with the A.B. degree. Besides teaching in the common schools of Lincoln County, she has taught in Adel High School, Norman Park Institute, Forsyth High School, Ashburn High School, and Lincolnton High School, all being located in Georgia. At present she is teaching in Rockmart High School, Rockmart, GA.

Miss Belle Hawes, daughter of James N. and Jennie (Marshall) Hawes. Received her elementary education in common schools of Lincoln County. Graduated with the A.B. degree at Bessie Tift College. Beside teaching in the common schools of Lincoln and Columbia counties, she has taught in a number of high schools, among which are Carrollton, Washington, Lincolnton and Tate. Is not teaching at present.

Miss Ruth Sale, daughter of P. Wyatt and Annie (Green) Sale. Elementary education was received in Lincolnton High School, the Washington High School, and St. Joseph's Academy, Washington, GA. Graduate of the State Normal School, now State Teachers College. Spent several summers studying at the University of Georgia. Taught one year at Jesup, GA. For a number of years she has been teaching in the City Schools of Columbus, GA, which is a fine tribute to her ability as a teacher.

Miss Blanche Hogan, daughter of Thomas B. and Lucy (Graves) Hogan. Received her elementary education in the common schools of Lincoln County and at the Tenth District Agricultural School, Granite Hill, GA. Received her A.B. degree at Meridian College, MS. Taught several years at Soperton, GA, three years at Millstead, GA, and for a number of years has been teaching in the City Schools of Clarksburg, W. VA, where she also teaches private classes in Expression. Has spent two summers studying at Columbia University, NY.

Miss Bernice Legg, daughter of Homer and Hattie (Deaver) Legg. Elementary education was received in Lincolnton High School. Graduated at the Georgia State College for Women, at Milledgeville, and then attended the University of Georgia, from which she received the M.A. degree. She is a young lady filling her first position, teaching in the Georgia State College for Women.

Many ladies, before marriage, and a number of gentlemen, before entering other lines of endeavor, made impressive records as teachers, and some of the ladies, since marriage, are still following the profession and are sustaining a deserved reputation in their work. The sons of Lincoln are occupying excellent positions, as superintendents or principals, in various high schools, and other schools of repute, throughout this end and other states, and who, by their conscientious and efficient services, are not only attaining prominence, but are reflecting great credit upon the county. And, besides, there are many others, both male and female, including a number of young teachers, holding good positions in this and other States, who are forging to the front and making namesof which the county is proud.

A NOBLE AND INDUSTRIOUS PEOPLE

Agriculture being the chief industry, the county, from its organization, has been blessed with a fine type of progressive farmers who have kept pace with the scientific development and the improved methods of farming, and who have taken pride in attractive and well-kept premises and in an abundant yield. Some of them, as at present, were large land owners and farmed on an extensive scale. Moreover, they have taken a keen interest in current events, have kept highly informed on political issues, and, throughout the years, have been leaders in county affairs.

Until recent years thriving country stores existed in each section of the county. The merchants, as a rule, were good substantial citizens, worthy of confidence, and outstanding for fair dealings. The stores were popular centers, loyally patronized by the community, and, besides being a great convenience to the people, they insured a prosperous business to the merchants. With the advent of good roads, the automobile and the railroad, they were gradually abandoned till now only a few remain. The mercantile establishments of the county are now largely centered in Lincolnton where, with its high-class and enterprising merchants, a large volume of business is done.

Many sons of Lincoln, seeking larger fields for their business genius, have gone forth and made their mark in various lines of endeavor, among the oldest of whom are James N. Bussey, Sr., William W. Bussey, Porter Fleming, William N. Mercier, A.W. Blanchard, Rem Remsen, Sr., John P. Dill, William W. Ramsey, E.J. Lyon, D.M. Lyon, B.W. Lyon, George W. Wright and T. Newton Hogan, of Augusta, GA; Peyton Hawes, Samuel Hawes, and A.S. Hawes, of Elberton, GA; George C. Hogan, of Washington, GA; Alex. P. Dunaway, of Smithsonia, GA; Caleb R. Ramsey, of Danburg, GA; William L. Hawes and Joe H. Hawes, of Norwood, GA; C.D. (Tony) Anthony, of Memphis, TN; Edgar Spires, of Knoxville, TN; George B. Perryman, of Greenwood, SC; W.O. Sturkey and M.L.B. Sturkey, of McCormick, SC; Alexander Parks, of

Newberry, SC; and Dr. E.H. Parks, formerly of Anderson, SC, and late of Lincolnton, GA. And numbers of younger sons and daughters, too, are scattered throughout this and other states, who are making good and reflecting credit on the county.

The county has a splendid citizenship. The people are intelligent, law-abiding and God-fearing, neighborly, generous and charitable, with a traditional hospitality, for which they are widely noted; and, in the practice of all the virtues which make a noble people, they are not surpassed by those of any other county in the state.

BIOGRAPHICAL SKETCHES

BIOGRAPHICAL SKETCHES

THOMAS P. ASHMORE. Many geniuses live in times congenial to the use of their superior abilities and shine in their full-orbed intellectual splendor; others, equally gifted, live ahead of their times and pass away with their merits obscured by the shadows of an unenlightened sense of appreciation, except to a limited few, and advancing knowledge alone must dispel the clouds and reveal their brilliance. Of this latter class was Thomas P. Ashmore, a genius in mathematics and astronomy, who, had he lived in the present scientific age, would doubtless have been a star of the first magnitude.

Thomas P. Ashmore was born in Lincoln County, April 25, 1812, about two miles southeast of Lincolnton, on the old Ashmore Place. He was the son of Peter and Elizabeth (Howard) Ashmore, whose ancestors on the father's siide came from England to Virginia long before the Revolution. His grandfather, Frederick, moved to Columbia County, Georgia, about 1768. His parents left Columbia County and settled in Lincolnton about the close of the eighteenth century. His father was a skillful carpenter, and built and owned the old Ferguson, or Nash, house in the town of Lincolnton, which was destroyed by fire in January, 1931, and he also built the old Fleming or Blanchard house and the old jail in the same town. in 1809, his father bought and occupied the place southeast of Lincolnton on which Thomas P. was born. In 1819, he built a dwelling on it which is still well preserved.

Educational facilities were meager, the country was new and schools were few. Altogether, Thomas attended school about two years. He had a wonderfully vigorous mind and a burning thirst for knowledge, and through years of hard study he became an accomplished scholar. He read Latin, Greek and French fluently and was one of the best mathematicians in the South. Entirely unaided, except by a few books, he mastered the science of astronomy. About 1837 he began making calculations for an almanac, and in 1848, when Robert Grier died, he began making astronomical calculations for Grier's Almanac, and continued this work until 1882, when his failing health caused him to give it up. Nearly fifty years before it occurred, he predicted the great total eclipse of the sun on May 28, 1900, the track of which passed over his grave; and, while it was not his privilege to witness it, yet there is no doubt that he often visualized and reveled in the sublimity of this awe-inspiring spectacle. His nephew, Otis Ashmore, has this prediction in his possession.

For many years he taught school in South Georgia, in Alabama, in Texas and in his native county. He was a skilled civil engineer, and was the first to lay out the railroad from Augusta to Greenwood, South Carolina. He took his pay in stock of the road, and when the company failed lost all compensation for his services. In 1869 he taught a special class in surveying and higher mathematics on the old Spires place, in Lincoln County, near the Pine Grove settlement, consisting of six young men, Alex B. Sims, T. B. Hollenshead, Alex Parks, Thomas Fortson, Pickens L. Sturkey and Otis Ashmore - all of whom, except the last named, have now joined him in the ranks of the dead. This closed his career as a teacher.

It would not be inaccurate to say of his mental calibre that he possessed a gigantic and constructive intellect, and had he lived in the present era he would have found kindred spirits in Milliken and Einstein.

He was never married, and while very deferential to ladies, he did not seek or enjoy their company. He lived most of his time with relatives in a most simple and unostentatious manner. In fact, he was almost a recluse, seldom appearing in public. He was a great reader and had a remarkable memory. He enjoyed seclusion and deep thinking upon his favorite studies. He cared but little for society or for the conventionalities of mankind, but withal he was one of the gentlest and most harmless of men. It was difficult to engage him in conversation except upon some subject in natural science or astronomy, but once this subject was touched one was charmed with the sparking stream of knowledge that poured from the reservoir of his powerful intellect. He had a most exalted conception of the majesty and sublimity of Nature. Sir Isaac Newton and LaPlace were his great ideals. He had little respect for American mathematics.

He had no patience with sham and hypocrisy in any form. He was not a member of the church, but his religion was very close to Nature. For nearly all of his life he was not in accord with the prevailing religious opinions of the world generally. He had his own opinions about religion, but he did not often discuss them.

He practiced the simple life. He used the greatest simplicity in his food and dress, often approaching to oddness. He never ate desserts. Though using tobacco moderately, he never used intoxicating beverages.

In person he was of medium statue, and weighed about 180 pounds. His head was very large but well proportioned and symmetrical. His eyes were grayish-blue. His hair was dark. He was always clean shaven. By great care of his teeth, he had them all at the age of seventy.

In his later years he lived with his nephew, George Ashmore, near New Hope Church, who at the time occupied the old Cartledge residence, the same in whch Dr. J. L. M. Curry was born. Here on February 4, 1884, he died. His body is buried in the old Ashmore grave-yard, within one hundred feet of the spot where he was born. His grave is unmarked.

His nephew, Honorable Otis Ashmore, of Savannah, who knew him well and could speak with accuracy about his life and character pays him the following tribute: "The remarkable thing about this remarkable man is that he should have mastered so many difficult subjects in the domain of human knowledge by his own efforts, for he was a self-made man. He was a bold and original thinker, and one of the most modest and unobtrusive of men. He loved learning for its own sake only, and he cared nothing for the wealth and honors of the world. He was a child of Nature, and was content to revel alone in the contemplation of her beauties and sublimities. If his mind was eccentric, it dwelt in the lofty atmosphere of grandeur. His life was simple and his fame obscure, but he was a philosopher, and he was profoundly respected by all who knew him. He lived close to the God of Nature, and in his daily dealings with his fellow man, his character and good name were as pure and unsullied as the stars he loved so well. He belonged to that class of men who lived before their times, and while his body was bound to this earth by the clay bonds of his mortality, his spirit soared among the stars."

---

*The author is indebted to Honorable Otis Ashmore, of Savannah, Georgia, for the facts in the above sketch, many of which he quoted literally.

OTIS ASHMORE. Of the noted men reflecting credit upon Lincoln County by a successful and honorable life, Otis Ashmore holds a place in the first ranks. Wherever located whatever his position or attainments, he has always retained a warm attachment for his native county, loved her people, and taken pride in her advancement. Lincoln County is proud of him.

Otis Ashmore, educator and astronomer, was born in Lincoln County, March 6, 1853, about two miles southeast of Lincolnton, on the old Ashmore place. He is the son of Jeremiah and Malinda J. (Wright) Ashmore. His father was the brother of Thomas P. Ashmore, the astronomer, whose ancestry has been given in a preceding sketch of which he is the subject. Jeremiah Ashmore was born at Lincolnton, Ga., September 20, 1808, and died on his plantation near there, May 4, 1883. Malinda J. (Wright) Ashmore was born in Lincoln County, Ga., June 12, 1819, and died in the town of Lincolnton, Ga., October 20, 1901. Both are buried in the old Ashmore grave-yard. The father of Otis Ashmore was a well informed man and a lover opf books, and, while primarily a farmer, he was at different times a school teacher, a merchant and Tax Receiver of Lincoln County. His mother was an estimable woman of high intelligence and strong personality.

The boyhood days of Otis Ashmore were spent on the farm in the slavery time amid the tragic scenes of the War Between the States. His father shared the common ruin that engulfed the fortunes of the people of the South, and from which he could not recover. The opportunities for acquiring an education were poor. Work on the farm by day and study of books by night was largely the rule for the ambitious boy. Of his earlier days as a boy he says: "My childhood years were mingled with the great Civil conflict which desolated the South. Not only was our material fortune swept away but our schools and the opportuniities for obtaining an education were nearly all destroyed. I began school in January, 1881, and for thirteen years I dragged through frequent interruptions, poor teaching, and night study. This was interspersed with work on the farm until I was nearly twenty years old."

In the summer of 1869, he, together with five other boys studied trigonometry and surveying for two or three months under his uncle, Thomas P. Ashmore, in Lincoln County, during which time he learned to survey accurately, and for many years afterward he was a popular surveyor in Lincoln and adjoining counties. "Here again," he says, "my experience with the problems in trigonometry prepared my mind for those problems in spherical trigonometry, calculus and astronomy which I was to encounter later."

In 1873, at the age of twenty, he accepted a small school at Lincolnton, and this began his career as a teacher. The proceeds of this year's work amounted to about $350.00. He was offered the school for the following year, but declined, deciding, instead, to use his earnings to acquire more education.

During the years 1874 and 1875, he attended Gainesville College, which was under the presidency of George C. Looney, a masterful teacher. Here his progress was very rapid. The curiculum of study included a full course in Latin and Greek and a thorough course in plane and spherical geometry, plane and spherical trigonometry, algebra, analytical geometry, and differential and integral calculus.

After two years at Gainesville College, he taught a high grade school for two years in Wilkes County, Ga., about nine miles from Washington, in which he was given a fine opportunity to review his later school work. He next taught two more years (1878-79) at Lincolnton, where his work was highly impressive. For the next four years (1880-84) he taught a large and flourishing school at Harlem, Ga. It was here that the illustrious Alexander H. Stephens made (1881) the commencement address before the largest assembly ever gathered at that place, making it a notable occasion. He then accepted the Presidency of Middle Georgia College, at Jonesboro, Ga., where he remained for two years (1885-86), when he moved to Savannah to teach Science in the High School. After ably filling this position for ten years, he was (1896) elected Superintendent of the Public Schools of Savannah and Chatham County.

Upon assuming his new position, he set himself to the task of reorganizing and improving the entire school system. A number of new and modern school buildings were provided, the teaching force was greatly improved, the course of study was vastly broadened, and the whole system was rendered more efficient. Through the erection of a new High School building in 1908, the departmental plan made it possible to introduce a number of new subjects and greatly to enrich the course of study.

In 1916, after twenty years of strenuous service as Superintendent, he voluntarily resigned his office to spend the remainder of his life in rest and retirement. Since that time he has devoted himself to rest and freedom from the cares and responsibilities inseparable from official life, and to such literary and scientific work that pleases his taste. He lives in Savannah were the best of his life work was spent.

In 1884 he was married to Miss Editha G. Collins, of Harlem, Ga., who is still living. One child was born of this marriage, Frederick Ashmore, who died in 1892 at the age of six years.

In 1889 he took a course in analytical chemistry in the University of Georgia, and for this and other work he received the Master of Arts.

Aside from his duties as a teacher, he was deeply interested in the progress of education. He has been a member of The Georgia Education Association since 1880, and twice elected President of that body. The Association in recognition of his long services to the cause of education in the state presented him with a gold medal, and granted him an honorary and life membership in the Association, which gives him the unique distinction of being the only living member so honored. He was among the first to advocate the establishment of Normal Schools in Georgia for the training of teachers. He is one of the earliest members of the National Education Association, and, in the study of educational matters, he has visited nearly every state in the Union from Maine to California, and has an extensive acquaintance with the prominent educators of the country. He has delivered many lectures on educational subjects both in Georgia and other states, and has contributed many articles to various educational and scientific magazines. He is the author of A Manual of Pronunciation, which is an authority on the subject of English pronunciation, and of several monographs on educational subjects. For more than thirty years he was Secretary of the Georgia Historical Society, and for more than forty years one of its Curators, during which time he contributed many papers and articles to the history of Georgia. He has been a member of the Telfair Academy of Arts and Sciences, of Savannah, for more than forty years, and he has been for many years a member of its Board of Managers.

In length of service and in the extent of acquaintance with the distinguished men of the state, he, perhaps, stands first. He has had a warm personal acquaintance with every State Superintendent of Schools of Georgia since the organization of the Public Schools in the State. He has personally known nearly all of the prominent school men and women of Georgia for the last fifty years, and he numbers his old pupils by the thousands in every walk of life.

While education has been the vocation or life work of Otis Ashmore, his avocation has been astronomy, and, like his distinguished uncle, Thomas P. Ashmore, he was self-taught in this field. He succeeded his Uncle in 1882 as the maker of the astronomical calculations for Grier's Almanac, that familiar and popular publication which hangs by the fireside of nearly every home in the South, and for half a century he has annually made these calculations, a period exceeding that of either of his predecessors. The 1931 edition of that publication contains a sketch of the life of Otis Ashmore, with portrait, and is called the "Ashmore Anniversary Edition," in recognition of his long and efficient service - a service that requires great knowledge and skill in a most difficult subject.

Of his interest in astronomy he says: *"During my life I have visited many of the largest astronomical observatories in this country, and many of the leading astronomers. In addition to the Naval Observatory at Washington, I have visited the observatory of Harvard College, the Chamberlain Observatory at Dever and the famous Lick Obsrvatory in California. At the latter place I met the well known astronomer, E. S. Holden, as well as Prof. E. Barnard who laster discovered the Fifth Satelite of Jupiter. I spent the greater part of one night looking through the largest telescope in the world, with Prof. Barnard at my side."

At the time of the great total eclipse of the sun, May 28, 1900, he was invited by the Naval Observatory to join a party of eminent astronomers from that institution to observe the phenomenon at Barnesville, Ga. He was assigned to the work of observing with a telescope the corona, the shadow bands and the contacts of the moon with the sun. All these were successfully made. He made a large crayon sketch of the corona during totality, the first ever made in eclipse work, and the original of this drawing still hangs in the observatory room in Washington. His report of the eclipse was published by the Naval Observatory.

The eminence he has attained, both as an educator and as an astronomer, is attested by the number of leading biographical publications containing sketches of his life, among which are the following: A CYCLOPEDIA OF GEORGIA; MEN OF MARK IN GEORGIA; LIBRARY OF SOUTHERN LITERATURE; WHO'S WHO IN AMERICA; and Herringshaw's CYCLOPEDIA OF AMERICAN BIOGRAPHY.

Otis Ashmore is a man of striking personality. In statue, he is slightly above medium height with a fine well proportioned physique. His head is large and symmetrical, and his features classical. His eyes are grayish-blue and reflect the mind of the student and scholar. Before the coming of age, his hair was dark and his figure erect. His bearing is dignified but is combined with the charm of refined manners and an affable spirit. In his personal appearance, he is scrupulously neat, and he dresses with becoming taste. One would mark him as a man of distinction anywhere.

He does not use tobacco in any form, and has never indulged in spirituous liquors. His life is singularly free of all vices which would mar its beauty and harmony. In addition to his temperate habits, he has always been systematic in his life.

He is not a member of any church, or of any secret society.

On November 22, 1921, he suffered a partial stroke of paralysis, from which he has partially recovered. However, he cannot write at all with a pen, but does his writing and astgronomical work with his left hand on the typewriter. His general health is good at this time (1931), and he weighs 185 pounds.

In the study of his life, one cannot but be impressed with the grim determination of young Otis Ashmore to overcome the difficulties which challenged his quest for knowledge and the success which rewarded his efforts. Naturally endowed with a vigorous mind, he refused to be conquered by adverse circumstances, but moved by the urge of an impelling ambition, he pressed forward to extract from the rich mines of treasured lore the golden gems which yield only to the earnest seeker. How well he wrought is attested by his abundant life. The plough-boy forged onward till learning, proud of her votary, opened wide her doors and made him a welcome guest in the house of elegance and culture. The country school teacher drank deep of the Pierian spring an her magic waters lifted him to higher positions of honor and made him the intellectual companion of master minds. The curious lad, studying the phenomina of earth, caught a vision of the beauty and grandeur of a sublimer realm, and, penetrating, in maturer years, the cerulean blue, he became friendly with the stars, observed their movements, charted their courses, learned their secrets and gave them to his fellowman, in Genesis accuracy, "for signs, and for serasons, and for days, and years."

Though his scholastic attainments made him famous - an honor he richly deserves, - he is best remembered as a gifted and beloved teacher. Under the influence of his winning personality and refined life, his pupils caught higher visions, dreamed loftier dreams, were ennobled, enriched, inspired, and made resolutions to be worth while In him the backward found a patient helper, the brilliant a wise adviser, and both a master guide. Affection wound her golden strands around the heart of both teacher and pupil and time has not broken or weakened them. While his just distinction is not to be diminished, his real glory is written in the lives of literally thousands of his old pupils who felt the touch of his guiding genius.

*"Record of Otis Ashmore," GRIER'S ALMANAC (1931).

Note: By special request, Mr. Otis Ashmore furnished an outline of his life to the author, which has been used freely in the preparation of this sketch. Being acquainted with him, other facts are given from the author's personal knowledge. The comments on the life of this distinguised man are those of the author.

JAMES HAMILTON BOYKIN. Born in Edgefield County, SC, on 2-17-1879, he is the son of James Fleming Boykin (born in Kershaw County, SC) and Isabelle (Abney) Boykin (born in Edgefield Co., SC) and the grandson of Hamilton Boykin and of Dr. W.M. and Caroline (Blocker) Abney of Edgefield County, SC. His elementary education was received in Edgefield High School, and, while he did not receive collegiate training, his wide reading and close study supplied this deficiency and gave him a broad culture. He is unmarried. In politics, he is a Democrat, fraternally, he is a Mason, and, while he is not affiliated with any church, he has the greatest respect for religion and attends the services and contributes to the support of the local denominations. He is a man of pleasing personality, with features which reveal firmness of character and a strong mentality. He has a sociable disposition, and, in affability and courtesy, he exhibits those fine manners typical of the southern gentleman.

He located in Lincolnton, Georgia, in 1896, after having accpeted the position of publisher of THE LINCOLN HOME JOURNAL, a paper established by the leading Populists of the county, for the work of which he had received experience in his native State, and since then it has been his permanent residence. In 1898 he purchased the paper and changed its name to THE LINCOLN JOURNAL. A few years later, he built the JOURNAL a neat brick home and equipped it with a modern printing plant. He not only ably discussed matters of local interest, for which he kept his columns open to others, but he dealt learnedly with matters of state importance. His clear, terse and brilliant style, with his ability to wield a trenchant pen when occasion demanded, attracted popular attention and made the paper state-wide in influence with a subscription list of around 10,000. In 1924 he sold the JOURNAL and retired from newspaper work.

He is a progressive business man. He has been President of the Farmers State Bank, of Lincolnton, since its organization in 1911, and he takes a deep interest, as well as pride, in its successful operation. For several years he was engaged in the lumber industry with Burton-Pitt Lumber Company, a local firm, of which he was president till he sold his interest in 1931. He is also interested in agriculture, being the owner of a splendid farm in the county.

His popularity is attested by the number and length of the official positions he has filled. He served as Mayor of Lincolnton for five terms, was Chairman of the County Democratic Executive Committee for the years 1904-08, 1914-20 and 1929, was a member of the State Democratic Executive Committee during the years 1923-4 and 1929, was a member of the Georgia House of Representatives during the years 1902-06 and 1929-30, and was a member of the State Senate, from the 29th District, during the years 1921-22, 1927-28, which position he now occupies, having been elected for the years 1933-34.

It was in the realm of state politics that Mr. Boykin was given an opportunity to display his splendid talents. Being a close student of political economy and a clear thinker, he thoroughly analyzed all measures affecting the welfare of Georgia , and, if convinced they were beneficial, he gave them his loyal support, but, if found to be inimical, he fought them with untiring energy. In 1906 he was the author and secured the passage of the "Boykin Bucket Shop Bill," dealing with transaction in futures, which gave him state-wide prominence. Its constitutionality was vigorously attacked in the courts, but its validity was sustained. He was an unyielding advocate of a balanced budget for the state government and ardently opposed excessive appropriations, believing that it was as dangerous for the state as for an individual to allow its expenditures to exceed its income, and, though often overcome by those of shallow views, time has vindicated the correctness of his position, as shown by the staggering deficit in revenue which the present legislature is laboring to raise to meet the state's obligations. While his name is associated with much constructive legislation, that, perhaps, for which he will be best remembered, and which has given him an honored and permanent place in the legislative history of the state, is the "Boykin State Income Tax Law," enacted in 1929, of which he was the author. The constitutionality of this law was warmly attacked in the courts, from every angle, by brilliant lawyers, but, like the Bucket Shop Bill, its validity was upheld. In 1930 he proposed certain changes in the law, making it broader in its scope, which were enacted, and since it has been unchallenged. He was also the author of the legislative Resolution, providing for the selection by the Grand Jury of each county of some competent person of the county to prepare a history of the county by Georgia Day, February 12, 1933, and to deposit it, on that date, in the State's Department of Archives and History to be preserved for the information of future citizens, prospective biographers and historians. His vision and the desirable end in view met with the most favorable general response, and he received much laudatory comment from the press of the state. The resolution makes no provision for compensation, and in many counties the historian's work is purely patriotic, while in others the work is sponsored by various organizations, and, in some instance, by the counties themselves, but in every county it was nobly responded to. The story of Georgia will be greatly enriched by much new, valuable and neglected information in this extensive work, and, as a tribute to the worthy purpose which inspired it, each history will be a lasting monument to Mr. Boykin's memory.

He was President of the Tom Watson Memorial Association, organized for the purpose of raising funds to provide a suitable memorial to Mr. Watson, and he put much time and effort in this undertaking. On December 3, 1932, an impressive marble statue of the distinguished statesman was unveiled on the grounds of the State's Capital, with elaborate ceremonies in which he, as Master, paid a beautiful tribute to the deceased, and in which Ex-Senator Thos. J. Heflin, Senator Walter F. George, and many other notables participated.

During the past few years, Mr. Boykin has not sought political preferment, feeling that the county had generously given him of her honors and that he should retire and not compete with other aspirants. It was with great reluctance that he yielded to the solicitations of his many friends to become a candidate for the present senate, consenting only, after being repeatedly impressed, that now, if ever, the state needed the ablest and most experienced legislators to untangle and relieve her financial condition; and he was elected without opposition.

Mr. Boykin is an upright citizen who has always stood for and advocated that which was for the best interest and progress of the county and encouraged the practice of noble virtues among her people. In the affairs of state, he has fearlessly and conscientiously discharged his duties, and, during his long tenure of office, he ahas kept his escutcheon bright and his name above reproach. His wise and constructive statesmanship has not only reflected great credit upon his county, but upon the entire State.

ELIJAH CLARKE. The subject of this sketch was born in North Carolina, the date of which is indefinite. Knight, in GEORGIA'S LANDMARKS, MEMORIALS AND LEGENDS, states that he was born in Edgecombe County, N.C., in 1733, but on the monument erected to his memory the year is given as 1738. Little is known of his early life, except as reflected by his character and disposition. He was evidently reared amid rugged mountains and vast forest, Nature's school, which developed his firm self-reliant traits and his dominant temperament. He came from Craven County, North Carolina, to Wilkes County, Georgia, in September, 1773, with his wife Hannah (Arrington) Clarke, and one son and three daughters, from the ages of seven to two years, and was granted one hundred fifty acres of land, by the Land Court, on Red Lick Creek. (See record of Land Court on file in the office of the Clerk of the Superior Court of Green County, Ga., a typewritten copy of which is on file in the office of the Ordinary of Wilkes County, Ga.) Mr. James A. LeConte, of Atlanta, Ga., who made the typewritten copy referred to, states that the last record he could find of him in North Carolina was in Anson County, during the Regulator troubles, in 1768-71, as shown by the North Carolina Colonial Records.

While he was unlettered, he was a bold resolute character, hardy and strong, active in body and mind, with a commanding appearance, a natural leader of men. He was one of the greatest, if not the greatest, heroes Georgia contributed to the Revolution. White, in his GEORGIA STATISTICS, says: "When Georgia and South Carolina were evacuated by their governments, and the forces of the United States withdrawn from them, Clarke alone kept the field, and his name spread terror through the whole line of British posts, from the Catawba to the Creek nation. Justice has not been done to this meritorious officer. 'The first action,' says the late General James Jacks in his manuscripts, 'in which the militia were brought to disregard the bayonets of the British, was gained by him over a British detachment in South Carolina, at the Enoree; and yet the credit has been given to Colonel Williams, who left the ground.' It is proper that Georgians should be made familiar with the history of those who, in ˜the times that tried men's souls,' devoted themselves to the cause of freedom, and at the expense of their fortunes and lives, purchased the blessings which we now enjoy."

With actual and threatened incursions by the Indians along the frontier, incited by British agents, and with marauding bands of Tories constantly invading this section of the State, devastating it by fire and sword, inflicting outrages upon the inhabitants and practicing savage cruelties, this Revolutionary period in which he lived required a leader of an iron will and dauntless courage. This was a time that put the patriotism of men to the acid test. White says: "Colonel Clarke's house was pillaged and burnt, and his family ordered to leave the State. Mrs. Clarke with her two daughters departed for the North, with no other means of conveyance than a small pony of little value; but even this was taken away after they had proceeded but a short way on their journey. The love of freedom, a persuasion that Heaven would favor the righteous cause of the Americans, inspired Clarke with hope; and the loss of his property, and the indignities offered to the helpless females of his family, did not in the least intimidate him, but nerved him to renewed action." His hatred of British and Tories became an obsession. Riding night and day with his faithful followers, often spending days in the swamps and woods with scarcely any food, marching mile after mile here, there and yonder, where he could strike an effective blow, there was no personal sacrifice he was unwilling to make in behalf of Freedom.

The history of this famous old soldier, connected with this section, has been given in the chapters devoted to the American Revolution and will not be reiterated in this sketch. His military career began in Georgia, in 1776, when, as captain of a company entrusted with the care of wagons loaded with provisions for the army, he repulsed a body of Indians who attacked him while he was on his way to the confluence of Broad and Savannah Rivers, in which attack he was wounded. He was with General Howe in his expedition against East Florida, and, in a battle with the British, he was severely wounded, which caused him to be away from his command for several weeks. In a stiff encounter with the British under General Ennis, near Musgrove's Mill, on the frontier, he defeated the enemy, killing sixty-three men and taking one hundred sixty prisoners, not without receiving, however, two sabre wounds on the back of the neck. At Blackstock's house, in South Carolina, he took a leading part in defeating the enemy. White quotes a letter from one of the commanders at Blackstock's, in which he says: "At Blackstock's, at the heed of his Wilkes riflemen,m Clarke charged and drove the British light infantry in an open field, where, although he did not command, he might be said to have insured the day, by turning the enemy's right flank. This also, as well as the merits of his compatriot, General Twiggs, who commanded two-thirds of that action, and gained it after General Sumter was wounded, Dr. Ramsay has accorded to South Carolina." He was serving under General Wayne when Savannah was evacuated, and had the satisfaction of seeing Georgia relieved of British control. He had several encounters with the Indians, the principal of which was at Jack's Creek, near the present town of Monroe, Georgia, in which he defeated the Creeks. It is said the battle was named in honor of his son, John Clarke, who was called "Jack" by his friends. He also took a prominent part in adjusting difference with the Indians. He signed the treaty with the Cherokee, at Augusta, in 1783, the treaty with the Creeks in the same year, and the treaty with the Creeks at Galphinton, in 1785. As a reward for his distinguished services in the Revolution, the State of Georgia gave him a commission as a Major-General.

After the war, General Clarke allowed his self-will and independence to involve him in two enterprises which cast a shadow over his illustrious career - his connivance with the French government and his attempt to establish a trans-Oconee republic on the Indian side of the Oconee River, - but which, in the light of surrounding circumstances, show no dishonorable motives, even though they seem to smack of treason. In 1794, when Citizen Genet, the French emissary, attempted to arouse popular hostility towards Spain, he found him a ready sympathizer. The purpose of the French was to take him to Florida and to recover Louisiana from the Spaniards. The Spaniards had been old enemies of Georgia and he hated them with all the ardor of his resolute nature. He knew nothing of diplomacy and never thought of the international complications that such a course might bring about, but, doubtless, believed he would be rendering a patriotic service. He accepted a commission as Major-General in the service of France, according to the historians Stevens and White, with a salary of $10,000 a year. Commissions were turned over to him for subordinate officers. He was recognized throughout the country as the leader in the movement. Inspired by the glory of the adventure and the fame of the leader, men from Georgia and South Carolina thronged to his standard, and especially, from the Huguenot element of the latter State, who wished to show their gratitude for French aid during the Revolution. Their places of gathering were along the Oconee River. The money and means furnished by the French were too limited for such a great undertaking, and, besides, General Clarke was acting arbitrarily, without consulting the Federal authorities. The enterprise met with the emphatic disapproval of President Washington and the National government. Genet's activities were outlawed, neutrality toward Spain was fully maintained, the movement collapsed, and, as a result, Clarke was left flat and humiliated on the banks of the Oconee.

Being thwarted in his purpose and finding himself at the head of a large army, he saw no reason why he should not seize the rich lands of the Creek Indians on the west side of the Oconee and establish a republic. Had not the Indians along the border been a menace to Georgia? Had they not been allies of the British? Had they not made treaties only to brek them? Were they not friendly to Spain? Would they not be a constant source of trouble to the State? Would not Georgia need this territory for her expansion and development? Was not now the accepted time to get rid of a troublesome enemy? No doubt, such thoughts as these filled the mind of the old warrior as he embarked upon this bold enterprise. It can scarcely be believed that he intended to form a permanent government, but that, on the contrary, his purpose was to take complete control of this extensive territory, open it to settlement by the whites, free it of Indian dangers, and then, at the proper time, annex it to Georgia. His dominant disposition led him into the unfortunate error of not counselling with the State authorities and of running counter to the treaty of New York, by which these lands had been allotted to the Indians. In the summer of 1794, he took charge of this area. A written constitution was adopted, he was made civil and military chief, and a Committee of Safety was organized to enact laws. Whether the new government was honored with a name is not known, but it is historically called the trans-Oconee Republic.

This undertaking met with popular disfavor and censure. The State and National governments, acting in concert, forced its abandonment, but not without drastic action. On July 28, 1794, Governor Matthews issued a proclamation in which he condemned this unlawful act of General Clarke, and commanded and required all officers and good citizens of the State "to be diligent in aiding and assisting to apprehend the said Elijah Clarke and his adherents, in order that they may severally be brought to justice." Upon learning of this proclamation, he returned to Wilkes County and surrendered to the authorities, where, after a trial in the court, he was unanimously acquitted. He then returned to his command.

Governor Matthews was authorized by President Washington to call out the militia and, if necessary, Federal troops to deal with the situation, but, in the hope of averting a conflict, he opened negotiations with General Clarke, through Generals Twiggs and Irwin. Clarke was unyielding and the negotiations came to naught. Thereupon State and Federal troops were concentrated along the border for action, many of whom were his old friends and comrades. He had organized his army to fight Indians and Spaniards and not his own people. He saw his error, and, under assurances of immunity for himself and his men, he surrendered his posts and disbanded his followers without the loss of a drop of blood. General Twiggs states in his report that on September 28th the posts were set on fire by State troops, together with fort Defiance, and several other garrisoned places were completely demolished. Thus came to an end the ill-fated trans-Oconee Republic.

Following this event, General Clarke retired to his plantation in the northern part of Lincoln County, on Savannah River, to spend the remainder of his life in peace and quiet amid rustic scenes reminiscent of the school of Nature in which he had received his hardy training. Here he passed away, on December 15th, 1799, and was buried on a knoll overlooking a beautiful valley of the Savannah, to be joined twenty-eight years later by his devoted wife, who had shared the joys and sorrows of his eventful career.

In "Book of Wills, Inventories and Appraisements from 1796 to 1808," pages 28-31, in the office of the Ordinary of Lincoln County, are recorded copies of two memorandums, dated March 3rd and March 5th, 1799, respectively, in which General Clarke specified how he wished his property disposed of in the event he should die without making a will; and also copies of two agreements, entered into on February 4th, 1800, by Hannah Clark, John Clark, J. Walton, Jesse Thompson, Polly Williamson, Gibson Clarke, John Clark, for his brother Elijah Clark, and B. Smith, the heirs and relatives of General Clarke, by which they adopted the memoranda as his last will and testament. As shown by the same book, John Clark, his son, and later Governor of Georgia, acted as executor of the will.

On page 32 of the same book, the following appraisement of his personal estate, by Peyton Wyatt, John Moses and William Clements, appears:

"Thirty-two negroes appraised to	$5318.00
Nine horses $484.30 and 40 head of cattle $199.50	683.80
Eight goats $12. 22 head of sheep $38.50.	50.50
Seventy hogs $107.25. 71 geese $33.00.	140.25
Wagon and gear $50. 4 plows $6.	56.00
6 hoes and 4 axes $9. 5 beds and mattresses $183.75	192.75
Other household furniture $77.75. 1 rifle gun $26.	103.75
1 small sword	40.00
	$6585.05

Some historians state that he was a resident of Wilkes County at his death, but these records settle definitely and finally that he was a resident of Lincoln.

On December 5th, 1801, the Legislature created a county and named it "Clarke" in honor of this old hero. In the City of Athens, the county seat, a beautiful monument has been erected to his memory which bears the following inscription:

"General Elijah Clarke, 1736-1799. Erected by
Elijah Clarke Chapter, Daughters American
Revolution, 1904."

In 1924 an impressive joint marker to his and his wife's memory was unveiled at their graves in this county, with appropriate ceremonies, at which Hon. Horace M. Holden, a former Justice of the Supreme Court of Georgia, was the orator, and on which the following inscription is lettered:

"Erected to the memory of Gen. Elijah Clarke,
Revolutionary soldier and patriot, 1736-1799,
and his wife Hannah Arrington, 1737-1827, by
Elijah Clarke Chapter, Athens, Georgia, and
the Hannah Clarke Chapter, Quitman, Georgia,
Daughters of the American Revolution. 1924."

Of the noted leaders furnished by the State during the Revolutionary period, Elijah Clarke is the most distinguished. Bold, relentless, defiant, a stranger to fear, impelled by this flaming love for Georgia and his burning hatred of her foes, the admiration of his followers and the terror of his enemies, he moved, a rugged knight, sword in hand, striking for Freedom, among the stirring scenes of that tragic era the most colorful figure of them all. Led into error by his dominant nature, he was ever guided by the star of patriotism, and, to turn to the course of right, he needed only to be shown its gleam. His name is permanently enshrined among Georgia's illustrious heroes, and Lincoln County is proud to have his ashes rest within her soil.

WILLIAM BEALL CRAWFORD. William Beall Crawford, M.D., was born in Lincoln County, Ga., on August 22, 1866. His father was Nathan Anderson Crawford (born in Columbia County, Georgia), a prominent and influential citizen of

Lincoln who represented the county in the House of Representatives for the years 1875 and 1876, and who for fourteen years before his death was County School Commissioner, and his mother was Harriet (Beall) Crawford, a cultured lady, who was reared at Dalton, Ga. Dr. Crawford's ancestry on his paternal side may be traced back as far as the year 1127 to the Earl of Crawford, of Kilbirnie, Ayrshire, Scotland, who fought valiantly against the enemies of the Scottish king. A number of the Earl's descendants received royal honors in recognition of distinguished services. Sir John Crawford, of Ayrshire, during the reign of King Charles I of England, was created a Baronet and presented with a Coat-of-Arms bearing the inscription "Sine labe nota," (Distinction without a stain), which became a family heritage. In 1643 another John Crawford emigrated to Virginia, and became the ancestor of the Kilbirnie Crawfords in the United States. Dr. Crawford belonged to a branch of this family which settled in Columbia County, as did William H. Crawford, statesman, Cabinet member, ambassador and jurist, and George W. Crawford, attorney-general, congressman and Governor.

Dr. Crawford received his elementary education in the common schools of the county and at Lincolnton Academy, and his academic education at the University of Georgia, from which he graduated in 1887. He dropped out of college for one year and taught school at Preston, Ga., and among his pupils was Walter F. George, one of the present U. S. Seanators of Georgia. After his graduation, he taught school at Midville and at Bairdstown, Ga. Aspiring to be a physician, he gave up teaching and entered the University of Louisville, Kentucky, at which he graduated in 1892 with the M.D. degree. He immediately located in Augusta, Ga., where he practiced a year or two, when he was engaged by the Plant System of Railroads as a surgeon with headquarters at Waycross, Ga. After a few years he resigned this position, preferring the general practice of medicine, and located permanently at Lincolnton.

The people of his county were not long in recognizing his skill as a physician, and he was soon enjoying a wide and lucrative practice, which increased with the years. He kept up with the progress of medicine and his ability was recognized by the profession, being called upon several times by the District and State Medical Associations to address them on certain branches of the science. In 1920 he organized the Crawford & Breazeale Drug Store, which did a flourishing business, and which is still operating under that name.

On September 18, 1912, he married Miss Sue Tom Hogan of Agnes, Lincoln County, and this union were three children, William B. Jr., Harriet Emily and Rebecca Marshall.

Dr. Crawford took an active interest in politics, and in this field, as in his profession, he enjoyed a wide popularity. For many years he served either as Mayor of Lincolnton, or as a member of council, or as a trustee of the Lincolnton High School, was often Chairman of the County Democractic Executive Coimmittee, was several times a member of the State Democratic Executive Committee, and, in 1904, was a delegate to the National Democratic Convention at St. Louis. In 1908 he succeeded his father as County School Commissioner and filled this office through 1916, during which time much progress was made in the schools under his efficient administration. He was also deeply interested in the progress of his town and county, giving his approval and support to all public enterprises, and in the establishment of educational and religious institutions, he contributed freely for their advancement.

Religiously, he was a Presbyterian, supported the church liberally, and, for many years prior to his death, he was an elder and clerk of the session. Fraternally, he was a Mason, devoted to its order, and bearing the reputation of being more deeply versed in its principles than any one in this section of the state. For a number of years he was Worshipful Master of the Lincolnton Lodge. His enlarged picture hangs in the lodge-room placed there by the local order as an expresssion of the esteem in which he was held by his brethren. Occasionally, he made public addresses on the principles of Masonry, which were remarkable for their clarity of thought and beauty of style.

Dr. Crawford was of a social dispositon and was an admirable conversationalist, with the happy faculty of expressing himself fluently. He enjoyed literature, had a good library, read much, and was blessed with a remarkably retentive memory. He was a man of wide influence, had the confidence of the people, and, by his prominence as a physician and his life as a citizen, he reflected great credit upon his native county.

He passed away on the 10th day of July, 1927, and was buried in Lincolnton cemetery in the presence of a large concourse of friends from Lincoln and adjoining counties.

THOMAS REMSEN CRAWFORD. Thomas Remsen Crawford, the son of Nathan A. and Harriet (Beall) Crawford, was born in Lincoln County, Georgia, on March 29, 1868. He was a brother of Dr. William B. Crawford whose ancestry was given in the preceding sketch of his life. He grew up on the farm, attended the common schools of his community, Lincolnton Academy, and later the University of Georgia, from which he graduated with the A. B. degree in 1888.

Being of a literary trend of mind, he was attracted to journalism as an inviting field. He boarded with the mother of Henry W. Grady while at college and formed a close friendship with the noted editor and orator who, upon his graduation, engaged him as a reporter for the Atlanta Constitution. His intelligence and pleasing personality soon made him socially popular and gave him an intimate acquaintance with the leading people of Atlanta. After serving in this position for about a year, he located in Athens, Ga., where he was editor of the Athens Banner for a short while, after which he returned to his former position with the Constitution. In 1891, while he was with this publication, he delivered a masterly literary address at the closing exercises of Lincolnton Academy before a large and appreciative audience. He remained with the Constitution for serveral years and then accepted a position as reporter for the New York World, where he was given a greater opportunity for the display of his genius. During his reportorial work he also contributed many articles on timely topics to magazines and to the press. In the latter part of 1907, he retired from newspaper work, and on December 26, 1907, he married Miss Winifred Wlliams, of Moncton, Canada, and settled on the large ancestral estate in Columbia County, a part of which he inherited, to engage in farming.

In his new venture Mr. Crawford was not successful, he had been trained to the pen and not to the plow, and, after a few years of heavy losses, he abandoned the enterprise and moved to Lincolnton, where he contributed an occasional article to the press and edited a column in the local paper. In a few years the urge for his old field came upon him, and he returned to New York where he did special work for various dailies and contributed to magazines. During the latter years of his life he spent much time on Ellis Island, the door through which foreign immigrants have to pass before admittance into our country, and there he saw and studied that colorful mass of aliens swarming to our shores and was impressed that thousands of them were undesirables and should not be admitted. He centered his efforts against the open-door policy of the United States, and, through the press and magazines, he rendered invaluable service in arousing public sentiment against the system, which resulted in the passage of Congress of restricted immigration laws. He told the author that he regarded this as the most outstanding work of his life.

While Mr. Crawford interviewed many distinguished persons during his reportorial career, the last one of note was Thomas A. Edison in 1930, a favor the old electrical wizard rarely ever granted, but he had interviewed him thirty years before and knew the proper method of approach. The article containing the a interview was published in the Saturday Evening Post, for which he received $1,000.

Broken in health and suffering from an incurable throat trouble, he returned to Lincolnton the latter part of 1931 and made his home with his brother-in-law Judge S. L. Wilkes. For his own pleasure and that of his friends he edited "A Candle in the Corner" column in the Lincoln Journal till his strength failed. While he enjoyed the companionship of friends, his efforts in conversation gave him pain and aggravated his trouble, causing him to refrain from much social intercourse. Nearly all of his time was spent in the quietude of the home.

Mr. Crawford was a man of impressive personality. He was of medium height, slender and erect, with a well-proportioned head and classical features, and with a grace of dignity and manner that added charme to his appearance. He was highly sociable, was a brilliant and entertaining conversationalist, witty, humorous and a master in storytelling, and he possessed the rare faculty of being able to adapt himself to any company whether ignorant or learned. His culture, wide experience and his interest in people gave him an almost inexhaustible supply of material to suit each occasion. He attracted people and they sought his company.

As a writer his style was terse and clear. He knew what he wanted to say and he said it. There was no fog to becloud his meaning. Nor was there any pedantic display of learning. He knew the art of writing and his articles were interesting and instructive.

At times, Mr. Crawford expressed himself in verse, not so much for publication as to satisfy a dominant sentiment. Some of his poems, however, were published in leading magazines. One of local interest is entitled, "The Village Oak," and refers to the ancient white oak standing in the yard of Mrs. Hugh Green. This was published in the Lincoln Journal in May, 1911. Just a few months prior to his death, the author asked him for one of his poems to be used with a sketch of his life, and he promptly requested that "A Toast to Old Lincoln" be used. Its sentiment is lofty and it is a fitting as a last tribute to his beloved country by this gifted son who was evidently conscious of the approach of the grim Reaper. In obedience to his request it is given below.

"Lincoln, oh, Lincoln, dear land of my birth;
  Rarest and fairest old garden of Earth;
Furrowed and fruitful, oh, blest be your sod
  Which came as a heritage straightway from God.
Nestling so tranquilly 'neath the blue skies,
  Cradled by rivers which croon lullabies -
    Saved from seclusion,
    From alien transfusion,
  Your blood is the purest,
    Your birthright securest -
So, here's to you, Lincoln! I'll call myself blest
When life's dream is over to sleep on your breast!"

He died on June 25, 1932, leaving his widow and two children, Nathan and Thomas William, and he was buried in Lincolnton cemetery in the bosom of the county he loved so well.

JABEZ LAMAR MONROE CURRY. Jabez Lamar Monroe Curry, educator, congressman, Baptist minister and diplomat, was born in what Longstreet was pleased to term the "Dark Corner" of Lincoln County, Georgia, on June 5, 1825, died February 12, 1903, at Asheville, N.C., and was buried in Richmond, Va. He was the son of William and Susan (Winn) Curry, the former a wealthy planter of Lincoln, who, with his family, emigrated to Alabama, in 1838, and settled on a large tract of land he owned in Talledega County, about six miles from the city of the same name; the grandson of Thomas Curry, whose wife was a Miss Walker, and of Richard F. and Prudence (Lamar) Winn; and a great-grandson of John and Dorothy (Wright) Winn and of Basil Lamar. The blood of three nationalities, at least, flowed through his veins; Scotch through the Currys; Welsh, through the Winn; and French through the Lamars. He received his early education in the "old field" schools of Lincoln County, as he himself stated in an address in the old Lincolnton Baptist Church, in 1895, when he paid his last visit to his native county, and he further stated that he well remembered sitting on puncheon benches in school, with his feet swinging down, studying "Webster's Blue Black Speller." His academic education was received at the University of Georgia, from which he graduated, in 1843, and which bestowed the degree of L.L.D. upon him, in 1887. His legal education was received at Harvard University, from which he graduated in 1845. Returning to Talledega, after graduating in law, he entered the law office of Judge Samuel F. Rice, and was admitted to the bar, in 1846. During the same year he joined the Texas Rangers and served with distinction for a short while in the Mexican War. On March 4, 1847, he married Ann Alexander, end of the issue of this marriage were two children, Susan Lamar, who married John B. Turpin, and Manly B., who married the daughter of A. O. Bacon, late U. S. Senator from Georgia. His wife having died, he was married, on June 25, 1867, to Marty Wortham, whose father was a wealthy tobacco dealer of Richmond, Va.

Seeing in him a young man of marked ability, the voters of Talledega County elected him to the legislature, in 1847, in 1853, and in 1855, which launched him on his public career. While in this service, he was actively interested in all measures for the advancement of education. In 1856 he was a Buchanan and Breckinridge elector. He was further honored by being elected to congress, in 1857, filling this position till 1861, when he resigned, with other southern members, to cast his fortune with the seceding States. In 1861 he was elected a delegate to the Provisional Confederate Congress at Montgomery, and later he was elected to the first Confederate Congress in Richmond. Two years later he was defeated for re-election. In 1864 he entered the Confederate service as lieutenant colonel of the 5th Alabama Calvary Regiment, with which he served till the close of the war.

He accepted the result of the War Between the States philosophically. The issue had been contested by a resort to arms and the North had won. Though a firm believer in the right of the states to secede, a belief he never renounced, he was not the type of man to harbor hatred or sectional feelings. Like the peerless Lee, with the conflict ended, he turned his energies and magnanimous spirit to the building of the southland as a part of the great united nation; and, like his leader, he believed that could best be done by the training and education of her children. His great soul caught a vision. "It was a vision," says Dr. E. A. Alderman, his biographer, in "Library of Southern Literature," "of many millions of children standing impoverished and untaught amid new duties, new occasions, new needs, appealing to the grown-up strength of their generation to know why they should not have a country to love, an age to serve, a work to do, and training for that work. The vision was life-unconquered, tumultuous, renewing, regenerative young life. The elders had had their day. Here stood undefeated youth asking a chance to live worthily in its world and time." The old order had passed - had passed with a tremendous crash - leaving the young generation bewildered amid its wreckage and in a different and unfamiliar environment. The work of training them, both in mind and heart, for noble service in the new order and in constructive adjustment to changed conditions became his ruling passion.

On December 5, 1865, he accepted the presidency of Howard College, then located at Marion, Ala., where he remained for three years, when he was made a professor in Richmond College, Va., filling at different times the chair of English and the chair of Philosophy, and lecturing for a period on constitutional and international law. He served this college till 1881, when an opportunity came to him to widen his sphere of usefulness throughout the southland in promoting better educational facilities for her youth. George Peabody, of Massachusetts, caught a vision of the stricken South, with her neglected youth, and, rising above sectional prejudice in a beautiful spirit of philanthrophy rarely, if ever, equalled in our land, he donated several of his millions to aid in providing better educational systems within her states. On February 3, 1881, he was made general agent for the Peabody Fund, and he entered enthusiastically into the work for which it had been given. His progress at first was slow, popular prejudices had to be overcome and the people had to be impressed with its merits. At last public opinion was awakened and his efforts met with increasing success. His activities brought national recognition, and, on March 27, 1885, he was honored by being offered the position of Commissioner of the Bureau of Education, but declined to accept it. He did, however, interrupt his work to accept the appointment by President Cleveland, on September 23, 1885 as ambassador to Spain.

In his new role as diplomat, he was very popular at the Spanish court and was held in high esteem by the nobility and the royal house. In his address at Lincolnton, referred to above, he stated that he was in Madrid when Alfonso XIII, the recently deposed king of Spain, was born and had the honor of seeing the unadorned little sovereign within an hour of his birth as he was presented on a platter of gold in the hall of the palace. He resigned this post, August 20, 1888, and returned to the United States to assume his former position as general agent of the Peabody Fund, the office, it is stated, having been kept open for him during his absence.

On October 20, 1890, he was also made general agent for the Slater Fund, a donation by a wealthy New Yorker to advance the education of the negro in the South, especially in normal and industrial training. He favored the education of the negro, as well as of the whites, believing that progress increases as ignorance decreases, and this fund was wisely administered. He was re-elected general agent of the Peabody Fund, in 1894, in 1896, and in 1902. This last named year brought to a close his splendid activities, but he had the satisfaction of seeing a good system of free public schools in each southern state, with new institutions of higher learning established and old ones revived - all sustained by general and local taxation and backed by a healthy, ever-growing educational sentiment. Approximately two and one-half million dollars of this fund were spent in the South under his wise direction and that of the board of trustees, but the good it accomplished is incalculable.

So favorable was the impression Doctor Curry made on the Spanish court while he was ambassador, that a special request was made on the President of the United States, by the royal family, for him to be commissioned to attend the coronation of Alfonso XIII, in May 1902. Graciously complying with the request, President Roosevelt, on April 7, 1902, appointed his ambassador extraordinary to attend the ceremonies. It is said that of the many compliments he received, at home and abroad, he cherished as one of the highest this tribute paid him by the House of Hapsburg. While there he was further honored by being decorated with the Royal Order of Charles III.

He was a Baptist minister of prominence, and, while he did not serve regular pastorates, he took a deep interest in advancing the Kingdom of God. In November, 1865, he was elected president of the State Baptist Convention (Alabama), and in 1871, he received the degree of D.D. from Rochester University, N.Y.

He was a member of the leading historical societies throughout the nation and a member of the American Society for Extension of University Training, the Evangelical Alliance for the United States, the American Colonization Society, the Northwest Literary and Historical Society, and of the Phi Sigma and Phi Beta Kappa college fraternities.

In the midst of his other activities he found time for authorship. He is the author of "Constitutional Government in Spain," "Establishment and Disestablishment in America," "William Ewart Gladstone," "The Southern States of the American Union," and "The Civil History of the Government of the Confederate States, with Some Personal Remiscences." And, besides, he frequently contributed articles to newspapers and magazines.

He was a man of distinguished appearance, who would be noted as a man of mark in any gathering. His frank, open countenance portrayed his noble character and a serene mind that dwelt in the realm of lofty thought. He had the fine manners and the social graces of the southern gentleman of the old school, but, while he possessed the elegance and refinement of the aristocrat, he, like Thomas Jefferson, was first, last and always a democrat, ever laboring for the betterment and elevation of the struggling masses.

Doctor Curry lived a rich and beautiful life. He understood and loved people, knew their longings, their hopes, their needs, and he gave full measure of his splendid talents for their uplift and encouragement. His long and honorable career was one of active devoted service to his fellowman, and from it he experienced the enriching joy that comes from the performance of worthy deeds. He wrought nobly, and his work was glorified by the beautiful Christian spirit that pervaded his activities. It is not surprising that such a man as he was favored with many signal honors: he was prepared in heart and mind and soul to receive them and to wear them worthily.

In recognition of his long and distinguished services as an educator, the Legislature of Alabama, in 1903, designated Doctor Curry as one of the State's noted men whose statue should be placed in National Statuary Hall, Washington City. In 1906 his statue was unveiled, with impressive ceremonies, in that shrine of the Capitol where bronze and marble perpetuate the memories of many of the Nation's illustrious dead.

JOHN DOOLY. John Dooly, Revolutionary patriot, was born in North Carolina, the date of which is unknown. As shown by the records of the Land Court, on file in the office of the clerk of the superior court of Greene County, a typewritten copy of which is on file in the office of the ordinary of Wilkes County, he came from South Carolina to Georgia, October 15, 1773, with his wife, three sons, from one to four years of age, and was granted five hundred acres of land, in what is now Lincoln County, on Savannah River, on which he settled. There is no evidence that he lived in South Carolina for any length of time. It is quite probable that he and Elijah Clarke left their native state about the same time and merely sojourned in South Carolina till plans could be perfected to enter the "Ceded Lands." His home, a log structure, was located between the present residence of Mr. Benj. Fortson and Fortson's Ferry, every vestige of which has gone. Nothing is known of his prior life, but he was a brave, positive and rugged character.

At the beginning of the Revolution, he received a commission as Captain in the Georgia continental brigade. He was patriotic to the core, and against the Indians, on the one hand, and the Tories, on the other, he struck many an effective blow for freedom. The brutal murder of his brother, Captain Thomas Dooly, by the Indians, on July 22, 1776, after he was wounded and captured in a skirmish, near the Oconee River, filled his heart with implacable hatred toward them, and he became a terror to them throughout the State. So determined was he to take vengeance upon the Indians for killing his brother that he planned an attack upon them at Galphinton while negotiations for peace were in progress by the proper authorities. His scheme was discovered and he was placed under arrest. General Elbert was ordered to call a general court-martial for his trial. His request to resign his commission as Captain was granted and that ended the proceeding. But his services as a courageous leader were too valuable for him to be a private. He was soon made a Colonel of militia in Wilkes County, and, cooperating with Generals Clarke and Pickens, he waged a relentless war upon the Tories, which was interspersed with an occasional brush with the Indians. The main features have already been covered in the chapters on the American Revolution.

Colonel Dooly not only fought Tories on the battlefield, but he fought them in the court-house with legal processes. He was appointed attorney for the State to serve at a term of the Superior Court of Wilkes County, held August 25, 1779, probably the first in the county, and, under his vigorous prosecution, nine of them were convicted and sentenced to be hanged for treason. His name was a terror to Tories and he became a marked man.

After Augusta was re-occupied by the enemy, in May, 1780, General Brown, the notorious Tory officer in command, subjected all of the inhabitants of the surrounding territory, who would not take the oath of allegiance to the British crown, to bitter persecutions, through bands of Tories, who applied the torch to their property, imprisoned or hanged or murdered the defenseless males, insulted the helpless women, and committed acts of barbarous cruelty. One of these bands, under Captain Corker, sneaked up to the house of Colonel Dooly, in the dead of night, forced an entrance and brutally murdered him in the presence of his wife and children. Thus passed, through cowardly vengeance, a bold and fearless leader, a pillar of strength to American freedom. He was buried near his home, but time has erased all trace of his resting place.

After the murder, the Tories proceeded to Broad River. Several of them crossed over and went to the cabin of Nancy Hart where they were captured by her and immediately executed by her husband and a band of patriots; those who remained on this side of the river were captured by another body of patriots and brought back to a pond, about three-quarters of a mile from Dooly's home, and hanged to a red oak tree. The place thereafter was called Tory Pond. About twenty years ago, the pond was drained and the land put under cultivation.

On May 15, 1821, the Legislature of Georgia created a county and named it "Dooly" in his honor.

THOMAS DOOLY. Thomas Dooly was born in North Carolina, the date of which is not known, and settled in what is now Lincoln County in 1773. Nothing is known of his early life or of his ancestry. He was a brother of John Dooly, a colonel of militia in Wilkes County, during the Revolutionary War. At the outbreak of the war, he was commissioned as Captain in the Georgia continental brigade. As he was returning from Virginia, with about twenty enlisted men for the continental brigade, he came upon a body of Indians encamped near the Oconee River, in Georgia. Though greatly outnumbered, he determined to advance upon them, but the Indians were on the alert and laid an ambuscade along the path of his approach. On the morning of July 22, 1776, as he was making his way through a canebrake, he was attacked on the front and flank by the enemy who were covered by the cane. The bones in one of his legs above the ankle were broken by an enemy bullet, but indifferent to his sufferings, he continued to encourage his men, and fired twice at the enemy after he was wounded. Seeing that he had fallen, the Indians rushed out to capture him. His junior officer, Lieutenant Cunningham, intent on his own safety, made no effort to remove him from his perilous position, but was among the first to leave the ground. Captain Dooly begged his men not leave him in the hands of the enemy, but fearful for their own lives, they took the course of their lieutenant and left him to his fate, and when last seen, though he could not stand, was trying to defend himself with the butt end of his gun. He and three of his men were captured by the Indians and murdered. Lieutenant Cunningham was afterwards tried for cowardice by a general court-martial, but was acquitted.

JOHN MITCHELL DOOLY. John Mitchell Dooly was the son of Colonel John Dooly, of Revolutionary fame, and, when a mere lad, had the horrifying experience of witnessing the brutal murder of his father by the Tories. Whether he was born in Georgia or North Carolina is uncertain. Some historians state that he was born about the year 1772, in what is now Lincoln County, but that is inaccurate, as the records show that his father did not settle in Georgia till October 15, 1773. It is probable that he was one of the three sons who were brought by their parents to Wilkes County, now Lincoln, at the time of their immigration; however, he may have been born after that date. Like those who have written of him, the author has been unable to learn anything of his early life, where he was educated, when he read law, or when he was admitted to the bar. Doubtless, he received his educational training in the local common schools and from his parents; for, had he attended an institution of higher learning, it would have come to light before now. He read law at Washington, Ga. In "The Bench and Bar of Georgia," by Miller, Judge Garnett Andrews, of that place, says: "I have been told by the old people who knew him when a student with Matthews in this place, that he was a little, swallow, pot-gutted lad, rather than a man, in his appearance...I have heard the judge say that he was so badly clad that he was ashamed to come into town. The office was just out of town." He married Elizabeth Walton, but there is a tradition among some of her relatives that she was a Harris. Miss Nancy Murray, of this county, says that she was Elizabeth Harris, an orphan child, and a niece of Thomas Murray by whom she was reared. The old marriage records of Wilkes County were destroyed by fire, wiping out any information from that source. There was no issue of this marriage. He lived in a large two-story house, with beautiful hand-carved mantels and panel work, which he had erected on his plantation about seven miles northeast of Lincolnton, near Savannah River, and which was called "The White House," a name it bears at present, because it was the first house in Lincoln County to be painted white.

His public career began when he was elected to the General Assembly of Georgia in 1799 and in 1800. On September 2, 1802, he was appointed Solicitor General of the Western Circuit to fill a vacancy, and, on November 22, 1804, he was elected by the Legislature to succeed himself. He represented the county in the State Senate during the years 1811, 1813 and 1815. In 1816 he was elected Judge of the Western Circuit; in 1822 he was elected the first Judge of the Northern Circuit, and in 1825 he was re-elected to that office. These positions cover his official life.

His contemporaries have left the following composite pen-picture of Judge Dooly: *"His stature was about medium size, erect and well-proportioned. He had a large head, with a bold, elevated forehead, heavy eyebrows, prominent nose, a small, compressed mouth, large, vivid, sparkling eyes, with long eyelashes, which, frequently opening and shutting, gave his countenance an expression as if under the influence of an electric battery. His features were of the finest cast. His complexion was florid. His large protruding black eyes indicated to any one who looked into them his extraordinary genius. He had a sharp and discordant voice, but there was a point, a spice, a felicity of expression, in all he said, marked with a conciseness which showed him at once to advantage, and which drew all other tongues into silence when he spoke. He was extremely volatile and social in his disposition, and was much admired for his constant flow of good-humor and pleasantry. The learned and the ignorant, the old and the young, all felt his power to please, and did him honor. He was quick and brilliant in repartee. His wit, keen satire, quick perception, and extraordinary speaking capacity were never surpassed by any one in Georgia. He was as simple and unostentatious in his manners and habits as a little child and was above the aristocratic nonsense of the times in which he lived."

While Judge Dooly had brilliant abilities, he also had serious faults, the most pronounced of which were his fondness for gambling and for intoxicating drink, which he made no pretense of trying to cover, but which, at times, he made the subject of jest. It is said that he could play a better game of poker and drink a stouter glass of ale than almost any of the hardened offenders who received his sentence from the bench. He did not, however, indulge in these habits as freely while he was a judge as he did while practicing law. It is said that he often appeared in court, as a lawyer, in an intoxicated state, but was always able, despite his condition, to conduct his cases in a masterly manner. There is no doubt but that these failings prevented his attaining higher positions of honor.

As an advocate at the bar, he was bold and independent, witty and sarcastic, logical and forcible, vivid and cogent in delivery, and, when provoked by an opponent, he would turn loose upon him a burning, withering charge of sarcasm, yet without guile, in which he was unsurpassed. He rose to the top of his profession, much dreaded as an advocate at the bar by opposing counsel, and enjoyed a wide practice not only in his own circuit, but in the surrounding circuits and in the upper districts of South Carolina. It is said that some of the aristocractic gentlemen of the profession in South Carolina would not notice Dooly, and that he took such great delight in ridiculing them at every opportunity and so successfully that they abandoned the practice in those districts.

As a Judge, he made an enviable record. He was fearless in the discharge of his duty, but he was warm-hearted and often shed the sympathetic tear. His mind was clear and quick, and his deep knowledge of the law gave him a ready grasp of the case on trial, however complicated.

Very few exceptions were taken to his rulings or to his charges to the jury. He was beloved by the young members of the bar for the protecting shield he threw around them when being overpowered by older and merciless opponents. Crowds flocked to his courts with the assurance that, in connection with the trial of cases and pleas of counsel, the proceedings would be enlivened by frequent flashes of his sparkling wit.

He was a member of the Clark party and gave it his warm and whole hearted support. It is said that on one occasion, however, he adroitly secured the support of the Troup followers in the legislature. He was in Milledgeville in the interest of his own campaign for the judgeship. Governor Troup was being criticized by some of his friends for his war-like message to that body then in session, it being referred to as an act of madness. Dooly remarked that if Governor Troup was mad when he wrote that message he wished the same dog would bite him. This got circulated among the Governor's friends, and when the election came on Dooly was an easy winner.

He aspired to higher office, but never rose higher than the judgeship. It is a matter of tradition that his speeches and debates on the stump were remarkable for their brilliance, wit and sarcasm, and it is unfortunate that none of them were preserved for the enjoyment and edification of succeeding generations.

An outstanding virtue possessed by Judge Dooly was his warm charity. His purse was ever open to the poor and needy. He said "that he was early taught, from refusing to give to an unfortunate widow in Savannah, never to let the devil cheat him out of another opportunity of bestowing charity; that he determined to err on the safe side after, and to give something in all cases of doubt."

While Judge Dooly was a singularly gifted lawyer and an able jurist, entitled to a place among the first of the State, his memory has been best perpetuated by the blazing wit with which it is invested. His contemporaries have left a record of well-authenticated incidents which illustrate that wonderful faculty of this unique character.

The most familiar anecdote is that of the tactful and humorous manner in which he avoided a duel with Judge Tait, who had a wooden leg. He and Tait became engaged in a controversy, which grew so bitter that Tait challenged him to settle their differences according to the code duello. Dooly was a man of peace, and not war, and he wanted to avoid an acceptance of the challenge, and, at the same time, not be thought a coward. Seizing upon Tait's wooden leg as an excuse, he replied that, inasmuch as his foe had had the misfortune of losing one of his legs, he did not think they could fight on equal terms, and that from all he had ever heard of his distinguished adversary he believed he would not seek a fight except on equal terms. This answer exasperated Tait, and he sent a hot reply, insinuating that Dooly's refusal to fight was due to cowardice rather than a reluctance to shed the blood of an unfortunate cripple. But Dooly was not to be cornered. He answered, stating that his adversary was mistaken in supposing that he would not meet him on terms of equality, that he would certainly meet him any day, at any place to be agreed upon, and exchange shots with him, if Tait would let him put one of his legs in a bee-gum. Tait was indignant when he saw Dooly was making a farce of the matter, and that it was creating much amusement throughout the State, and he wrote him a blistering letter, stating that he would publish him in the newspaper as a coward. Whereupon Dooly calmly wrote him to go ahead and do so, that he would rather fill a dozen newspapers than one coffin.

During a session of court in Hancock County, two men were before him to be fined for riot. He called for some paper from the clerk on which to write the sentence. The clerk, who was rigidly economical in the use of paper, after much stirring around, handed him a small, dirty piece. The Judge turned it over and over, and then suddenly threw it down contemptuously on the bald head of the clerk and said, "I would not fine a dog on such a piece of paper as that. Go, gentlemen, and sin no more, or I will see to it next time that you are fined upon gilt-edged paper."

At the close of a term of court in one of the counties of his circuit, as he was ready to depart, he came from his room with a very small pillow under his arm, the one that had been on his bed during his stay. Upon being asked by some one what he was going to do with it, he replied, "I am going to plant it in some rich soil, that it may grow larger by next court.

A certain lawyer in Lincoln County was making the race for a seat in the Legislature. When asked by the judge what he thought his chances were for election, he replied that he was fearful of the outcome, as the people were averse to voting for a lawyer. "If that is all, " replied the judge, "I will aid you, for you can get a certificate from me at any time that you are no lawyer."

An impressive hint was given to a landloard who honored him by presenting on the table, at each meal, during a term of court, a half-grown hog in the shape of a baked stuffed pig. Each meal he remained uninjured, neither fork pierced him nor knife cut him. Upon being asked if he would take some of the pig, he replied that he was certainly a well-grown pig, and was much larger and in better shape than any of his fattening hogs. He called the sheriff to him after the last meal, and ordered him to discharge the pig on his own recognizance, to be and appear at the next term of the court, with the thanks of the court for his prompt and faithful atendance.

While Judge Dooly was stopping at the McCombs hotel, in Milledgeville, on one occasion, an egotistical young man made himself conspicious by complaining the country was disgraced by the election of such a man as Adams for president over such a man as Crawford; that even Jackson, with all his shortcomings, was more desirable than the successful candidate; and that the country would face ruin and dishonor, in his deliberate judgment, under the administration of Adams. During this time, Judge Dooly was sitting before the fire with his head drooped on the back of his chair, attentively listening. Lifting up his head and looking at the complainer, he said, "Young man, does Mr. Adams know that you are opposed to him?" "No, sir," was the reply, "I wish he did know how little I thought of him." "Then," said Dooly, with twinkling eyes and cutting tone, "suppose I write on to let Mr. Adams know that you are dissatisfied with his election. Perhaps he will resign." Completely unhorsed, and withering under the stinging taunt, the young politician made his exit amid the roar of laughter of the assembled guests.

Reference has been made in this sketch to Judge Dooly's making jests of his failings. This anecdote is illustrative of his fondness for gambling. At the close of one of his courts in Wilkes County, he had retired to rest, but, being disturbed by the noise of a faro-table in an adjoining room, he got up, dressed and went in and told the players that he had tried legal methods to break them and failed, and now he was going to use another plan. He joined the game and before the night was over had broken the bank. Upon being twitted the next day by some of his friends for his inconsistency, he explained that the had fully made up his mind to end this vicious practice in the county, but having failed to do so by juries, he had decided to do it in person.

Now one illustrating his fondness for drink. During a protracted trial of a criminal case in Hancock County, he noticed one of the lawyers constantly drinking from a suspicious looking little pitcher which sat on the table before him. Becoming suddenly thirsty, he asked the sheriff to bring him a drink of water. Going to the pail, which sat in a corner, he brought him a glass of his contents. On its being presented, the Judge shook his head, and, in a manner understood by all, requested a drink out of the pitcher from which the lawyer drank. The sheriff immediately complied with his request. Having tasted it copiously, for it was apple brandy, he smacked his lips approvingly and said, "Mr. Sheriff, that is decidedly the best water I have drunk since I have been in this village, and hereafter, when the court calls for water, I want you to get it from that same spring."

It is regrettable that this wonderfully gifted man was subject to the influence of two demoralizing habits; for, otherwise, he, doubtless, would have been an eminent leader in the political affairs of the State. Governor Gilmer, in, GEORGIANS, p. 210, states: "His capacity was sufficient for any attainment if it had been properly directed and actively employed. Unfortunately for himself and society, he was, when young, under the influence of idle, drunken, gambling associates . . . He was a lawyer, and would have been the most successful at the Georgia bar if his habits had corresponded with his talents . . . Mr. Forsyth was his only countryman who equalled him in polemic party debate. They were never pitted against each other so that their debating powers could be compared."

Judge Dooly died on May 26, 1827, and was buried on his plantation in Lincoln County, about fifty yards from his home. His grave is unmarked. (*Pen-picture was made from descriptions of Judge Dooly by his contemporaries, as found in THE BENCH & BAR OF GEORGIA, by Stephen F. Miller).

BEN HILL DUNAWAY was born in Lincoln County, Georgia, July 1, 1875, and is the son of John L. and Lucinda (Parks) Dunaway. His education was received in the public schools of the county and at John Gibson Institute, Bowman, Georgia. On May 25, 1904, he was married to Miss Mildred Sims, of Leverett, Lincoln County, Georgia, and of this union are two children, Lucile and Marjorie (now Mrs. T.R. Powell of Lincolnton). After teaching school several years in the county, he devoted his attention to his large farming interests, in connection with which he operated a general mercantile business, and was one of the outstanding farmers and merchants of the county. In 1916 he was honored by the electorate with the position of Ordinary of Lincoln County, which he filled creditably for one term, declining to offer for re-election. On May 15, 1923, he was appointed Superintendent of the Georgia State Prison Farm, at Milledgeville, which position he now holds, though he retains his citizenship in his native county, in whose progress he takes great interest. Politically, he is a Democrat; fraternally, he is a Knight of Pythias, a Mason and a Shriner; and religiously, he is a Baptist.

Judge Dunaway is a fine specimen of manhood, erect with a splendid bearing, and being six feet four inches tall and weighing slightly more than 300 pounds. He is very sociable and amiable in his disposition, blended with a fine courtesy, which makes him a magnetic and agreeable associate. His friends are legion throughout the State.

The State was fortunate in selecting him for his present position. Being a practical and experienced farmer, the farm as a whole has been greatly improved and the infertile and worn lands have been built up to a high state of productivity under his supervision, and its affairs have been conducted justly, intelligently and economically under his administration. And he is admirably suited by temperament and character for this office. While firm in requiring obedience to the rules and regulations of the institution, he is a man of a tender heart and broad sympathies, and he deals with its inmates as human beings with sensibilities and soul-longings and uses his influence to reclaim them for society. They look upon him as their friend, and, in response to his kindly treatment, they, with few exceptions, are too honorable to violate the rules. It is, indeed, a credit to the State to have such a practical, intelligent, just and humane man at the head of this penal institution.

DR. LOREE FLORENCE, the daughter of W. Thomas and Lessie (Wellmaker) Florence, was born in Lincoln County, Ga., about six miles west of Lincolnton. Her elementary education was received in the public schools of Lincoln and in Washington, Ga., High School, and her academic training was received at Shorter College, Rome, Ga., from which she graduated with the A.B. degree in 1915. Aspiring to be a physician, she took a two year pre-medical course at the University of Georgia, after which she entered the State Medical College in Augusta, Ga. She graduated from this institution, after taking the required four year course, with the degree of Doctor of Medicine in 1926 with the distinction of being the first woman graduate of the college and the first woman in the state to receive an M.D. degree.

Upon finishing her course at the State Medical College she did post-graduate work in Woman's College in Philadelphia, after which she acted as intern at Bellevue Hospital, New York. She was next engaged as physician at Smith College, North Hampton, Mass., were she remained one year, after which she taught one year at the State Medical College, her Alma Mater. She is now connected with Grassland Hospital, in Valhalla, New York.

Dr. Florence is a young woman of rare charm and of pleasing personality. Cultured both classically and in the science of medicine, she is advancing rapidly in her profession and is destined to occupy an eminent place among the physicians of our country.

JAMES ROBERT HOGAN, the son of Rev. John and Priscilla (Ware) Hogan, was born in Lincoln County, 9-24-1850. He grew up on the farm and received his educational training in the common schools of his community. The financial ruin of the South, following the War Between The States, which all of her people experienced, no doubt, prevented his college training, as it did thousands of other young men of that era, but he possessed a strong mentality and was blessed with a high degree of practical and common sense. On September 22, 1869, he united with New Hope Baptist Church, which was served by his father, and on November 17, 1877, he was ordained as a deacon, which office he filled till his death. On December 19, 1869, he married Miss Mollie R. Hawes, of Lincoln County, and of this union were seven children -- Luther Rice, J. Mercer, Nancy Jane, now Mrs. R.L. Colvin, Emma, now Mrs. J.Z. Colvin, Graves and Patrick H. After his first wife's death, he married her sister, Miss Emma J. Hawes, and, after her death, he married another sister, Miss Lula M. Hawes. Upon his first marriage, he settled on his farm, within a mile of where he was reared, and made it his home for life. From time to time he extended his operations till he became one of the leading and most successful planters of the county.

Mr. Hogan was an enthusiast on the subject of education and gave liberally to that cause, both of his time and of his money. For a number of years he was chairman of the board of eduation of Lincoln County, a member of the board of trustees of the Tenth Congressional District A&M School, and a member of the board of trustees of the State Normal School at Athens, in all of which bodies he was noted for his liberal and progressive ideas.

Not only was he interested in education, but he took an active interest in political affairs. With the formation of the Populist party, he became the recognized leader in his county and was elected as the candidate of that party to the Georgia House of Representatives from 1890 through 1897, where he served with distinction. In 1898 he was the Populist candidate for Governor and made a creditable race. The Populist and Democratic parties in the county having fused, he was again elected to the House on the fusion ticket for the years 1900-01. In 1905-06 he was a member of the State Senate from the 29th Senatorial District, having been elected on the Democraic ticket. In his political career he was distinguished for his broad-minded views and his earnest support of all measures for the progress of the State, and he was popular with and had the confidence of both the Populist and the Democratic members of the legislature.

One of his crowning virtues was his noble charity. Anyone who had suffered misfortune or who was in need found ready and willing aid at his hands. He was known throughout the county foir his philanthropy and his love of the poor, and it is said that a tramp hungry was never turned from his door.

Mr. Hogan died on September 16, 1916, and was buried in the cemetery at New Hope Baptist Church.

WILLIAM AMBROSE HOGAN, Baptist minister, stands among the foremost of the brilliant luminaries whose lives, characters and works have shed luster on Lincoln County, and he holds first place, Judge Dooly not excepted, in giving prominence to his county throughout the State. When one mentions in other sections of Georgia that he is from Lincoln, he is often met with the response, "Oh yes, that is the home of Am Hogan." The light of others, with few exceptions, is reflected from different settings; his is a radiance shining from his native heath.

He was born February 1, 1869, about six miles southeast of Lincolnton, near New Hope Church. His father was Rev. John Hogan, of sturdy Irish lineage, a prominent Baptist minister of the county, whose ancestors came from North Carolina just prior to, or immediately following, the Revolution and settled in Wilkes County. His mother was Priscilla (Ware) Hogan, a devout Christian lady, a descendant of the noted Ware family, and a relative of Nicholas Ware, U.S. Senator, for whom Ware County was named. He was reared on a farm and received his elementary education in the common schools of the neighborhood. At the age of eleven, he united with New Hope Baptist Church, which his father was serving as pastor. When he was fifteen he entered Mercer University, at which he graduated, in 1887, with the A.B. degree, and by which he was awarded the degree of D.D. in 1909. In 1898 he attended the Southern Baptist Theological Seminary, at Louisville, Kentucky. Following his graduation at Mercer, he taught in the public schools of his community for fifteen years--a number at Liberty Hill School of his community and several at Lincolnton--during which he made an enviable reputation as a masterful teacher and attracted many boys and girls from other sections of the county to be prepared for college.

On November 26, 1891, he was married to Miss Minnie F. Davis, of Greensboro, Ga., who has been an ideal help-meet in his work. On this union are four children--Ada Ruth, Georgia Katharine, now Mrs. W.G. Robertson, Wayne A., and Mary Rachael, now Mrs. C.V. Bentley.

It was the earnest hope and prayer of his devoted father that his gifted son would follow him into the ministry, and it must have been one of the happiest days of his life when he assisted in ordaining him to that service in December, 1895, at New Hope. With his preparation, both of mind and heart, he was destined to become an outstanding leader in that calling. Due to failing health his father retired from the active ministry in 1896, and he was called to two of his churches --New Hope and Rehoboth--which he has served continuously for 36 years. Later he was called by Danburg, which he has served for 33 years, by Double Branches, which he has served 29 years, and by Lincolnton, which he has served 26 years. He also served Hephzibah, Sharon, Greenwood and Goshen from 7 to 11 years each. So popular is he as a minister that, combining afternoon services, he has often served from 5 to 8 churches at the same time. Early in his ministry he gave up teaching, as much as he loved it, to devote his energies to his increasing pastoral duties. In recent years he resigned several of his charges and now serves only Lincolnton, New Hope, Double Branches, Danburg and Rehoboth. He believes that God should be honored not only with beautiful lives, but with attractive houses of worship. During his ministry, New Hope and Rehoboth have erected imposing wooden buildings and Lincolnton an elegant brick structure. In 1920 he sold his home and farm near New Hope and purchased a residence in Lincolnton, near his church, where he and his family now reside.

Some years ago his churches granted him a three months vacation in order that he might visit the Holy Land and other foreign countries. His description of his travels are wonderfully interesting.

Dr. Hogan never preaches without preparation. In the language of another, "he prepares himself prayerfully and thoroughly and takes beaten oil to the sanctuary and feeds and enlightens the people who throng to hear him."* Modernism has made no innovations on his faith. He believes the Bible and preaches the Word. As a pulpit orator, it is doubtful that he has a peer in the State. He speaks fluently and earnestly, and his gestures, contenance and voice harmonize perfectly with the thought expressed. His messages are live, vibrant, gripping, fittingly illustrated to drive home their main points, and his congregations are thrilled, moved, inspired, by their eloquent appeal. It is the privilege of few men to be so wonderfully endowed with such gifts of speech. It is said that the late Senator Watson, nationally famous orator as he was, envied his voice. A high tribute from one whose eloquence swayed thousands. In 1910 he preached the baccalaureate sermon for Mercer University, in 1912 for Shorter College, and in 1925 the annual sermon before the Georgia Baptist Convention at Savannah, in each of which his audience was held in enraptured attention by his thrilling eloquence, and each of which received laudatory comment in the secular and the religious press of the State. He is besieged each year with requests to preach commencement sermons and to make literary addresses, and the school or college, securing his services, is fortunate, knowing that he will deliver a masterpiece and draw a packed house.

He has received deserved recognition from his denomination. He has been a Trustee of Mercer University since 1905, and Moderator of the Georgia Baptist

Association since 1908. In 1913 he was vice-President of the Georgia Baptist Convention, and, in 1928, was vice-President of the Southern Baptist Convention. He is among the leading Baptist ministers of the South and is worthy of any honor bestowed upon him.

Not only is he a distinguished man, but he has a distinguished appearance. He is slightly below medium in stature, heavy-set and erect, with well-formed features, brilliant black eyes and a prominent forehead, which, in earlier days, was crowned with cold black hair, and he is scrupulously neat in dress, goes clean-shaved and has an easy dignity which graces his bearing. His attractions of person are emphasized by his genial disposition, his pleasant conversation, his friendly greetings, his words of good cheer and his radiant optimism. One feels brighter by having been in his presence. It would be more accurate to describe him as a man of magnetic personality.

Dr. Hogan has never resided elsewhere than in Lincoln. He has had many attractive calls from other churches in villages and cities, but he has chosen to dwell among his own people to whom he is bound by ties of kinship and of deep affection. He, no doubt, would have done great work in other places, but no other people would have loved him more. So firmly is he rooted in this field and in the hearts of the people that it is impossible to think of him apart from the county. His ministry has been abundantly fruitful. Thousands have been uplifted by his Gospel messages, and he has experienced the joy of leading large numbers into the Kingdom of God. And his light shineth afar. While he is far past the meridian of life, his bouyant health gives promise of many golden years yet in the vineyard of the Lord. He loves his county, and in all matters affecting her welfare his influence is on the side of progress, social betterment and civic righteousness. His unselfish service, his consecrated ministry, his ideal citizenship, has been and is a blessing to Lincoln, regardless of creed, and she takes a genuine pride in claiming him as her own.

Dr. Hogan died in Washington (Ga.) Hospital on March 28, 1938, and was buried in the cemetary at New Hope Church, Lincoln County, on March 30, 1938, at 11:00 a.m. It is estimated that several thousand people attended the funeral.

*Baptist Biography - Graham, p. 198.

LUTHER RICE HOGAN. Luther Rice Hogan, educator and Baptist minister, the son of James R. and Mollie R. (Hawes) Hogan, was born in Lincoln, County, Ga., six miles southeast of Lincolnton, on February 16, 1873. His elementary education was received at Liberty Hill School of his community, and his academic training was received at Mercer University, from which he graduated with the A.B. degree in 1894. On June 25, 1919, he married Miss Lila S. Fuller, of Edgefield, S.C., and of this union are two children, Lillie Rebekah and Luther Rice, Jr.

He chose teaching as his life work, and his ability and efficiency have called him into many positions of prominence during a long and successful career in that profession. His first position was Superintendent of Sisson (Ga.) School, Wilkes County, after which he was Superintendent of Lithonia (Ga.) High School and then Vice-president of Locust Grove Institute. He was next called to teach Bible, Psychology and Philosophy at Bessie Tift College, and since then he has been a professor in those branches at Shorter College and at Ottawa University, Kan., Dean of Meridian College, Miss., which conferred the honorary degree of D. D. upon him in 1920, and a professor at Union University, Tenn. He is now professor of Education at Oglethorpe College, but he has recently been elected Dean of Cox College, College Park, Ga.

Besides his distinction as an educator, he is a Baptist minister of prominence, having served as pastor of churches in connection with his position in college work. Among the churches he has served as supply pastor at First Baptist of Forysth, Ga., of Rome, Ga., of Ottawa, Kan., of Jackson, Tenn., and of Shreveport, La. He is frequently called upon by the leading Baptist ministers of the state to fill their pulpits. He has a profound knowledge of the Scriptures, and his messages are fraught with stimulating thoughts pleasingly delivered.

He is a student, and, at different periods in his professional life, he has taken time to pursue his studies in high institutions of learning, having spent two years at the University of Chicago, one year at Columbia University and six months at Union Theological Seminary, and in addition, having traveled and studied for several months in Europe. He is a gentleman of broad culture, an oranament to his profession and one of the leading educators of the state.

Professor Hogan's home is in Atlanta, but he has farming interests in Lincoln. He loves his native county, is proud of her people, both of the past and of the present, and he feels a deep interest in her progress.

JAMES THOMAS HUDSON. James Thomas Hudson was born in Elbert County, Georgia, May 19, 1860, and died January 14, 1929. He was the son of James M. and Sarah (Wilkins) Hudson, the former being a Baptist minister. In early manhood he located in Lincoln County and made it his residence for life. His education was received in the public schools of Wilkes and Lincoln Counties. He never had the advantage of collegiate training, but he had a bright mind, and, during his last years at school, he had the privilege of being taught by Otis Ashmore and other teachers of prominence. He had a good educational foundation, and this was built upon by private study and wide reading. He was well-informed, had a keen sense of humor, and, except for an impediment in his speech, would have been a brilliant conversationalist. In 1890 he married Miss Theodosia C. Crook of Wilkes County, who preceded him in death by six months. Of the issue of this marriage were several sons and daughters.

During the 80's he was connected with the Lincolnton News, the first newspaper established in the county, and his writings indicated a literary trend of mind. After a few years he gave up this work and engaged in teaching school in this and Wilkes County. Upon his marriage, he located on his farm near Graves Mountain and engaged in both teaching and farming till the latter years of his life. In 1925 he served as Clerk of the Court of Ordinary of Lincoln County, after which he retired to his farm where he spent the remainder of his years.

In the midst of his other duties, he found time to devote to writing. While he contributed articles of local interest to the county paper under the non de plume of "Hoosier," his main efforts were in the realm of poetry. He wrote a number of beautiful poems, some of which were accepted by leading magazines. Most of them dealt with melancholy themes, reflecting a mind given to much thought on the future state of existence. He was fond of mythology and the classics, and, in much of his writings, expressions and illustrations are used from that ancient source. He will be best remembered as Lincoln's poet. His son kindly furnished one of his unpublished poems entitled, "The Vale of Rest," to be used with this sketch.

"Oft times the soul, tired with strife,
  From fitful turmoil seeks surcease,
And from the battle-fields of life
  Turns recreant and sues for peace.

Like Noah's dove, it seeks afar
  From Mt. Ararat's towering crest,
Some quiet spot, 'yond cliff and scar,
  Some peaceful quiet Vale of Rest.

In that fair nook - that calm retreat,
  It lives apart. From chains of creeds,
It loosens then the fettered feet,
  That long have groped. The lover needs
The loving sympathy that binds
  The noblest souls that long have wrought.
It likes to dwell with kindred minds,
  Sequestered in this Vale of Thought.

For what is Fame? A meteor's flash
  Athwart a storm-cast horizon,
A moment flickers, then 'twill dash
  Into a bleak oblivion.
'Tis but the clamor that proclaims,
  "The man of Nazareth passeth by!"
The mob who greet with loud acclaims
  Will cry tomorrow, "Crucify!"

O restful Vale! O calm abode!
  O Sabbath of the mind and soul!
Here would I lay my heavy load -
  Here from my heart the sorrow roll,
Here I would 'bide far from the strife,
  Nor wish, nor seeks a higher boon
Where from the warring fields of life,
  I'd with my better self commune.

>   Come! Leave, O soul, thy Olivet!
>   Abandon bleak Gethsemane!
>   Thy dream of indolence forget!
>   Not yet the restful Vale for thee!
>   The sun-kissed heights, they beckon thee.
>   Come! Leave the sordid lowly plain!
>   Let none a dastard reckon thee!
>   Gird on, O soul, thy sword again!
>
>   Leave for the bats thy hermit cell,
>   Thy vigils cease, pale anchorite!
>   Come with thy brother man to dwell,
>   With him to strive and nobly fight
>   With sabre thrust or tongue or pen,
>   Nor let thy spirit quail.
>   The night is coming fast and then
>   For thee the Restful Vale."

RALPH WILBUR HUMPHREYS, the son of Dr. Thomas S. & Althea (Hollenshead) Humphreys, was born in Lincolnton, Ga., on March 6, 1884. He was a bright, apt child, and early in life showed a fondness for books. He attended the public schools of the county in which he was always among the leading students. When he was thirteen years of age, he entered the University of Florida, then located at Lake City, from which he graduated five years later in the A.B. course with the first honor. Upon his graduation, he returned to Lincolnton and was appointed the first rural mail carrier in his county, the duties of which he effeciently performed for eight and a half years. This was before the days of the automobile, and the excellent care he gave to "Butler," his faithful horse, which served him throughout this period and was more vigorous at its close than at the beginning, was a matter of general comment.

Aspiring to follow the profession of his father who was a prominent physician, he entered the medical department of Tulane University at New Orleans, in the fall of 1910, and four years later graduated with second honor. After his graduation he remained in New Orleans for two years, serving as intern at Charity Hospital.

A short while before our country entered the World War, England sent out a call for young physicians to enter the Red Cross service. Dr. Humphreys responded to the call and returned to Lincolnton to await orders. On August 4, 1917, he received orders to report to the Commandant of the Army Medical School at Washington City. On August 6, he left Lincolnton for Washington, and during the month sailed to England for active duty in foreign service. After remaining in England a few weeks, he was sent to France, as 1st Lieutenant of the Medical Officers Reserve Corps, to do surgical work behind the trenches with the 16th Division Field Ambulance Corps.

His work called him to perilous positions, where the battle was hottest--at Cambrai, at Villers-Gouslains and at other places--where the air resounded with an almost incessant roar of cannon, patter of machine guns and of bursting shells where almost each evening closed on a scene of awful carnage and of fields drenched in blood; but he sought no easy situation; he went to do his duty as a loyal American and to do it with credit and honor. In the great German drive of March 21, 1918, he lost his hat and clothing by an exploding shell, but sustained no personal injury. One of his comrades, an English officer, in writing of him, stated: "I recall with what unconcern and fine spirit he would take up his work in the dangerous places. He did it so quietly in such a matter of fact way we scarcely thought of the consistent heroism of his life. He seemed to represent the fine ideals for which your country stands." In recognition of his faithful and valiant services, he was promoted to a captaincy.

On October 18, 1918, during one of the last battles of the war, the improvised hospital in which he was stationed was struck by a gas shell and he received some of its poisonous fumes. At first he did not think his condition was serious, and he continued in the discharge of his duties. When he became conscious of his condition, he started to Yorkshire, England, where he had friends, but was not able to proceed further than Le Harve, France, where he was placed in a hospital and treated by two of the most eminent specialists in that country. He seemed to improve and the chances for his recovery looked very favorable, but the gas had done its deadly work. In a short while he began to decline, and on the morning of November 1, 1918, his spirit took its flight while he was peacefully sleeping. He was laid to rest with due military honors by the Americans on the cemetery at St. Marie, at Le Havre, in the section set apart for the Allied soldiers.

Captain Humphreys was a member of Lincolnton Presbyterian Church, of which he was a deacon for a number of years prior to his death, and he not only loyally supported it, but took a leading part in its various Christian activities. He showed his faith by his works, and lived a clean, upright life. Upon learning of his death, a gold star was hung on the wall of the church as a tribute to his supreme sacrifice, and on Sunday, January 19, 1919, appropriate memorial exercises in his honor were held in the packed church under the direction of that Christian lady, Miss Natalie Crawford, of lamented memory, who gave a sketch of his life, from which some of the material for this sketch was gathered.

It is lamentable that one of his talents and of such excellent preparation should have been cut off just as the prospects were roseate for a successful and honorable career in his chosen profession, but his life was not spent in vain. He followed the star of patriotism and died nobly for his land. Hundreds from foreign fields could speak of his skill in repairing their shell-torn bodies, and others who passed on, if it were possible, could praise him for easing their last dying moments by his faithful ministrations. As the people gather each year to honor their dead in St. Marie, may some gentle hand place the lilies of France upon the grave of this gallant young officer who gave his life in the service of humanity.

COLONEL PETER LAMAR. Peter Lamar, the son of Basil Lamar who settled in what is now Lincoln County following the Revolutionary War, was born in what is now Lincoln County, October 1, 1786, and died in Lincolnton, Georgia, February 6, 1847. His grave is in the walled family burial ground, near the center of the town, on his old home place which is now owned by the E. R. Perryman estate. he was a well educated man, though there is apparently no record showing where he received his educational training. He married Miss Sarah Cobb Benning, of Columbia, County, Georgia, a lady of culture who represented two prominent families of the state - the Cobbs and the Bennings, of this union were one son and four daughters.

He was one of the pioneers of Lincolnton; in fact, it may be said that he was the founder of the town. He was a wealthy planter and owned much land in and around where the town is located. He gave the land for the court-house square, on which the Confederate monument now stands, and for the jail, and, when the town was incorporated, he was one of its three first commissioners. In 1823 he gave three acres of land, on which Union Church and the cemetery are located, for educational and religious purposes, and for such other uses as would not interfere with these purposes. He was a faithful member of the Presbyterian Church which he served many years as ruling elder and as clerk of the session. He was public-spirited and took a great interest in the development of the town, but, under prevailing conditions of his day, its progress was slow. His residence, which was one of the old land-marks of Lincolnton, was destroyed by fire in July, 1888.

His popularity throughout the county and his interest in politics called him into public life. In 1811-12 he represented his county in the House of Representatives; from 1816 to 1834, he was Clerk of the Superior Court of Lincoln County; and from 1834 to 1838 he represented the county in the State Senate.

Colonel Lamar, as he was called, belonged to one of the most illustrious families of the state. He was related to Miribeau B. Lamar, the second President of the Republic of Texas, to L.Q.C.Lamar, U.S. Senator from Mississippi and Associate Justice of the Supreme Court of the United States, and to Joseph R. Lamar, Associate Justice of the Supreme Court of Georgia, and later of the U.S. Supreme Court. He was a great uncle of Dr. J.L.M.Curry, educator, statesman, diplomat and Baptist minister, and of Richard F. Lyon, Associate Justice of the Supreme Court of Georgia; and he was the great grandfather of Dr. Lucian Lamar Knight, the noted author and orator and Historian, Emeritus of Georgia.

LAFAYETTE LAMAR. LaFayette Lamar, the son of Peter and Sarah Cobb (Benning) Lamar, was born in Lincolnton, Lincoln County, Ga., in 1818. It is not known where he received his early education, but his parents were wealthy and cultured, and, no doubt, he had excellent advantages. He graduated at the University of Georgia in the early forties, being a college-mate of his kinsman, J.L.M. Curry.

It is said that he was a brilliant and gifted man. On February 18, 1851, he married Miss Mary Ann Dallis, who lived but a short while; on November 4, 1852, he married Miss Mary A. Simmons, who passed away in a few years; and on February 9, 1858, he married Miss Frances Ann Sale, - all of whom were residents of Lincoln County. Of these unions there were no children. After his first marriage, he lived at Goshen, north of Lincolnton, where he farmed successfully on a large scale.

He was a delegate to the Secession Convention at Milledgeville, Ga., in January, 1861, and ardently supported the ordinance. At the outbreak of the War Between the States, he organized a company from his county, the first organized, of which he was captain, and went to the front. At Warrenton, Va., he was taken ill and was placed in a local hospital, at which he died in November, 1881.

His remains were brought back to his county and buried in the Sale-Simmons-Lamar private burying lot, near Goshen, and his tomb bears the following inscription:

"In Memoriam, LaFayette Lamar, Capt. Co. C. 15th Georgia Regiment. In the service of his country, November 17, 1861, aged 43 years. He had the qualities which adorn our nature. At the time of his death he was an officer-bearer in the church of which he was a member. Though his race was short, he did run well. `Blessed are the dead which did in the Lord.'"

He was popular and influential and was slated for congress when the war interfered, and there is little doubt but that he would have sustained the reputation of the Lamars in public life.

RICHARD FRANCIS LYON. Richard Francis Lyon, lawyer and jurist, the son of Thomas and Mary (Winn) Lyon, was born in Lincoln County, Georgia, on September 9, 1817, in the same section in which his first cousin, J.L.M. Curry, was later born. His father was a hardy, substantial farmer of Lincoln, of strong natural intellect, though somewhat eccentric, and his mother, who was a grand daughter of Basil Lamar, was a woman of fine intelligence. His early educational advantages were limited to the "old field schools" of his community. When nearing majority, he left his father's farm and attended for one year Dr. C.P. Beman's famous school, at Midway, in Liberty County, Georgia, and, during that period, under the guidance of that good and masterful teacher, he made rapid progress. Upon leaving Midway, he taught school for one year at Traveller's Rest in Dooly County, where he fell in love with and married one of his pupils, Miss Ruth Knowles, who was his faithful and devoted companion for more than half a century.

Aspiring to be a lawyer, he gave up teaching and studied law in the office of Col. Joseph Henry Lumpkin of Lexington, Ga., who later became Chief Justice of the Supreme Court of Georgia. He was admitted to the bar in 1839, and located at Starkville, in Lee County, Ga., for the practice of his profession. After remaining here a few years, he located at Albany and later at Macon, in each of which places he was associated with eminent lawyers as partners, and in each of which he enjoyed a lucrative practice. He was a rugged, positive character, impatient of criticism or contradiction, impetuous in action, dogmatic in the expression of his opinions, and indefatigable worker, and an uncompromising fighter. Convinced that his client's cause was right, he made it his own and contested every inch of ground like a gladiator. This trait insured him a large clientele, for they knew they would have in him a champion who would fight to the last ditch. While he was not an eloquent or polished orator, he expressed himself clearly and effectively before the court or jury. In the rough and tumble of court-house practice he had few equals in the state. And he was deeply versed in law.

In 1860 he was elected a Justice of the Supreme Court of Georgia, which office he held for a term of six years, the only official position he ever filled, though some years before he had sought congressional honors as a Whig candidate and had come in 105 votes of being elected. His associates on the bench were Joseph Henry Lumpkin, his old preceptor, Linton Stephens and Charles J. Jenkins. his judicial opinions, while not remarkable for elegance of style, were clear, logical and to the point, and were held in high esteem by the members of the bar. He thoroughly analyzed the controlling questions in a case, and, in his discussion of them, he neither strayed nor wandered, leaving no devious ways for the mind to travel before arriving at his meaning. He appreciated the law for its strength and utility, and for that reason, perhaps, his decisions lack the fine finish of those of a jurist who appreciated it for its glory and majesty. His record was that of a strong and able judge.

After leaving the bench, he returned to Macon where he again resumed the practice of law, with different distinguished lawyers, at times, as partners. He was associated with the noted criminal lawyer, John R. Cooper, at the time of his death on the 25th day of April, 1893.

Judge Lyon inherited some of the peculiarities of his father, notably his disposition to refrain from easy and free social intercourse with people and to envelop himself in a cloak of mystery, but those who knew him best state that when drawn out from his reserve, he was vivacious, entertaining, full of good humor, and that he was an agreeable associate. He was, however, a man of marked individuality. *The committee which prepared a sketch of his life for memorial exercises in the Supreme Court, on May 26, 1894, states: "He was affected less by his environment than any man we ever knew. Neither persons nor places nor occupations nor associations had much influence over him. Nature made him as you know him, and art added little to her handiwork; like a huge stone, rough from the quarry in the mountains and hardly touched by the chisel of the sculptor....Elevation of office, however high, did not effect his bearing towards others. He was the same in his intercourse with his fellowmen, whether in or out of office." He loved the country, with its freer and easier life, whose habits and ways he had never relinquished, and he always welcomed the opportunity to escape the conventionalities of city life.

His manner often impressed those who did not know him well that he was self-centered and lacking in sympathy, but when they understood him they found they had misjudged him. He was tender-hearted and was exceedingly generous and charitable to the unfortunate. Moreover, he was a man of fine sense of honor. If, under the impulse of the moment, he was discourteous to or wounded the sensibilities of a brother of the bar he was prompt to make a satisfactory apology. No man was readier to amend a wrong he had done another. One who knew him states that he had seen him, with tears streaming from his eyes, ask forgiveness of one he had wronged.

*93 Georgia Reports, p. 831.

THOMAS WALTON MURRAY. Thomas Walton Murray, legislator, was born in what is now Lincoln County, Georgia, in 1790, and he was the son of David Murray, who came from Prince Edward County, Virginia, and settled in what was then Wilkes County immediately after the Revolutionary War. His education was received at Dr. Moses Waddell's School, at Willington, Abbeville County, South Carolina, - a school noted for its number of students who became famous, including John C. Calhoun, George McDuffie, Hugh Swinton Legare and others. He studied law in the office of George Cook, in Elberton, Georgia. On August 8, 1819, he married Miss Elizabeth Harper, of Lincoln County, and of the issue of this marriage were three children, one son, John Dooly, and two daughters.

At the age of twenty-eight, he entered public life and gained distinction, not so much for his brilliant talents, as for his industry, his independence and his unquestionable honesty. He served in the Georgia House of Representatives from Lincoln, from 1818 through 1822, from 1824 through 1826. and from 1830 through 1831. In 1825 he was Speaker of the House and presided with great dignity and impartiality. In politics he was affiliated with the Clarke party, though he did not always support it. He formed his own opinions after careful deliberation and adhered to them regardless of party. His fine sense of honor lifted him above the petty schemes of designing politicians, and he lent no encouragement to questionable methods for political success. He recognized that integrity could be found among enemies, and he treated them with fairness. In the early forties, he was an unopposed candidate for Congress, but he died before the election.

Little is known of the personal appearance of Mr. Murray. It is recorded that he was five feet eleven inches in stature, and that he had remarkably large features, but beyond that the record is silent.

In recognition of his popularity and high character, Murray County was named for him while he was still living, a signal honor that has come to few men.

MISS MINNIE THADDEUS PERRYMAN. Miss Minnie Thaddeus Perryman, the daughter of Edwin R. and Martha (Bouchillon) Perryman, was born at Bordeaux, Abbeville County, South Carolina, January 22, 1862, where she spent most of her girlhood days and attended the common schools of her community. In 1878 her parents moved to Lincolnton, Ga., where she has since resided. She completed her elementary education under such eminent teachers as Otis Ashmore, W.L.C. Palmer and Rev. T.A. Nash. Her high record as a student and her pleasing manner of meeting and dealing with people impressed a number of parents in and around Lincolnton and she was engaged to teach a private school, which she conducted for a year in a large room of her home. A school building was then erected for her use on the plantation of Mr. Houston Glaze, near the town, and called Independence Academy, in which she taught several years, and which was largely attended by pupils from Lincolnton as well as from the surrounding community. This was the beginning of thirty-three years of service in teaching, during which she taught in a number of rural schools in Lincoln, Wilkes and Columbia Counties, including one year at Bordeau, S.C., and several years at Lincolnton. While teaching in the latter place in 1920, her health gave way and she retired from the work. She is now the oldest living teacher of the county.

She never received full collegiate training, but she did special work at Erskine College, Due West, S.C., and at the State Normal School, Athens, Ga. She was a close student, which largely overcame this disadvantage, and she kept up with all of the improved methods of teaching.

To her teaching was a calling, as sacred as the ministry, and she sought not only to impart to pupils information contained in their books, but to inspire them with noble ideals of life, believing that true education consists in a trained intellect fortified by a Christian character. In that spirit she wrought, and hundreds in the various walks of life, who were her pupils, hold her in loving remembrance for her faithful services. After she retired from teaching, Professor Ashmore paid her this tribute in a letter, "You have done your part, and done it well, and you deserve a rest. May you live long to enjoy the fine reputation and the enduring friendships which you have made in the years gone by."

Her mother died in 1892, leaving several children of immature years, and being the oldest daughter, she took, as far as possible, the place of a mother to them and in looking after the affairs of the home. This responsibility changed some of her cherished plans, but she willingly and lovingly accepted it and made many sacrifices in faithfulness to her trust. She and her brother and sister live at the old home, where for so many years she has ministered with tender care.

Not for herself, but for others has been the principle of her life not only in the home, but in her school work, and her labors have not been in vain. She has experienced the satisfaction of seeing many worthy results of her sacrifices. And now, in the evening of life, her heart is often cheered by messages, letters, visits and occasional gifts from numbers of her old pupils who hold her in deep affection.

ADOLPHUS ERASTUS STROTHER, son of William Francis and Nancy (Griffin) Strother, was born near Amity, in Lincoln County, Ga., March 10, 1844, and died at his home in that county on March 12, 1933. His ancestry may be traced to Alan-Del Strother, Lord of Northcumberland, England, who, during the reign of Edward III, was Sheriff of Northcumberland and Warden of the Scottish border in 1354. William Strother, the son of Alan-Del Strother, emigrated to Virginia, and from him sprung the American branch of the family to which the subject of this sketch belonged. Mr. Strother grew up on the farm and attended the common schools of his community. He was not college trained, but he was a great reader and was well-informed.

In February, 1862, he answered the call of the Confederacy for volunteers and enlisted in Company A, Cutt's Battalion. He was in a number of important battles and served with distinction throughout the conflict. On April 2, 1865, seven days before Lee surrendered, he was taken prisoner in the Battle of Ft. Gregg and was held for some time. He reached home on July 4, 1865.

A short while after his return from the war, he married Miss Eugenia Holliday, and of this union were five children--Clara H., who married Samuel R. Edmunds, Maude O., who married Joseph G. Fanning, William J., J. Sidney, and Josephus A.

Mr. Strother took up farming as his life work, and he was one of the country's most successful planters. He took an active interest in the affairs of his county and state. For a number of years he was a member of the County Board of Education, represented the county in the House during 1880 and 1881, and was senator from the 29th District during 1896 and 1897, filling each position with credit. In 1927 he was elected Messenger of the State Senate and held this place for several terms.

"Uncle Babe," as he was called, was of a happy, genial disposition, a veritable apostle of sunshine. Depressive feelings melted in his presence like the mist before the sun-rise. He was a certain cure for the blues. He was a great talker and an entertainer and at ease in any company. His violin was one of his great assets in which he found genuine enjoyment, and, before age interfered with the smoothness of his bow, he was frequently called upon to play at both private and public entertainments. He was especially fond of young people--liked to be at their gatherings, entered into their amusements, played for their dances, and entertained them with violin and humorous songs. They knew he was their friend and they all loved him. He was a welcome guest wherever he went. Enjoying hospitality himself, he practiced it; his home was always open for the entertainment of his friends. He appeared to get the best out of life himself, and he made a substantial contribution to the happiness of others by filling them with good cheer and in causing them to see the silver lining without the cloud. He was looked upon as "Lincoln's

grand old man," and his memory will be long revered.
"Uncle Babe" was a Mason and a member of Greenwood Baptist Church to which he was faithful. He was buried, with Masonic honors, in the cemetery at Pierce's Chapel, in Wilkes County, by the side of his devoted wife, who had preceded him some years before.

WELCOME TALMADGE SMALLEY was born in Lincoln County, Ga., January 21, 1885, and he is the son of Charles D. and Mary E. (Hogan) Smalley. He received his elementary education at Liberty Hill School, in Lincoln County, and at Locust Grove Institute. After graduating at the latter institution, he entered Mercer University, from which he received the A.B. degree in 1913. After teaching a number of years, he took summer courses at Columbia University, N.Y., from which he received the M.A. degree in 1927. On June 8, 1921, he married Miss Mabel Dickey, of Washington, Ga., and of the issue of this marriage are two children, Allison Kent and Mary June.

Mr. Smalley has made teaching his life work, and his efficiency as a teacher is attested by the number of years he has been retained by the same institutions. From 1913-23 inclusive, with the exception of one year, in France, as Secretary of the Y.M.C.A. and as a member of the Educational Corps of the A.E.F., he taught at Locust Grove Institute, and, from 1923-present, he has been Associate Professor of English at Mercer University.

In his childhood, Mr. Smalley had the misfortune of accidentally sticking a knife in his right eye, which destroyed its sight, but this defect, in later life, never chilled his ambition, nor impeded his quest for knowledge. In his youth he learned that the door of opportunity was ever open to those with rich and well-stored minds founded on Christian virtues, and he set out with firm resolve to make the entrance. He has wrought well. Not only does he hold a position of honor, but he is a cultured gentleman with a character above reproach.

WILLIAM DUNCAN TUTT, son of Benjamin and Mary A. (Fleming) Tutt, was born near Double Branches, in Lincoln County, Ga., on the 19th day of May, 1838, where his boyhood was spent. His elementary education was received in the common schools of Lincoln County. He attended Emory College, at Oxford, Ga., and graduated with the class of 1858. On March 26, 1872, he married Miss Susan Leonora Freeman, the daughter of Major Henry Freeman and _____ (Fleming) Freeman. Of the issue of this marriage were three sons, Lucien W., William Duncan and Carl.

Upon the outbreak of the War Between the States, he enlisted with the Clinch Rifles, of Augusta, Ga., but was shortly transferred to an Alabama regiment and was elected Lieutenant of his company. He was stationed at Pensacola, Fla., for some time and later saw active duty with the Army of the West. He was wounded in the battle of Franklin, Tenn., and he engaged in numerous fights in Ala., Ga., and Miss.

He read law in the office of Judge William M. Reese, of Washington, Ga., and about the year 1875, he moved to

Thomson, Ga., where he began the active practice of law, building up, in a short while, a large and lucrative circuit practice.

While residing in Thomson, he and Thomas E. Watson became engaged in a personal difficulty about a case, in which he received a pistol wound in the hand. He discouraged taking the matter into the courts and the incident was closed. Mr. Watson had a high regard for his ability, and at his death he paid him a beautiful tribute.

Colonel Tutt was not ambitious for public office, though his brilliant intellect and forensic abilities admirably fitted him for legislative halls. He did, however, serve in the Georgia House of Representatives, from Lincoln County, for the years 1873-4, and in the State Senate, from McDuffie County, for the years 1882-3.

In 1884 he removed to Augusta, Ga., where he formed a partnership with Fred T. Lockhart and continued to practice his profession until 1888, when he took up his residence at the old homestead in Lincoln County, devoting his time to the farm, for which he had quite a predelection. Here he remained until the year 1893, when he removed to Elberton, Ga., and resumed the practice of law with his son, William D. Tutt, which he continued until the year 1904, when he returned to his old home to pass his last years in peace amid the familiar scenes of childhood.

In the hey-day of his career he was an orator of acknowledged ability and power and held his own in many a forensic battle with the most gifted speakers of the times. Especially effective were his campaign speeches, and he was called numbers of times to take the stump for his friends, among whom were Alexander H. Stephens, Seaborn Reese and Senator A.O. Bacon. Lucien L. Knight, in his REMINISCENSES OF FAMOUS GEORGIANS, v2, p. 411-412, makes the following reference to him: "Among the eloquent Georgians whose voices still ring in memory above the din of more than three decades, the writer vividly recalls Fleming duBignon and Pope Barrow and W.D. Tutt and Lucius M. Lamar and Robert Falligant. . . But scarcely inferior to duBignon was W.D. Tutt. If less classical he was more vehement; and at times he made the walls tremble. Yet this intense orator, who seemed to have caught some of the sparks from the anvil of Demosthenes, has been content to bury himself in the woods of North Georgia."

On the 7th day of May, 1906, in the very room in which he had first seen the light of day 69 years before, he peacefully fell asleep. He is buried in the church-yard of Pine Grove in Lincoln County.

MISS LAVILLA A. WARD, the daughter of W. Cleveland and Rosa (Hawes) Ward, is a native of Lincoln County. Her elementary education was received in the public schools of her neighborhood, following which she graduated at the State Normal School, at Athens, Ga. Becoming interested in teaching the deaf, dumb, and blind and those of defective speech, she took special training in this work at Northampton, Mass., and at other outstanding schools. She was engaged to teach in the School for the Deaf and Dumb at Cave Springs, Ga., where she spent about ten years, following which she taught a number of years in the School for the Deaf and Dumb at Davenport, Iowa. She attained a wide reputation in her work and was called to a higher position. She is now Assistant-Superintendent of Public Instruction for the Deaf, Dumb, Blind and for Corrective Speech of the State of Wisconsin, with headquarters at Madison, which position she has been holding for the past eight years. Her work is largely supervisory and requires her to travel throughout the state giving lectures and seeing that the schools are being properly conducted.

Miss Ward is a versatile lady, an engaging conversationalist, with easy and polished manners, and is blessed with a sunny disposition. She loves her work and, with her splendid qualifications, she will, doubtless, rise to still higher positions of honor.

MISS NANNIE WARE was born in Lincoln County, Ga., about six miles west of Lincolnton, and is a descendant of an old and prominent family of the county. She is a daughter of the late Robert A. and Mary Long (Zellars) Ware, both of whom lived to a ripe old age. Her early education was received in the ungraded schools of Wilkes and Lincoln Counties. After finishing her work in these schools, she attended the Hawkinsville (Ga) High School for six months, when she entered sophomore class at the Georgia Normal and Industrial College at Milledgeville, now the Georgia State College for Women, where she studied for two years, after which, in the fall of 1895, she entered senior class at LaGrange College and graduated with the A.B. degree the following June.

Since her graduation, with the exception of two years when there was illness in the family, Miss Ware has been engaged in teaching. She taught a number of years in the county schools of Lincoln, Wilkes and Putnam Counties, where she is gratefully remembered for her faithful services. Since changing from this work, she has taught in the high school at Thomson, at Villa Rica, at Senoia and at Lincolnton, in each of which she made an enviable record. At present she is Principal of Avondale Grammar School, Avondale Estates, Ga. She is a conscientious, an efficient and a progressive teacher, devoted to her work and keenly alive to its best methods. In point of service, she is among the oldest teachers of the county, having followed this noble calling for thirty-five years, during which she has inspired hundreds of boys and girls to nobler lives and won an enduring place in their hearts. Lincoln County takes pride in her record.

Miss Ware is a loyal member of the Methodist Church - a church with which her forebears have been prominently connected through a long stretch of years, - takes part in its activities, and exercises much influence for good by her Christian example.

PETER ZELLARS, the son of John and Mary (Florence) Zellars, was born in Wilkes County, Ga., June 29, 1867, while his parents, who were residents of Lincoln, were temporarily residing with relatives of that county. He grew up on the farm and received his elementary education at Lincolnton Academy. His academic training was received at Mercer University, from which he gradated with the A.B. degree in 1886. On November 14, 1889, he married Miss Lucy Nash of Lincolnton, and to this union three children were born - John Thomas, now a Captain of infantry in the U.S. army, Reid Nash, now in New Jersey, and Macie Pete, now Mrs. Burt Paynter of Arkadelphia, Ark.

After his graduation, Mr. Zellars entered upon a long career as a teacher. His first position was at Cartersville, Ga., after which he taught at Excelsior, Lithonia, Lincolnton, John Gibson Institute, Elberton, Commerce, and then again at Lincolnton, in each of which he rendered excellent services and enjoyed a wide popularity. Upon the organization of the Bank of Lincolnton, in 1905, he was elected cashier and filled this place for seven years. In 1913 he accepted the chair of Greek and Latin in Quachita College in Arksdelphia, Ark., where he remained for nineteen years. In addition to his duties in the class-room, he was business manager of Quachita for several years during the administration of President S.Y. Jameson. While he was connected with the college, he took summer courses at Mercer leading to the A.M. degree. From his long connection with the institution and his intimate association with the students, he became affectionately known as "Uncle Pete."

Professor Zellars was one of Lincoln's outstanding teachers whose splendid record reflected credit on his county. He could number his friends by the hundreds among the students whom he had taught, many of whom have made a marked success, and some of whom have occupied and are occupying positions of honor. His long service at Quachita attests his efficiency and the high esteem in which he was held by the officers of the institution.

He was an active member of the Baptist church. For several years he was superintendent of the Sunday school at Lincolnton, and, while he was not an ordained minister, he was often called upon to fill the pulpit by the pastor at Lincolnton and other places. He was a pleasing and enthusiastic speaker, and his sermons were listened to with interest. For a number of years prior to his death, he was teacher of the Men's bible Class of the First Baptist Church at Arkadelphia.

He passed away on November 26, 1932, in Arkadelphia, after an illness of two years, and was buried in that city.

APPENDIX A

GRANTEES UNDER HEAD-RIGHT LAND WARRANTS ISSUED IN WILKES COUNTY TO LANDS NOW IN LINCOLN COUNTY.

1786	Arthur, Martha	200 a. on Soap Cr.
"	Arthur, William	400 a. on Soap Cr.
1787	" "	200 a. on Lloyd's Cr.
1789	Aaron, William	100 a. on Soap Cr.
1794	Blanton, Christopher	200 a. on Gray's Cr.
"	Bussey, Hezekiah	400 a. on Gray's Cr.
1784	Bentley, John	200 a. on Lloyd's Cr.
"	Bussey, Hezekiah	200 a. on Savannah R.
"	Bentley, Jeremiah	200 a. on Mill Cr.
1785	Bentley, John	200 a. on Gray's Cr.
"	Bentley, Jesse	200 a. on Little R.
"	Barnett, Daniel	350 a. on Soap Cr.
1786	Bosworth, Obediah	400 a. on Soap Cr.
1787	Bussey, Hezekiah	200 a. on Gray's Cr.
"	Benson, John	200 a. on Cherokee Cr.
"	Beard, Francis	200 a. on Fishing Cr.
"	Ballard, Joshua	160 a. on Lloyd's Cr.
1788	Bostich, William	200 a. on Morris's Cr.
"	Bohannan, John	283 a. on Little R.
1793	Burnett, John	400 a. on Gray's Cr.
1795	" "	850 a. on Broad R.
1802	Boler, Hanna	200 a. on Little R.
1784	Clarke, Elijah	1325 a. on Savannah R.
"	" "	600 a. on Fishing Cr.
1785	" "	450 a. on Pistol Cr.
1785	" "	600 a. on Fishing Cr.
1786	" "	600 a. on Soap Cr.
"	" "	500 a. on Broad R.
1785	Call, Richard	900 a. on Little R.
"	" "	500 a. on Gray's Cr.
1786	Clay, Jesse	450 a. on Little R.
1790	" "	200 a. on Little R.
1787	Clarke, Elijah	400 a. on Soap Cr.
"	Cunningham, John	300 a. on Mill Cr.
"	" "	200 a. on Soap Cr.
"	Curry, Thomas	200 a. on Gray's Cr.
"	Crutchfield, John	400 a. on Mill Cr.
"	Clancy, George	400 a. on Soap Cr.
"	Carter, Josiah	793 a. on Soap Cr.
"	Call, Richard	1936 a. on Broad R.
"	" "	5900 a. on Gray's Cr.
"	Cook, Mark	490 a. on Gray's Cr.
"	Ceath, James	350 a. on Gray's Cr.
1784	Davis, Absalom	83 a. on Savannah R.
"	" , Augustine	200 a. on Mill Cr.
"	" , Wiley	200 a. on Mill Cr.
"	Dooley, George	600 a. on Mill Cr.
"	" "	650 a. on Savannah R.
1791	" "	400 a. on Soap Cr.

1784	Dean, William	200 a.	on Savannah R.
1785	Douglass, William	200 a.	on Morris's Cr.
1786	" , George	550 a.	on Savannah R.
"	Dunn, Nehemiah	200 a.	on Little R.
1785	Davis, Lewis Coxson	200 a.	on Fishing Cr.
1790	" , Absalom	320 a.	on Mill Cr.
1788	Delaney, William	200 a.	on Mill Cr.
1799	Daltten, Thomas	200 a.	on Soap Cr.
"	Dooley, John (Heirs of)	350 a.	on Savannah R.
1785	Evans, William	200 a.	on Savannah R.
"	" , David	200 a.	on Savannah R.
"	Eades, John Sr.	200 a.	on Broad R.
1784	" , John	50 a.	on Broad R.
1785	" , Mary	150 a.	on Pistol Cr.
1789	Eager, Hugh	200 a.	on Well's Cr.
1784	Finley, James	400 a.	on Broad R.
1787	" , Thomas	420 a.	on Fishing Cr.
1785	Freeman, James	200 a.	on Savannah R.
"	Forrester, Thomas	400 a.	on Soap Cr.
1786	Florence, Thomas	200 a.	on Soap Cr.
1788	Franklin, Philemon	200 a.	on Soap Cr.
1784	Graves, James	400 a.	on Lloyd's Cr.
1786	Graves, Richard	300 a.	on Gray's Cr.
"	Graves, William	450 a.	on Little R.
1789	" "	665 a.	on Cherokee Cr.
"	" "	2291 a.	on Soap Cr.
"	" "	330 a.	on Lloyd's Cr.
"	" "	575 a.	on Gray's Cr.
1790	" "	271 a.	on Lloy's Cr.
1786	Golden, William	240 a.	on Soap Cr.
1788	Guys, Phillip	300 a.	on Soap Cr.
1790	Guise, John	200 a.	on Soap Cr.
1793	" "	200 a.	on Soap Cr.
1791	Gartrell, Francis	188 a.	on Lloyd's Cr.
1797	Graham, Thomas	107 a.	on Morris Cr.
1801	Grice, Phillip	100 a.	on Soap Cr.
1784	Holmes, John	200 a.	on Mill Cr.
1785	Harper, Samuel	200 a.	on Gray's Cr.
1786	" "	250 a.	on Lloy's Cr.
1790	Hammock, John	380 a.	on Lloy's Cr.
1793	Highsmith, Thomas	167 a.	on Soap Cr.
1797	Harnesberger, Stephen	300 a.	on Fishing Cr.
1802	Hughes, James	80 a.	on Savannah R.
1784	Jones, Richard	200 a.	on Savannah R.
1785	" , Phillip	287 a.	on Savannah R.
"	" , Henry	600 a.	on Savannah R.
1792	" "	191 a.	on Soap Cr.
1798	" "	27 a.	on Soap Cr.
1787	" , John	130 a.	on Savannah R.
1801	" , Gabriel	45 a.	on Soap Cr.
1787	Jamison, Robert	200 a.	on Cherokee Cr.
1788	" "	200 a.	on Cherokee Cr.
1787	Jordan, Baxton	200 a.	on Soap Cr.
1784	Kennebrew, Jacob	700 a.	on Lloyd's Cr.
1785	" "	150 a.	on Lloyd's Cr.
1784	Keating, Edward	200 a.	on Savannah R.
1786	Kelly, Hugh	200 a.	on Soap Cr.
1802	Kelly, John	50 a.	on Cherokee Cr.

1787	Kendall, Jeremiah	200 a.	on Little R.
1784	Lamar, Basil	200 a.	on Little R.
"	" "	250 a.	on Pistol Cr.
"	" "	400 a.	on Broad R.
"	" , Zacharia	700 a.	on Broad R.
1785	" "	400 a.	on Broad R.
1784	Laramore, John	300 a.	on Savannah R.
1786	Lessflore, Elenor	200 a.	on Soap Cr.
1790	Langford, John	300 a.	on Savannah R.
1791	Lockhart, Richard	200 a.	on Broad R.
1784	Middleton, John	200 a.	on Savannah R.
1790	" , Robert	130 a.	on Savannah R.
1784	Martin, Jacob	200 a.	on Cherokee Cr.
"	Mosley, Benjamin	600 a.	on Soap Cr.
1785	" , Thomas	200 a.	on Soap Cr.
1788	Mosley, William	200 a.	on Soap Cr.
1784	Moore, Joseph	400 a.	on Savannah R.
"	Moore, William	200 a.	on Savannah R.
1784	Mofett, Thomas	200 a.	on Cherokee Cr.
1786	Murphy, James	300 a.	on Soap Cr.
1786	Manning, Drury	200 a.	on Gray's Cr.
"	Mann, John	200 a.	on Soap Cr.
1787	McKlemuny, James	100 a.	on Soap Cr.
"	McKinney, Travis	200 a.	on Gray's Cr.
1790	Matthews, James	200 a.	on Gray's Cr.
1784	" , Moses	270 a.	on Lloyd's Cr.
1791	Murray, Thomas	110 a.	on Soap Cr.
1784	Nail, Joseph	200 a.	on Savannah R.
"	" , Julius	200 a.	on Savannah R.
"	" , Acquilla	200 a.	on Mill Cr.
1787	" , Julia	200 a.	on Savannah R.
1784	Nowland, William	200 a.	on Soap Cr.
1785	O'Neal, William	200 a.	on Gray's Cr.
1793	" "	9 a.	on Gray's Cr.
1786	Oliver, John	200 a.	on Savannah R.
1789	Odom, Solomon	220 a.	on Gray's Cr.
1784	Parks, Charles	300 a.	on Soap Cr.
"	Partee, Elizabeth	200 a.	on Soap Cr.
1785	Peteet, Richard	341 a.	on Soap Cr.
1786	Pendall, Sarah	400 a.	on Soap Cr.
"	Palmor, Solomon	400 a.	on Morris's Cr.
1794	Pharr, Samuel	385 a.	on Soap Cr.
1784	Ramsey, John	250 a.	on Soap Cr.
1784	Richardson, Walker	350 a.	on Soap Cr.
1788	Ratcliff, Robert	200 a.	on Soap Cr.
1790	" , William	33 a.	on Savannah R.
1791	Roquamore, James	300 a.	on Savannah R.
1783	Scott, Samuel	500 a.	on Savannah R.
1785	Scott, Alexander	300 a.	on Soap Cr.
1784	Smith, William	200 a.	on Cherokee Cr.
1785	" Henry	200 a.	on Cherokee Cr.
1786	" Drew	400 a.	on Soap Cr.
1787	" David	200 a.	on Savannah R.
"	" Peter	420 a.	on Lloyd's Cr.
1791	" Gabriel	100 a.	on Savannah R.
"	" Benajah	356 a.	on Soap Cr.
1795	" Nathaniel	275 a.	on Soap Cr.
1785	Stokes, William	500 a.	on Broad R.

Year	Name	Acres	Location
1787	Slaughter, Samuel	250 a.	on Cherokee Cr.
1788	Seal, Jarvis	200 a.	on Morris Cr.
"	" , Anthony	200 a.	on Morris Cr.
1790	Senders, Robert	55 a.	on Savannah R.
1785	Triplett, William	900 a.	on Savannah R.
1786	" "	1030 a.	on Little R.
"	" "	680 a.	on Lloyd's Cr.
1787	" "	200 a.	on Fishing Cr.
"	" "	600 a.	on Little R.
1786	Troy, John	200 a.	on Soap Cr.
"	Tatom, Abner	350 a.	on Soap Cr.
1791	" John	200 a.	on Fishing Cr.
1794	" Abel	200 a.	on Soap Cr.
1794	" John	250 a.	on Mill Cr.
1786	Talbott, John	1600 a.	on Soap Cr.
1787	" John, Jr.	242 a.	on Soap Cr.
1790	" Thomas	900 a.	on Gray's Cr.
1787	Todd, John	173 a.	on Fishing Cr.
1792	" "	200 a.	on Fishing Cr.
1794	Thompson, Samuel	80 a.	on Fishing Cr.
1792	Tullis, Moses	200 a.	on Soap Cr.
1787	Veasey, William	341 a.	on Soap Cr.
"	" " "	100 a.	on Little R.
1784	Ware, Henry	450 a.	on Savannah R.
1785	" "	250 a.	on Savannah R.
1787	" "	150 a.	on Savannah R.
1765	" Henry, Jr.	200 a.	on Soap Creek
1784	" Nicholas	200 a.	on Little River
"	" Robert	200 a.	on Savannah R.
1786	" "	400 a.	on Savannah R.
1784	Wadsworth, Thomas	200 a.	on Cherokee Cr.
1785	" "	100 a.	on Soap Cr.
"	Wooten, Thomas	200 a.	on Lloyd's Creek
"	Williamson, Micajah	400 a.	on Soap Cr.
"	Wallace, Marjery	200 a.	on Soap Cr.
1789	" William	300 a.	on Savannah R.
1787	Walker, Sanders	350 a.	on Lloyd's Cr.
1795	" Moses	173 a.	on Soap Cr.
1785	Walton, John	300 a.	on Savannah R.
1790	" Newell	327 a.	on Savannah R.
1788	Williams, Susannah and Elizabeth	200 a.	on Mill Cr.
"	Whatley, Michael, Jr.	200 a.	on Savannah R.
"	Williams, Charles	250 a.	on Soap Cr.
1790	Watkins, John	600 a.	on Soap Cr.
1793	" Benjamin	95 a.	on Soap Cr.
1785	Zachery, William	200 a.	on Savannah R.
1799	Zimmerman, Phillip	119 a.	(near Soap Cr.)

Note: As previously stated, many who received these grants did not settle here. There were a number of settlers here at the time Lincoln County was formed whose names do not appear on the above list. Many, no doubt, purchased land from non-settlers, while others may have held grants not listed because of lack of information as to location. At any rate they were outstanding citizens. For the names of other early settlers not listed above, see the list of jurors in the Chapter headed, "The Organization of

Lincoln County." C.J.P.

Note: Dr. Thomas Sandwich, a noted physician of Harrow-on-the-Hill, Scotland, was among the early settlers of Lincoln County.

APPENDIX B

HEAD-RIGHT LAND WARRANTS ISSUED BY THE LAND COURTS OF LINCOLN COUNTY

1796	Andrews, Benjamin	650 acres
"	Bussey, Benjamin	300 "
"	Barton, John	200 "
"	Cox, Haney, or Naney	100 "
"	Fowler, James	737 "
"	Green, William	200 "
"	Kennon, William	550 "
"	Lockhart, Joel	700 "
"	" John	200 "
"	Murray, David	900 "
"	Middleton, John	650 "
"	Stovall, Drury	200 "
"	Smith, Lewis	23
"	Warren, Lot	287 "
"	Ware, James	--- "
1797	Aycock, Richard	300 "
"	Burks, David	300 "
"	Bond, Thomas	200 "
"	Hardy, Jesse	50 "
"	Marshall, James	50 "
"	Russell, Thomas C.	28 "
"	Seal, Anthony	100 "
"	Tatom, Abel & Abner, Ext'rs.	165 "
1798	Bussey, Thomas	100 "
"	Bentley, John	50 "
"	Edwards, John	16 "
"	Murray, Thomas	400 "
"	Moffitt, Thomas	50 "
"	Woolridge, Gibson	100 "
"	Wallace, William	200 "
1802	Boler, Hannah, (Heirs of)	200 "
"	Booth, Abraham	264 "
"	Casey, Roger	100 "
"	Crofford, Claborn	200 "
"	Clark, Edward	275 "
"	Glaze, David	300 "
"	Kennon, William, Sr.	100 "
"	Lockhart, John	122 "
"	Langford, Joseph	100 "
"	Paradise, William	6 "
"	Thompson, Samuel	50 "
1803	Ashmore, Peter	300 "
"	Espey, James	105 "
"	Edmonds, James	200 "

Year	Name	Acres	
1803	Groce, Jared	60	"
"	Hardy, Jesse	100	"
"	Jones, Moses	25	"
"	Lockhart, John	8	"
"	Mays, William	215	"
"	McGill, Thomas	200	"
"	McCord, John	40	"
"	Spires, Hezekiah	115	"
"	Stokes, William	100	"
"	Winn, Richard	500	"
"	" " F.	203	"
"	Wallace, James	50	"
1804	Davis, Samuel	200	"
"	Golden, William	300	"
"	Hardy, John	400	"
"	Jones, Henry	250	"
"	Moss, John	80	"
"	Stovall, Ralph	200	"
1804	Wallace, Robert	50	"
1805	Clark, Edward	70	"
"	Lockhart, Joel	50	"
"	Seaggo, William	900	"
"	Stokes, William	30	"
"	Twitty, George	100	"
"	Walton, Robert, renewal of grant from Wilkes Co. in 1799	300	"
1806	Bates, John	300	"
"	Champ, Richard	300	"
"	Espey, James	82	"
"	Moss, John	75	"
"	Ware, James	300	"
1807	Dooly, John M.	200	"
"	Groce, Sheppard	55	"
"	Paschal, William	50	"
"	Walker, John H.	20	"
1808	Dooly, John M.	800	"
"	Hughes, Robert	50	"
"	Powell, Richard	15	"
"	Smith, James	10	"
"	Smart, Ezekiel	200	"
1809	Gorley, James	25	"
"	Moss, John, Sr.	75	"
"	Walton, John H.	100	"
"	Walton, Benton	100	"
1810	Arrant, William	50	"
"	Bennett, Jacob	200	"
"	Hollman, Edmond	300	"
"	Powell, Richard	300	"
"	Remson, Rem.	150	"
"	Willingham, James	200	"
"	York, John	100	"
1811	Davis, Samuel	152	"
"	Groce, Sheppard	55	"
"	Hollman, Edmond	100	"
"	Matthews, William	---	"
"	Smith, Austin	20	"
"	Zellars, Jacob	40	"
1812	Currey, James	200	"

Year	Name	Amount	
1812	Snow, James P.	200	"
1813	Booth, Alexander	400	"
"	Hughes, Alexander	150	"
"	Henderson, Joseph	200	"
"	Parks, Lewis	550	"
"	Stewart, James	400	"
1814	Curry, Thomas	450	"
1815	Covington, William	300	"
"	Crosson, John	200	"
"	Lee, Andrew	200	"
"	May, John W.	100	"
1816	Fleming, Samuel	200	"
"	Hardy, John	1000	"
"	Hammock, John	15	"
"	Lamar, Peter	100	"
"	Stovall, Stephen	25	"
1817	Ammons, Jacob	100	"
"	Bates, Daniel	240	"
"	Crosson, John	200	"
"	Jordon, John	600	"
"	Lockhart, Joel	250	"
"	Lee, Andrew, Sr.	50	"
"	Hardy, John	150	"
"	Moss, Alexander	500	"
"	Murray, Thomas	250	"
"	Ratliff, Richard	100	"
1817	Ratliff, Samuel	50	"
"	Snow, Delila	200	"
"	Wright, William	200	"
1818	Ammons, Jacob	500	"
"	Brown, Jacob	100	"
"	Bussey, Nathan	1000	"
"	Clark, John	400	"
"	Florence, Thomas	500	"
"	House, Lot	125	"
"	Hawes, Peyton	20	"
"	Jordan, John	960	"
"	Jennings, Thomas	525	"
"	Lee, Andrew	25	"
"	May, James A.	200	"
"	Ratliff, Thomas	125	"
"	Wadsworth, James	500	"
"	Wing, John	100	"
1819	Crosson, John	200	"
"	Dallis, Thomas	100	"
"	Frazer, Samuel	30	"
"	Golden, Allen	100	"
"	May, John W.	200	"
"	McClerney, John	2	"
"	Parker, Zionas	50	"
"	Ratliff, Hezekiah	100	"
"	Wing, John	128	"
1820	Boatwright, James	100	"
"	Kendrick, Sylvanus	100	"
"	Loverett, Matthew	50	"
"	Lee, Andrew	25	"
"	Sibert, John	300	"
1821	Mumford, Robert	400	"

Year	Name	Amount	
1821	Stribbling, Anthony	450	"
"	Quinn, William	400	"
1822	Frazer, Samuel	50	"
"	" John	50	"
"	Hardy, Henry	10	"
"	Holmes, Ichabod	268	"
1823	Bond, Mark	150	"
"	Cullars, Matthew	200	"
"	Florence, David	200	"
"	Lamar, Peter	50	"
"	Lee, Andrew, Jr.	20	"
"	Sibert, Frederick	200	"
"	Wright, William	100	"
"	Walker, Henry G.	100	"
1824	Rhodes, Eusten	100	"
"	Ratliff, Hexekiah	30	"
"	Tatom, Wiley G.	10	"
1825	Cullars, Matthew	25	"
"	Frazier, Arthur	20	"
"	Lockhart, James	30	"
"	Nally, Handly	20	"
"	Welborn, Arthur	100	"
1826	Cullars, Mathew	240	"
1827	Simmons, Sterne	100	"
"	York, David	20	"
1828	Brown, Robert	30	"
1830	Crosson, Felix	200	"
"	Jennings, James	300	"
"	Lockhart, James	50	"
1831	Eady, John	20	"
"	Lamar, Peter	50	"
1832	Lockhart, James	50	"
1834	Henderson, Robert	100	"
"	Hammond, John	100	"
"	Ullum, Francis	200	"
"	Wallace, James	100	"
1835	Walker, Malcom T.	500	"
1836	McGill, Robert	100	"
"	Powell, Francis	255	"
"	Stribbling, Thomas	25	"
"	Trammel, William, Jr.	300	"
1837	Henderson, Robert	200	"
"	Sistrunk, Goshn	50	"
1838	Psalmonds, Thomas L.	50	"
"	Barksdale, Beverly	75	"
1844	Barksdale, Nicholas G.	100	"
"	Hambrick, John W.	100	"
1845	Cartledge, James	100	"
"	Harper, George	50	"
1846	Harper, George	200	"
1847	Garnett, Eli.	50	"
"	Moncrief, James	50	"
1848	Sims, William	50	"
1850	Moss, John D.	150	"
1851	Cutliff, John M.	50	"
1854	Henderson, William	10	"
"	Lyon, Edmund J.	40	"
1855	Henderson, Robert	300	"

1821	Stribbling, Anthony	450	"
"	Quinn, William	400	"
1822	Frazer, Samuel	50	"
"	" John	50	"
"	Hardy, Henry	10	"
"	Holmes, Ichabod	268	"
1823	Bond, Mark	150	"
"	Cullars, Matthew	200	"
"	Florence, David	200	"
"	Lamar, Peter	50	"
"	Lee, Andrew, Jr.	20	"
"	Sibert, Frederick	200	"
"	Wright, William	100	"
"	Walker, Henry G.	100	"
1824	Rhodes, Eusten	100	"
"	Ratliff, Hexekiah	30	"
"	Tatom, Wiley G.	10	"
1825	Cullars, Matthew	25	"
"	Frazier, Arthur	20	"
"	Lockhart, James	30	"
"	Nally, Handly	20	"
"	Welborn, Arthur	100	"
1826	Cullars, Mathew	240	"
1827	Simmons, Sterne	100	"
"	York, David	20	"
1828	Brown, Robert	30	"
1830	Crosson, Felix	200	"
"	Jennings, James	300	"
"	Lockhart, James	50	"
1831	Eady, John	20	"
"	Lamar, Peter	50	"
1832	Lockhart, James	50	"
1834	Henderson, Robert	100	"
"	Hammond, John	100	"
"	Ullum, Francis	200	"
"	Wallace, James	100	"
1835	Walker, Malcom T.	500	"
1836	McGill, Robert	100	"
"	Powell, Francis	255	"
"	Stribbling, Thomas	25	"
"	Trammel, William, Jr.	300	"
1837	Henderson, Robert	200	"
"	Sistrunk, Goshn	50	"
1838	Psalmonds, Thomas L.	50	"
"	Barksdale, Beverly	75	"
1844	Barksdale, Nicholas G.	100	"
"	Hambrick, John W.	100	"
1845	Cartledge, James	100	"
"	Harper, George	50	"
1846	Harper, George	200	"
1847	Garnett, Eli.	50	"
"	Moncrief, James	50	"
1848	Sims, William	50	"
1850	Moss, John D.	150	"
1851	Cutliff, John M.	50	"
1854	Henderson, William	10	"
"	Lyon, Edmund J.	40	"
1855	Henderson, Robert	300	"

*The mames were alphabetically arranged by the author.

Note: This list, in addition to showing many of the early settlers, shows the long period embraced in the settlement of Lincoln County. The pages of the Land Court Records covering the years from 1838 to 1844 are missing. Several names were omitted because they were not legible. For the names of other early settlers, see the list of jurors in the chapter headed, "The Organization of Lincoln County." C.J.P.

INDEX

Aaron, William 145
Abbeville, S.C. 61, 62, 138, 139
Abney, Caroline 104
    Nathan 4
    Dr. W.M. 104
Adams, Rev. H.M. 32-35
Adel High School 95
Agnes, Lincoln Co. 112
Agnes Post Office 69
Agnes Section (Community) 3, 75, 76
Albany, Ga. 19, 137
Albea Family 37
Albea, E. H. 41
    G. E. 40
    T. T. 40
    Thomas 37, 57
    W.H. 57
Alderman, Dr. E. A. 116
Alexander, Ann 116
Alexander, General E. P. 62
Alfonso XIII 117, 118
Allen, Curtis 55
    G. P. 65
    Rev. M.C. 39
    Robert 77
Allendale, S.C. 85
Amer. Colonization Soc. 118
Amer. Soc. for Extension of Univ. Training 118
Amity Community 18, 69, 74-77, 140
Amity Post Office 69
Ammons, Jacob 151
Anderson, S.C. 97
Anderson Co., S.C. 92, 93
Anderson, Capt. Robert 9
Andrews, Benjamin 22, 23, 149
    Judge Garnett 121
    M.L. 58
    Roy W. 77
    Wyatt 77
Anson Co. 107
Anthony, C.D. (Tony) 96
Anthony's Chapel (Meth.) 38-40
Antietam, Battle of 55
Antioch Church 42
Antioch Meth. Ch. (Col'd) 46
Appalachicola, Fla. 91
Appling, town of 84
Appomattox, Battle of 55
Aquinaldo, Captain 73
Aramathea Ch. (Meth.) 41
Archives and History, State's Dept. of 106

Arkadelphia, Ark. 144
Armstrong, Rev. James 32, 33, 34
Armstrong, John 5
Army Medical School 133
Army of the West 141
Arnet, J.A. 58
Arnold, Rev. W.P. 38
Arrant, Peter 23
Arrant, William 150
Arrent, William 22
Arrington, Hannah 111
Arthur, Martha 145
Arthur, William 145
Ashburn High School 95
Ashe, General 19
Asheville, N.C. 115
Ashley, A.J. 55
Ashley, Charles 58
Ashley, J.R. 57
Ashmore Anniversary Edt. 102
Ashmore, Elizabeth 98
    Evans 74
    Frederick 98, 102
    George 99
    George P. 57
Ashmore Graveyard 99, 100
Ashmore, Jeremiah 51, 100
    Malinda J. 100
    Hon. Otis 50, 66, 94, 98-100, 103, 104, 131, 139
    Peter 50, 98, 149
    Peyton, 58
Ashmore Place, Old 98, 100
Ashmore, Richard 45
    Thomas P. 98, 100-102
Athens Banner 113
Athens, City Of 111, 113, 127, 139, 142
Atlanta, City of 70, 92, 93, 107, 113, 131
Atlanta Constitution 113, 114
Augusta Dist. (Meth.) 38
Augusta-Lincolnton Mail 69
Augusta Presbytery 44, 45
Augusta, 7-16, 30, 31, 51, 61, 68, 70, 96, 98, 108, 112, 120, 126, 141, 142
Avery, Isaac 23, 47
Avondale, Grammar Sch. 143
Avondale Estates 143
Aycock, Richard 149
Ayres Family 41
Ayres, Thomas 33

Bacon, Senator A.D. 116, 142
Bailey, Rev. G. H. 37
    John 23
Bairdstown, Ga. 112
Bales, Rev. S.A. 39
Ballard, Joshua 23, 145
Banks, George W. 77
    Johnnie O. 74
    Lewis 77
    Willie W. 74
    Wyatt 58
Barden, Randal 5
Barksdale, Beverly 152
    James W. 89, 91
    Mose 77
    Nicholas Giles 87, 90, 152
    Hon. R.O. 17, 61, 62
    Sirth (Sith) 85, 90
    Tom 63
Barksdale's Ferry 17, 31
Barnard, Prof. E. 103
Barnes, Virgilius Maro 87
Barnesville, Ga. 103
Barnett, Daniel 145
Barrett, Mr. Ed 85
    Rev. George W. 38
    W. R. 41
Barron, Thomas 22, 23
Barton, John 149
Bartram, William 1-3
Bates, Daniel 151
Bates, John 150
Battle, Argonne Forest 74
Beall, Asa 89
Beard, Dewey 77
    Edwin 74
    Francis 145
    Guss 77
Beck, Rev. T. J. 32-34
Bellevue Hosp., N.Y. 127
Bemis Heights, N.Y. 127
BENCH AND BAR OF GEORGIA, THE 121, 125
Bennett, Claude 66
Bennett Family 42
Bennett, Jacob 50
    W. Homer 88
    William (2nd Lieut) 57
Benning, Miss Sarah Cobb 135
Benson, John 145
Bentley, A. J. 58
    Dr. B. F. (Benjamin) 58, 92
    Balaam 51, 52
    Dr. Ben Sheats 93

Bentley, Dr. Ben S. 93
    Benjamin 87
    Mrs. C.V. 128
    Cary N. 77
    Charles M. 58
    D.B. 58
    Family 52
    Fred 74
    H.N. 58
    J.B. 55
    J.M. 57
    J.T. 58
    Jeremiah 145
    Jesse 145
    John 35, 50, 145, 149
    Dr. John 52, 92
    John C. 35
    W.P. 58
Berry, Rev. Paul V. 35
Bessie Tift College 95, 131
Bethany Meth. Ch. 40
Beulah Church 33
Bibb, William 22
Bird, Adolphus 58
Bivens Family 37
Bivens, J.B. 57
    John 57
Blackburn, Jesse H. 73, 76
    Jim 74
Blackstock 108
Blackwell, Box 77
    James 77
    Willie, 73, 80
Blair, Miss Ruth 88, 90, 91
Blakey, C.S. 58
    J.F. 58
    P.A. 58
Blanchard House 98
Blanchard, Rev. James 35
Blanton, Charles 23
    Christopher 145
Boatwright, James 151
Bobbit, Jacob 22
Bocock, Mrs. Harold 76
Bohanan, Duncan 22
    William 22
Bohannon, Duncan 47
    John 145
Bohler, Addie 77
Bohler Family 41
Bohler, John T. 57
Bohley, W.H. 58
Boler, Hanna 145, 149
Bolton, I.N. 33, 34
Bond, James 77
Bond, Mark 152

Bond, Thomas 149
Bonner, Rev. G. E. 37
    Harvey 66
    J. W. 58
    James   W.   74
BOOK OF WILLS, INVENTORIES AND APPRAISEMENTS FROM 1796 TO 1808 110
Booker, Cloves M. 74
    Titus, B. 73, 76
Booth, Abraham 149
    Alexander 151
Bordeaux, S.C. 139
Boring, Rev. W. H. 37
Borum, Rev. Wm. 35, 92
Bostich, William 145
Bosworth, Obediah 145
Bothwell, Eddie 73, 76
Bouchillon, L. D. 56
Bound, Brook 18
Bowling, Rev. Hugh 45
Bowman, Ga. 94, 126
Boyd, Colonel 8, 9
    Robert E. 74
Boyd, Wilie 77
"Boykin Bucket Shop Bill" 105, 106
Boykin, Hamilton 104
    Isabelle 104
    James Fleming 104
    James H. 69-71, 89, 91, 104-106
"Boykin State Income Tax Law" 106
Bradley, Abraham 22
    John 23
Brakefield, Isaac 86
Branham, Rev. H. F. 37
Breazeale, Homer D. 93
Briar Creek 15, 19
Broad River 1,3,4,8,9,11,17, 30,83,108,120,145,146,147
Broom, Solomon 58
Brown, Cleve 77
    Colonel (A Tory) 8,11, 12, 14, 15
    General 120
    Henry 77
    J. D. 40
    Jacob 151
    Leonard M. 74
    Marshall 57
    Mrs. Marshall 39
    Robert 23, 33, 152
    William 35
Bryant, Benjamin 23
Bull Run, Battle of 54, 55

Bullard, J. W. 58
Bunch & Harnesberger 7
Bunch, W. A. 71
Burch, Dr. A. W. 41, 9
Bureau of Education, Commissioner of 117
Burgess, Alvin 56
    Rev. P. B. 92
    Rev. P. F. 32, 33, 35, 36
    Rev. T. P. 45
Burke County 12
Burke, John A. 50
Burks, David 149
Burnett, John 145
Burton-Pitt Lumber Co. 71, 72, 10
Burton, T. C. 69, 71
    Thomas C. 74
Bussey, Benjamin 149
Bussey Community 74, 77
Bussey, David 22
    H. T. 42
    (Rev.?) Hezekiah 42, 145
Bussey, Sr., James N. 96
    James R. 55
    John M. 91
    John R. 55
    Joseph 77
    N. D. 57
    Nathan 88, 151
Bussey Post Office 69
Bussey, Thomas 22, 23, 149
    Will 77
    (Rev.?) William 42
    William W. 58, 96
Bute Co., N.C. 4
Butler, Rev. J. B. 34
Cade, Matthew 77
    Winslow 77
Cade's Water-Mill 30
Caither, Elijah 22
Calhoun, John C. 138
    Solomon 77
Call, Richard 145
Callahan, Arthur 74
    Rev. B. M. 34
    Enoch 34
    Rev. J. S. 34
Cambrai 133
Camp Ground Church (Meth.) 40, 42, 43
Campbell, C. A. 58
    Colonel 8-10
Candler, W. L. 38, 40
Cantelow, William B. 49, 87

Cantor, Cuthbert B. 22
Carnes, Judge E. W. P. 24
Carr's Fort 8
Carrol, J. W. 56
Carrollton High School 95
Carter, Rev. J. A. 35, 36
    Josiah 145
    William 22, 23
Cartersville, Ga. 144
Cartledge, Cleveland L. 74
    James 51, 152
    James T. 57
    Jesse M. 57, 74, 88
    Mrs. Lula M. 88
Cartledge Residence 99
Cartledge, Thomas 45
    W. T. 40, 58
    Walton, 57
    William H. 57
    William M. 70, 73, 88
Carver, Jacob 33, 50
Cary, Rev. C. C. 37
Casey - 5
Casey, Roger 149
Catawba Indians 107
Cave Springs, Ga. 142
Caver, Henry 58
    James 58
Ceath, Absalom 145
Ceded Lands 4
Chafin, Fred H. 74
    Jesse M. 74
Chamberlain Observatory at Denver 103
Chamberlain's Ferry 46
Champ, Richard 150
Chancellorsville, Battle of 55
Chappell, Absolam 23
Charity Hospital (New Orleans) 74, 133
Charles Hardy Place 82
Charleston, S.C. 11, 19
Charlotte, N.C. 92
Chatham, County of 101
Cheivers, Major 4
Chenault Family 63
Chenault Home 62
Chenault, Joe 77
    Mr. 63
    Mrs. 63
    Nicholas B. 89
Cherokee Academy 67
Cherokee Creek 1,84,145-148
Cherokee Ford 5, 9
Cherokee Hill 1

Cherokee Indians 1,7,12,108
Cherokee Meth. Church 42
Cherokee Road 5
Chicago, Univ. of 94, 131
Chickamauga, Battle of 55
Chivers, Gideon 4
Citizen, Genet 109
CIVIL HISTORY OF THE GOVERNMENT OF THE CONFEDERATE STATES, WITH SOME PERSONAL REMISCENCES 118
Clancy, George 145
Clark, Edward 149, 150
    Gibson 90
    John 151
    Elijah 145
    Col. Elijah 7,9,10, 12-16,107,108
    Gen. Elijah 52, 109, 110, 111, 119
    Gibson 110
    Hannah 107, 110
    Gen. John 52, 108, 110
    Jr., Elijah 90
    Mrs. Elijah 108
Clark's Creek 9
Clarksburg, W.Va. 95
Clary, B.C. 37
Clary Family 37
Clary, Harrison 57
    Henry 57
    James 57
    S. J. 57
    Thomas 57
    William 57
Class, Rev. L. P. 34
Clay Hill Community 69, 75,77
Clay Hill Post Office 69
Clay, Jesse 145
Clearwater, Fl. 93
Clements, William 21, 85, 111
Clemmons, Rev. W. B. 45
Cliatt, A. M. H. 74
    D. W. 58
    Edward J. 74
    Isaac 58
    John 58
    Lee 58
    Peter 56
    Thomas 58
Clinch Rifles 141
Cold Harbor, Battle of 55
Coleman, Rev. D. W. 38
Coleman, Lucius C. 89
College Park, Ga. 131
Colley, John D. 68
Collins, Miss Editha G. 102
Colquitt, Charlie 77

Columbia Co. 18,70,92,95,98
    112,114,135,139
Columbia, S.C. 70
Columbia Seminary 45
Columbia Univ., N.Y. 95,131,
    141
Columbus, Ga. 95
Colvin, Dr. F. Gilderoy 93
Colvin Family 42
Colvin, Mrs. J. Z. 127
Colvin, Mrs. R. L. 127
Comb, Sterling 23
Combs, Sterling 22
Commerce, Ga. 144
Committee of Safety 110
Company A, Cutt's Btn. 140
Company F, 22nd. Ga. Reg.
    54, 55
Company G, 15th Ga. Reg.
    54, 57
Company H, 37th Ga. Reg.
    54, 57
Company M, 41st Inf. 73
Congregational Holiness 45
Conner, E.J. 56
    James 56
    Jerry 58
    Micajah 23
    Shadrack 57
    W. G. 57
CONSTITUTIONAL GOVERNMENT
    IN SPAIN 118
Continental Army 15
Cook, George 138
    Mark 145
Coofer, John R. 137
Corker, Captain 11, 120
Cornwallis, Fort 15
Cornwallis, Lord 11, 16,
    18, 19
County Demo. Exec. Com.
    105, 112
Covin, R.L. 42
Covington, William 23, 151
Cowan, John 23
Cox, Clifton Mailon 74
Cox College 131
Cox, Henry 149
    John E. 58
    John T. 74
    John W. 56
    Nancy 149
    P.A. 56
Crauson, John 22
Craven County 107
Crawford & Breazeale 112
Crawford, Mrs. C.P. 45

Crawford, Earl of 112
Crawford, George W. 112
    Harriet Beall 112, 113
    Harriet Emily 112
    Hicks M. 74
    Sir John 112
    Miss Natalie 134
    Nathan A. 58, 89, 91,
        111, 113, 115
    Rebecca Marshall 112
    Thomas 57
    Thomas Remsen 113-115
    Thomas William 115
    Dr. William B. 73, 89,
        93, 111-113
    William B. Jr. 112
    William H. 52, 112
Crawfordville Bank 42
Creek Indians 1, 10, 107-109
Crim, Thomas 22
Crite, Sherman 77
Crofford, Claborn 149
Cromer, John O. 74
Crook, Florence M. 74
    Henry 56
    Horace A. 76
    Isaih 57
    Jamison 57
    Noah 56
    Theodosia C. 131
    William 56
Crosson, Felix 88, 152
    John 151
Crozier, Silas 56
Cruger, Col. 12
Crutchfield, John 145
Culberson, H.L. 91
    Henry L. 93
Cullars, Joe 77
    John B. 91
    Matthew 152
    R. Toombs 57, 89
    Robert W. 74
    T. Watson 84
    Thomas D. 88
Cunningham, John 145
    W.R. 55, 120-121
Currey, James 150
Curry, Abe 77
    Dooley 77
    Ephriam S. 77
    Dr. J.L.M. 29, 94, 99,
        115-19, 135-36
    Luther 77
    Susan Winn 115
    Thomas 86, 115, 145,
        151

Curry, William 90, 115
Cuthbert City Schools 94
Cuthbert, Ga. 94
Cutliff, John M. 152
A CYCLOPEDIA OF GA. 103
Dailey, Rev. S.A. 39
Dallas, Albert H. 74
    Fate 77
    Thomas Sr. 49, 151
    Z.B. 58
Dallis, Mary Ann 136
    William 87
Dalton, Ga. 112
Daltten, Thomas 146
Danburg, Ga. 96, 129
Daniel, Joshua 88
Dartmouth 4
D.A.R. 111
Davenport, Iowa 143
David Family 37
David, George Hays 91
Davie, Rev. R. 35
    Robert 58
    William 58
Davis, Absalom 145-146
    Alex 77
    Alexander 77
    Augustine 145
    Austin J. 52
    Rev. J.G. 37, 40
    Mrs. Jefferson 62
    Jesse 33
    Lewis Coxson 146
    Minnie F. 128
    President 54, 61
    Rev. Roscoe 38
    Samuel 86, 150
    Wiley 145
    Rev. Wm. H.
Davy, Randolph 33
Dawson, William 21, 85
Dean, William 4, 146
Deason, Harry 74
    Manley 74
Dedge, Guss 76
Delaney, William 146
Dempsey, Rev. E.F. 37
Dennis' Mill 14
D'Estaing, Count 19
Dexter 93
Dickey, Rev. C.H. 36
    Mabel 141
Dill, David 23
    J.M. 91
    John P. 96
    Joseph 58, 87

Dill, P.H. 58
    William P. 74
Dillard, Rev. M.H. 37
Doggett, Rev. M.W. 45
Dooley, George 145
    John 146
    Col. John (Dooly) 5-11, 16, 119-120, 138
    Capt. Thomas 7, 119, 120, 121
Dooly County 136
Dooly, Judge John M. 29, 40, 48, 89-91, 121-125, 128, 150
Double Branches Academy 50
Double Branches Baptist 85
Double Branches Ch. 33, 42, 129
Double Branches Community 70, 74-77, 84, 85, 129, 141
Double Branches Sch. Dist. 65
Douglas, Doss 77
Douglass, George 146
Douglass Island 4
Douglass, William 146
Dowsing, William Jr. 86, 90
Dozier Hotel 2
Dozier, W.Z. 58
Drayton, Henry 77
Drinkard, John P. 69
Drury Cade's Mill 17
DuBose, B.J. 58
Due West, SC 139
Duloney, William 4
Dunaway, Alex P. 96
    Ben Hill 88, 126
    John L. 57, 126
    Lucinda 126
    W. Tutt 88
Dunn, Rev. John 37, 92
    Nehemiah 146
    Willie R. 77
Dunnegan, Rev. E.G. 37
Dye, William H. 75
Eades, John 146
    John Sr. 146
    Mary 146
Eady, John 152
Early, Peter 23
Eaton, Major 15
Echols, Rev. A.D. 37, 40, 41
Edgecombe Co. NC 107
Edgefield Co. SC 93, 104, 130
Edgefield High Sch. 104
Edison, Thomas A. 114
Edmonds, James 149

Edmonds, James 149
Edmunds, Fred L. 75
    J. A. 58
    J. W. 41
    John C. 75
    Samuel Robert 75,14
    Willie Timmons 76
Edwards, Hogan 77
    John 23, 149
    M. D. 77
    Rev. W. C. 34
Elam, Floyd 77
    J. P. 58
    John B. 77
    Lincoln Patrick 76
    Paul 77
    William F. 58
Elbert Co. 4, 17, 93, 131
Elbert, General 119
Elberton District (Meth.) 38
Elberton, Town of 51, 70, 96, 138, 142, 144
Elijah Clarke Chapter 111
Ellenburg, Henry G. 75
Ellis Island 114
Elrod, Rev. R. F. 37
Emory College at Oxford, Ga. 141
Emory, Rev. H. C. 37, 40
Emory University 42
Ennis, General 108
Enterprise Street 72
Entzminger, Rev. M. D. 35
    W. D. 36
Erskine College 139
Espey, James 90, 149, 150
ESTABLISHMENT AND DISESTA-BLISHMENT IN AMERICA 118
Estes, W. H. 91
    Dr. William H. 93
Eubanks, William 56
Evangelical Alliance for the United States 118
Evans, - 61
    Rev. C. S. 45
Evans Community 13
Evans, David 146
    Rev. S. D. 37
    William 86, 146
Excelsior, Ga. 144
Fanning Co., Ga. 92
Fanning, Joseph G. 140
Farmers State Bank 70, 72
Farr, Samuel 22
Farrar, Barret 22, 23
Faulkner, Ambrose 56
    William 56

Ferguson, F. M. 77
Ferguson House 98
Ferguson, J. A. 41
    Dr. S. G. N. 92
    Walter L. 75
Ficklen, Jr., Mrs. Boyce 69
    Sr., Boyce
Fields, Claud 77
Alabama Cavalry Regiment (Fifth) 116
Fifth Satelite of Jupitar 103
Finley, James 146
    Thomas 146
First Bapt.Ch.at Arkadelphia 144
Fishing Creek 4,17,21,145, 146, 148
Flanigan, W. A.
Fleming, Francis F. 88
    Hill 58
Fleming House 98
Fleming, James L. 45
    John 89, 90
    John W. 77
    Porter 96
    Robert 33, 86
    Samuel 90, 151
Florence, David 152
    John 23
    Lessie 126
    Dr. Miss Loree 93, 126
    Thomas S. 75, 146, 151
    Rev. W. A. 72
    W. K. 58
    W. Thomas 126
Florida, Univ. of 133
Florney, Harrison 77
Ford, Willie 77
Foreman, Mr. B. F. 85
Forrester, Thomas 146
Forsyth, Ga. 131
Forsyth High School 95
Forsyth, Mr. - 125
Ft. Gregg, Battle of 140
Fort James 1, 3
Fort Sumter 54
Fortson, Benjamin 40, 119
Fortson Family 37
Fortson, Rev. J. H. 34
    Thomas 99
Fortson's Ferry 70, 119
Foster, J. H. 33
Fouche, Eddie Y. 77
Fouche, Jered 57

Four Point Consolidated
  School 66
Four Points Consolidated
  School District 65
Fowler, James 149
Fox, Nicholas 49
Franklin, Rev. J. L. (John)
  37, 38
Franklin, Philemon 146
Franklin, Tenn. 141
Frazer, Alexander 87
       Arthur
       John 86, 89, 152
       Samuel 151, 152
Frazier, Alexander 39
        Arthur 152
Fredericksburg, Battle of 55
Freedman's Bureau 62
Freeland, Clarence Earl 73,76
Freeland, Edgar 75
         Edgar H. 74
Freeman, H. N. 56
         Henry 51, 87
         Major Henry 141
         Henry H. 73
         James 146
         Robert L. 56
         Samuel 77
         Miss Susan Leonora
         141
         W. F. 58
Fuller, Miss Lila S. 130
Fullilove, Thomas 22
Gafford, Stephen 32
Gaines, Rev. W. S. 37, 40
Gainesville College 101
Galphinton 108, 119
Gant, Lunford 23
Garner, Prof. J. T. 67, 84
Garnett, Eli 35, 50, 152
         John M. 77
         Nathan 77
Garrett, Rev. H. G. 39
Gartrell, Francis 146
Gaskin, James Lafayette 76
Gassaway, John L. 65
          Patrick H. 75
Gates, General 18
General Assembly of Ga. 121
George, Senator Walter F.
  106, 112
Ga. Bapt. Assc. 129, 130
Ga. Bapt. Conv. 129, 130
Ga. Continental Brigade
  119, 120
Ga. Continental Telephone
  Co. 70
Ga. Copper Co. 82

Ga. Ed.Assc. 102
Ga. Female College (Wesleyan)
  49
Ga. House of Representatives
  105, 138, 142
GEORGIA'S LANDMARKS,MEMORIALS,
  AND LEGENDS 107
Ga. Normal and Industrial
  College 143
Ga., Province of 5
Ga. State College for Women
  95, 96, 143
Ga. State Prison Farm 126
Ga. State Teachers College 95
Ga., Univ. of 95,96,102,112,
  113, 116, 126, 135
Gettysburg, Battle of 55, 56
Gibson Hotel 66
Gibson, Cap't. John 54, 55
Gill, I. M. 58
Gillebeau, John Jacob 35, 59
          Rev. John Lucius
          34, 35
Gilmer, Governor 125
        John 22
Glascock Co. 93
Glaze, A. N. 41, 57
       Alford 56
       David 86, 149
       Houston 57, 139
       Peyton 77
       Thomas R. 57
       Watson 77
       Will 77
       Willie 77
Glenn, Rev. N. Z. 37
Glove, Hardy M. 23
Godard, Geo. D. 66
Gogan, W. A. 66
Golden, Allen 151
        William 146, 150
Golding, Mark 23
         Matthew 23
         William 23
Goldman, Jasper 56
         M. L. 56
         Marion 56
         Newton 56
         T. J. 58
         Thomas F. 56
         Welcome J. 75
Goodwin, George 23
         Henry 23
Gordon, Confederate Officer
  55
Gordon Institute 94
Gorley, James 150
Goshen Academy 50

162

Goshen Bapt. Ch.(Col'd) 46
Goshen Ch. 32,33,42,42,129
Goshen (Community of) 32,33
    82, 83, 136
Grady, Henry W.   113
Graham, Thomas 146
Granite Hill, Ga. 95
Grassland Hospital 127
Graves, Benjamin 35, 50
        George W. 59
        James 146
Graves Mountain 3, 36, 70,
    82, 83, 132
Graves, R. N. 57
        Richard 22, 146
        Thomas 23
        Wiulliam 146
Gray's Creek 145,146,147
Green, Rev. H. O. 37
        Mrs. Hugh 115
        Mrs. T. M. 61, 62
        Rev. W. H. (William)
        34, 36, 92
        William 32, 149
Greene County 4, 119
Greensboro, Ga. 85, 128
Greenwood Bapt. Ch. 32, 34,
    35, 129, 140
Greenwood, Town of (S.C.)
    32, 96, 98
Gresham, Elisha 37
        J. H. 57
        Wheeler 90
Grice, Phillip 146
Grier, Euclid 77
        Nathaniel 77
        Robert 98
Grier's Almanac 98,102,104
Grierson, Colonel 11,12,15
Grierson Fort 15
Griffin, J. L. 56
        John 23
        William 56
Groce, Jared E. 87, 150
        Sheppard 150
Gross, Dudley 56
Groves, C. L. 66, 70
        Dr. J. Coleman 93
        John W. 75
        Lucius C. 91, 92
        Dr. W. Hammond 93
Grovetown, Ga. 85
Guice, Philip 23
Guillebeau Hotel 72
Guillebeau Inn 66
Guillebeau, J. E. 66, 67
        Rev. J. Jacob 92
        Rev. John L. 92

Guillebeau, Joseph E. 94
        Len B. 92
        Nora 94
        R. Elam 93
        Robert F. 89, 91
        94
        William W. 75
Guise, John 146
Gunby, E. N. 73
Gunby Family 42
Gunn, Rev. Radford 33, 35
Gunter, George I. 75
Gunter, Rev. J. G. 34
Gustavous 4
Guys, Phillip 146
Hagerman, Harrison W. 87, 91
Hambrick, A. P. 56
Hamilton, Col. 8, 9
Hammock, John 32, 146, 151
Hammond, John 152
        William J. 89
Hamp, Robert 72
Hamrick, John W. 88, 152
Hancock, Rev. B. W. 38, 40
Hancock Co. 124, 125
Hannah Clarke Chapter 111
Hardy, Jesse 150
        John 150
Harrow-on-the-Hill 149
Hapsburg, House of 118
Hardaway, Olin Forest 76
        William G. 75
Hardy, Arron 37, 87, 91
        F. A. 37
Hardy Family 37
Hardy, Harrison 59
        Henry 152
        J. A. 59
        James 22
        James A. 37
        Jessee 22,23,149
        John 33, 59, 151
        Mrs. T. S. 38
        William F. 37
Harlem, Town of 84,101,102
Harmon, Anthony 59
        Doyle 73, 80
Harmony Bapt. Ch.(Col'd) 46
Harnesburger, Adam 57
        Henry 57
        J. T. 57, 71
        Stephen 23, 146
        Lt.Stephen 54,57
        Wyatt A. 92
Harper, Elizabeth 138
        George 152
        J. C. 59
        Philmore 78

163

Harper, Robert 22
    Samuel 146
    V. E. 59
    William 89, 91
    William H. 75
Harris, Bert Lee 75
    Buster 78
    Elizabth 121
    Henry 78
    James 23
    John C. 75
    Rev. Juriah 33,35
    Rev. R.E.L. 32,34
    Will 78
Harrison, Wiley S. 89
Hart, Nancy 11, 120
Hartman, Rev. F. G. 45
Harvard Univ. 116
Harwell, Rev. R. J. 38
Hawes, A. S. 96
Hawes, Dr. Albert S. 93
    Albert W. 78
    Burl 78
    Miss Emma J. 127
    Fred 78
    J. N. 59
    James L. 56
    Joe H. 96
    Dr. John B. 93
    Miss Lula M. 127
    Manley 66
    Miss Mollie R. 127
    Mosely (Mosley) 52,87
    Percy 78
    Peyton 86, 96, 151
    Samuel 96
    T. D. (Capt.) 96
    Ulysses 78
    William L. 96
    William Lafayette 35, 92
Hawk, Rev. I. T. 45
Hawk's Gulley 12
Hawkinsville High Sch. 143
Heflin, Thomas J. 106
Hemphill, Hiram 91
Henderson, Alex 78
    Ezekiel 59
    Frank 78
    James H. 57
    Joseph 151
    Pete 78
    Robert 152
    Rufus 78
    W. H. 56
    William 152
Henley, John 56
    Matthew 56

Henley, Micajah 88,89,90,91
Henry, Charley 78
Hephzibah Bapt. Ch. 36, 129
Herndon, Rev. V. L. 33, 36
HERRINGSHAW'S CYCLOPEDIA OF AMERICAN BIOGRAPHY 103
Hester, Benji 23
    James 22
Hicks, John 23
High Hill Fork 5
Highsmith, Thomas 146
Hill, Ben 78
    Dolphus 78
    E. E. 36
    Robert G. 75
Hillhouse, J. B. 45
Hillman, Winder 32
Hingham, Mass. 18,19,20
Hogan, Ada Ruth 128
    Blanchard 78
    Miss Blanche 95
    Boyce 36
    Emma 127
    Emmie 95
    George C. 96
    Georgia Katharine 128
    Graves 127
    Hatcher H. 92
    J. W. 67
    J. Mercer 127
    James 58
    James Robert 89, 91, 127, 128, 130
    Miss Jennie
    Rev. John 33,35,36,92, 127, 128
    John Walker 76
    Lillie Rebekah 130
    Lucy 95
    Luther 94
    Jr., Luther Rice 130
    Rev. Luther Rice 35, 92, 127, 130, 131
    Mary Rachael 128
    Mollie R. (Hawes) 130
    Nancy Jane 127
    Patrick H. 127
    Priscilla 127, 128
    Shadrack 22, 23
    Sim 78
    Simeon W. 95
    Miss Sue Tom 112
    T. Newton 96
    Thomas B. 95
    Rev. W.A. (Wm.Ambrose) 32-36, 92
    W. G. 59
    Walker H. 92

Hogan, Wayne A. 75, 128
    William 59, 78
    Dr. Wm. Ambrose 35,
      128, 129, 130
Holden, E.S. 103
    Hon. Horace M. 111
Holiness Ch. (Col'd) 46
Hollenshead, C . R. 57
      Charles R. 37
Hollenshead Family 37
Hollenshead, T.S.(Sergeant) 57
      Thomas B. 68, 88, 99
Holley Const. Co.Augusta 66
Holliday, Miss Eugenia 140
    P.J. 69
    Thomas 23
    William 23
Hollman, Edmond 150
Holloway, Rev. B. Paul 92
    Bonnie S. 75
Holmes, Ichabod 152
    John 146
Holsenback, Jacob 33
    Miss Minnie 36
Honora Community 74-77, 82
Honora Post Office 84
Hopkins, John 56
    William 56
House, Frank 78
House, Lot 151
Houston, Texas 92
Howard College 117
Howard, James Henry 76
    Thomas 23
    Zebulon 35, 92
Howe, General 108
Howell, Lewis 35
Howerton, Rev. G. M. 45
Hudson, Rev. J.M. (James) 36, 131
    James Thomas 94,131, 132
    Sarah (Wilkins)131
Huger, General 19
Hughes, Alexander 151
    Rev. Goodman 37, 38
    James 21,22,88,146
    Robert 88, 150
Hulme, Rev. G. W. 34
Humbert, H. B. 66
Humphreys, Althea (Hollenshead) 133
Humphreys, R. T. 66
    Capt. Ralph W. (Wilbur) 69, 74,76,133,134

Humphreys, Dr. Thomas S. 56, 91, 92, 133
Hunter, David 23
Huntingdon, In. 94
Independence Academy 139
Ingram, Albert E. 75
Interstate Commerce Commission 72
Irvin, Willis 68
    General 110
Ivey, J. M. 40
    Marion 59
    W. C. 40
Jack's Creek 108
Jacks, General James 107
Jackson, Major 15
    Stonewall 54, 55
Jackson, Tenn. 131
Jackson, Rev. Wychie 33-36
Jacksonville, Fl. 93
Jacobs Family 41
Jacobs, Joseph 41
Jameson, Pres. S.Y. 144
Jamison, Robert 146
Jasper, Ga. 19
Jefferson County 93
Jenkins, Amy 78
    Charles J. 157
Jennings, Charles 56, 88, 90
    Hoody 22
    James 87, 91, 152
    Robert 56
    Robert W. 78
    Sim 56
    Thomas 151
    Thomas A. 58
Jesup, Ga. 95
Jeter, Wylie 33
John Gibson Institute 126,144
Johnson, Frank E. 78
    George D. 78
    Henry 56
    Thomas 56
    Tommie 78
Johnston, Alexander 23,49,87, 88
Johnston, - Conf. Officer 55
Johnston, Joe 54
    Sidney 54
Jones, Ausey 73, 80
    E. C. 36
    Edward 22
    Erwin 78
    G. W. 59
    Gabriel 146
    Greenvillle 51
    Henry 86,88,146,150
    John 146

Jones, Joshua 57
    Moses 57, 150
    Philip 23, 146
    Richard 146
    Samuel A. 75
    Seaborn 57
    Toliver 17
    Tom 78
    W. J. 59
    William 90
    William M. 17, 86
Jonesboro, Ga. 101
Jordan, Baxton 146
    Charles 22
    John 151
Journal (home) 105
Justice, Jim C. 75
Keating, Lt. Edward 4,5,146
Kelley, George W. 78
    Henry 78
    James W. 73,89
Kelly, Hugh 146
    John 146
Kelsey, Rev. D. 37
Kendall, Jeremiah 147
Kendrick, Sylvanus 151
Kendricks, Nathaniel 78
Kenna School District 65
Kennebrew, Jacob 146
Kennebrow, Henry 23
Kennedy, Rev. A. L. 35
    Arthur 56
    Doyl 78
    Frank 78
    George 59
    H. C. 56
    Henry 5
Kennon, Micha 22
    William 149
    Sr., William 149
Kershaw Co., S.C. 104
Kettle Creek 9, 10
Kettle Creek Battle 52
Kilbirnie, Ayshire, Scotland 112
Kilbirnie Crawfords 112
Kinder, Rev. D. 35
    David 35
King Charles I of England 112
Kinney, B. Clark 95
Kirkland, Rev. J. R. 32, 33, 35, 36, 92
Knight, Dr. Lucian Lamar 61, 135, 142
Knowles, Miss Ruth 136
Knox, John 56
Knoxville, Tenn. 96

Klu Klux Klan 64
Kunk, Dr. 83
LaGrange College 143
Lake City 133
Lamar, Basille (Basil) 22, 85, 115, 135, 136, 147
    Dr. Ezekiel 92
Lamar Faction 47
Lamar, Joseph R. 135
    L. Q. C. 135
    Capt. Lafayette 51, 54,57,87,135
    Miribeau B. 135
    Peter 89,90,151,152
    Col. Peter 44,47,48, 49,66,87,88,135
    Susan 116
    Thomas 90
    Jr., Thomas 4
    Zacharia 83, 147
Lampkin, John 90
    William M. 50
Land Court 107
Land, Henry J. 91
Landers Family 41
Landers, John 41
Lane, Dr. G. Mitchell 93
    Henry G. 75
    John A. 57
    Dr. L. Simeon 92
Lane, Rev. M. A. 33-35
Lang, Henry J. 51,52,59,89,91
    Miller 59
    R. Bruce 89
Langford, Rev. F. P. 37
    John 147
    Joseph 149
LaPrade, Jr., Rev. W.H. 38
Laramare, John 147
Laurens Co., S.C. 93
Lazenby, Rev. A. J. 34
Leah, GA. 94
Leake, Rev. Sanford 37
Leathersville Community 51, 69, 74, 76, 77
Leathersville Post Office 69
LeConte, James A. 4, 107
Lee, Andrew 151
    Jr., Andrew 152
    Sr., Andrew 151
Lee Co. 136
Lee, General 55
    Col. Henry 15
    Rev. R. E. 35, 36
    Robert E. 15, 116, 140
    Sam 78
    Will 78
Lee's Old Place 5

Legare, Hugh Swinton 138
Legg, Miss Bernice 95
    Hattie 95
    Homer 88, 92, 95
Legislature of Alabama 119
Le Harve, France 74, 134
LeRoy, Hester 66
    Rev. J. E. 33-36
    Rev. Joseph E. 92
Lessflore, Elenor 147
Lester, Rev. A. 37
Leverett, A. J. 56
    C. R. 59
Leverett Community 45,46, 76, 77
    Ed 98
Leverett Family 37
Leverett, George W. 78
    Hardy 87,88
    John 59
    John P. 75
    L. B. 73, 80
    Lonnie 78
    Lum 75
    Pat 78
Leverett Post Office 69
Leverett, Remus 78
    Sam J. 78
    T. B. 78
    Thomas H. 76
    Thomass 78
    Zederick 78
Leverette, Ollie 59
    Robert C. 56
    W. A. 56
    Rev. Z. M. 34, 35
Levitt, Sol 78
Lewis, James 78
    John H. 78
    Richard Esley 73, 76
    Jr., Robert T. 93
Lexington, Ga. 136
Liberty County 136
Liberty Hill Sch. 128,130,141
Library of Southern Lit. 103
Lick Observatory 103
Lincoln, General Benjamin 10, 11, 18, 19, 20
Lincoln Co. 1,4,6,7,17,18,21, 22,29,30,32,51,61,65,82,83, 84,92,93,94,95,98-101,110, 110-113,115,119,120,121, 124-128,130,131,132,135, 136,138,139,140,141,142, 143,144,145,148,149,153
Lincoln Co. Courthouse 67

Lincoln Co. Jail 50
Lincoln Co. Schools 65
LINCOLN HOME JOURNAL 69,105, 114, 115
Lincoln Lodge No. 78 (Masonic) 52
Lincoln, President 54
Lincolnton Academy 48, 112, 113, 114, 144
Lincolnton, Bank of 70, 144
Lincolnton Bapt. Ch. 34, 116
Lincolnton Bapt. Ch.(Col'd)46
Lincolnton Cemetery 45
Lincolnton Charge (Meth.) 37, 38, 40, 41, 42
Lincolnton Female Academy 49
Lincolnton H.Sch. 94,95,112
Lincolnton Hotel 54
Lincolnton Lodge 113
Lincolnton Masonic Lodge 66
Lincolnton, Mayor of 105
Lincolnton-Metasville Star Route 69
Lincolnton Meth. Ch. 38
LINCOLNTON NEWS 68, L3L
Lincolnton-Plum Branch Star Route 69
Lincolnton Post Office 69
Lincolnton Presbyterian Ch. 44, 134, 135
Lincolnton School 66, 67
Lincolnton-Thomson Star Route 69
Lincolnton, Town of 2,17,18, 21,24,31,36,37,39-42,44,45, 47,48,51,61,66,67,68,70-72, 74-77,81-85,93,96,97,98, 100,101,105,112,114,117, 121,126,128,129,130,133, 135,136,139,143,144
Linenkohl, Lewis E. 75
Lisbon Post Office 69
Lisbon, Town of 61,70,76, 77, 82, 83
Lithonia, Ga. 144
Lithonia High School 131
Little, John H. 35, 51
Little-Cleckler Const. Co. (Anniston, Ala.) 67
Little River 1,3,4,5,9,13,14, 17,30,31,70,81,145-148
Lloy's Creek 146
Lloyd's Creek 145-148
Lockhart, Asa 59
    Britain 23
    Eliel 88,89,91
    Fred T. 142

Lockhart, James 152
    Joel 56, 149-151
    John 23,47,86,149, 150
    Richard 147
    Vincent 90
Lockhart's Ferry 31
Lockhart's Mill 30
Loco Baptist 80
Loco Community 69,70,75,76
Loco Post Office 40, 69
Locust Grove Institute 94, 131, 141
Loflin, George 23
    James 59
    W. P. 59
Long Cane 14
Long, George R. 75
Longstreet - 29, 33
Longstreet, General 55
Looney, George C. 101
Lord, Rev. W. H. 32, 35
Louisville, Kentucky 128
Louisville, Univ. of 112
Lovelace Chapel (Col'd) 46
Lovelace Lumber Co. 71
Lovelace, Ralph A. 75
    Dr. T. B. 71
Lovelace Village 38, 71
Loverett, Matthew 151
Lovern, Rev. I. J. 39
Low, Ebenezer 5
Lowe, William 22, 23
Lower Trading Path 5
Luker, William 23
Lumpkin, Col. Joseph Henry 136, 137
Lupo, Rev. J. L. 38
Lyon, B. W. 96
    D. M. 96
    Edmund J. 96, 152
Lyon Family 37
Lyon, Mary Winn 136
Lyon, Judge Richard Francis 29, 91, 135-138
Macon, Ga. 137
Madison Co. 93
Madison, Platt 63, 91
Madison, Wisconsin 143
Mahoney, John 73, 80
Maitland, General 19
Mallet, James 56
Maloof, Joe 75
Malvern, Battle of 56
Manassas, Battle of 56
Maness, Rev. Arthur 37, 40
Manila Bay 73
Mann, John 147

Manning, Drury 14
A MANUAL OF PRONUNCIATION 102
Marbury & Crawford's DIGEST OF GEORGIA 6, 83
Marigay, Dan 73, 74, 80
Marion, Ala. 117
Markey, G. H. 67
Marshall, Abram 32
Marshall, Grant 78
Marshall, Rev. J. P. 32,35,36
Marshall, James 149
    John 23
Martin, Rev. C. S. 39
    Clifford E. 75
Martin Family 37
Martin, Jacob 147
    Jim 78
    John C. 75
    L. C. 56
    R. A. 59
    W. E. 56
    W. Q. 59
    William G. 57
Martin's Cross Roads 45, 65, 66
Mason, Nathan 78
    William T. 78
Mathews, Jr., James 33
    Sr., James 33
    Thomas A. 75
    Wesley W. 75
    Williams 22, 23
Mathis, Rev. J. E. 34
Matthews, Dan 78
    Governor 110
    J. E. 42
    James 147
    John W. 59
    Joseph 59
    Moses 147
    Sr., Moses 23
    William 150
Maxim Community 75
Maxim School District 65
Maxwell, Rev. J. H. 39
May, C. Julian 94
    Dr. Ellis R. 93
    James A. 151
    John W. 151
    Rev. J. C. 32-34,36,66
    William 22, 150
M. E. Church, Lincolnton 37
Memphis, Tn. 96
MEN OF MARK IN GEORGIA 103
Mercer Univ. 94, 128-130, 141, 144
Mercier, Frank 75

Mercier, 3rd Lt. J.N. 55
    Jim 78
    William N. 56, 96
Meridian College 95, 131
Metasville, Ga. 30, 48, 94
Meth., Gen. Conf. 42
Mexican War 116
Miami, Fla. 92
Miami High School 94
Middle Ga. College 101
Middlebrooks, Rev. T. b. 39
Middleton, Hugh 4, 5
    John 23, 147, 149
    Robert 147
Midville, Ga. 112
Midway, Ga. 136
Midway Meth. Ch. 41
Miles, John 22
Mill Creek 145-148
Milledgeville, Ga. 96, 123, 124, 126, 143
Miller, Stephen F. 121, 125
Mills, Alexander 5
Millstead, Ga. 95
Mims, Eunice D. 74, 75, 93
Mitchell, T. P. 91
    Dr. Thomas P. 93
Modoc, S. C. 69
Mofett, Thomas 147
Moffitt, Thomas 149
Moncrief, Elijah 22
    James 152
    John 59
    John C. 89
    Joseph 58
Moncton, Canada 114
Monk's Corner 19
Monroe, Ga. 108
Montcrief, Wiley 35
    William 32
Montgomery, Ala. 54, 116
Moore, Benning B. 89, 92
    James R. 75
    Joseph 147
    William 22, 147
Morgan, John M. 75
    William 59
Morris Creek 17, 145-148
Moseley, B. J. 56
    Benjamin 4, 22
    Henry 58
    James 59
    Johnathan 22, 23
    L. E. 56
    P. N. 59
    S. T. 59
    William 23, 59
Moses 13

Mosley, Benjamin 147
    Thomas 147
    William 147
Moss, Alexander 151
Moss Home 61, 62
Moss, John 47, 87, 150
    John D. 152
    Sr., John 150
    Roy L. 75
    Walter T. 65
    William Caesar 76
Motes, P. A. 36
Moultrie, Col. 19
Moultrie Fort 19
Mt. Carmel, S. C. 69
Mt. Zion Bapt. Ch. (Col'd) 46
Mulberry Meth. Ch. (Col'd) 46
Mumford, J. J. 59
    R. D. 57
Murfreeesboro, Battle of 55
Murphrey, Thomas 56
Murphry, A. J. 59
Murphy, George P. 89
    James 147
Murray, Aaron 79
    Aggie 78
    B. Frank 93
    Britt 79
    Clephus 79
Murray County 138
Murray, Dan 79
    Dandy 79
    David 23, 138, 149
    Dr. Delon L. 79
Murray Faction 47
Murray, Dr. George H. 93
    Harrison 79
    Harry M. 75
    Henry 88
    Isiah 79
    James H. 59
    James W. 87, 93
    Jim J. 79
    John 79
    Morris 79
    Miss Nancy 121
    Nathaniel 79
    Thomas 149, 150
    Thomas Walton 23, 79, 86, 90, 91, 121, 138, 147
    W. T. 59
    Will 79
    William T. 79
    Willie 79
Musgrove's Mill 108
Myer, Rev. W. L. 45
    Rev. Pat M. 92

MacLemurray, James 5
    Patrick 4, 5
McBean, Ga. 93
McBrayer, Rev. N.E. 37
McCall, Col. 12-14
McCallie, S.W. 82
McClenon, Samuel 23
McClerney, John 151
McCombs Hotel 124
McConly, William H. 88
McCord Family 42
McCord, Harvey E. 78
    John 35, 50, 150
    L. Pearl 42
    Lloyd 78
    R.W. 59
McCorkle, Arch 58
McCorkle Family 42
McCorkle, Hezekiah 58
    John 58
    Matthew 56
McCormick, SC. 69, 70, 96
McCurry, Andrew 78
McDowell, John 50, 86, 88, 90
McDuffie Co. 4, 18, 142
McDuffie, George 138
McDuffie Gold Belt 82
McGee, James E. 75
McGill, Robert 152
    Thomas 150
McGilvery 10
McGirth, Col. 8, 9
McGowan, R.G. 68
McGruder Gold Mines 82
McKinney, Francis 42
    Travis 147
    W.A. 69
    William G. 75
McKlemuny, James 147
McLendon, William H. 93
McMahan, A.L. 44, 45
McMurray, Will 78
McWhorter, Billie 85
    Fred A. 73, 75, 84, 85, 91, 92
    Fred A. Jr. 84
    Nina 84
    Sarah 85
Nail, Acquilla 147
    Joseph 147
    Julia 147
    Julius 147
    Presley 22
Nally, Handly 152
Nanney, Spurgeon 75
Nash, George 79
Nash House 98

Nash, J.H. 58
    Lucy 144
    R.C. 70
    T.A. 66
    Rev. T.A. 32-36, 92, 139
National Demo. Conv. 113
National Ed. Assoc. 102
National Statuary Hall 119
Naval Observatory 103
Neal, James Briscoe 87
Neese, Rev. L.P. 38
Neil, James B. 91
New Hope Academy 51
New Hope Baptist Church 35-36, 127-129
New Hope Church 99, 128, 130
New Hope Meth. Ch. 42
New Hope School Dist. 65
New Hope Section 3
New Jersey 18
New Orleans 133
New Tabernacle Bapt. Ch. 46
New York 18, 19
New York World 114
Newberry Bapt. Ch. 46
Newberry, James 75
Newberry, SC 97
Newell, Walton 21
Nolachuckie River 13
Noland, William 23
Normal School In Ga. 102
Norman, Cliff 79
    G.E. 33
    George 79, 88
    George W. 57
    Jake 79
    Jesse 74, 80
    Jim 79
    Johnnie 79
    P.C. 79
Norman Park Institute 95
Norman, Peyton 57
    Robert T. 75
    Toombs A. 75
    Rev. W.C. 37
    W.T. 41
    Rev. W.T. 38
    William 42
    William H. 88
N.C. Colonial Records 107
Northern Circuit Judge 121
Northhampton, Mass. 93, 127, 142
NW Literary & Hist. Soc. 118
Norwood, GA. 96
Novell, T.B. 56
Nowland, William 147
Nunally, John E. 79

Ocilla 93
Oconee River 7,109,119-20
Odom, Solomon 147
Oglethorpe College 131
O'Hara, Gen. 19
Old Union Church 49
Oliver, John 147
O'Neal, Benjamin 51
    Benjamin P. 87
    William 23, 147
O'Neal's Path 5
Ordinary, Lincoln Co. 6
Ordinary, Wilkes Co. 6
Orlando, Fla. 92
Oslin, Rev. W.W. 37
Ottawa, Kansas 131
Ottawa, Univ. 131
Overstreet, William 22, 23
Owens, Arthur 22
Pace, Rev. H.D. 39
Palmer, W.L. 66, 139
Palmor, Solomon 147
Palmore, Rev. Elisha 34,35
Par, John 23
Paradise, A.G. 56
    Albert W. 75
    Fred A. 92
    Howard H. 75
    J.C. 56
    J.V.M. 36
    John Alvin 76
    Marshall 75
    Moody 92
    Pink 75
    William 149
Parham, C.V. 67
Paris, France 74
Paris Treaty 16
Park, Rev. G.R. 38
    John 59
Parker, James R. 59
    Zionas 151
Parks, Alex 99
    Alexander 96
    Ben 79
    Charles 147
    Collie 79
Parks Family 37
    Dr. E.H. 59, 97
    Jabe 59
    John 86, 89
    Lewis 87, 151
    Louis 59
    Louis Sr. 37
    W.E. 59
    William 86, 89
Parson, Edward E. 93
Partee, Elizabeth 147

Partelow, Robert 79
    Tom 74, 80
Pascal, William 59
Paschal Place 82
Paschal, William 42, 150
Patten, Jacob 5
Patterson, George W. 68
Paynter, Mrs. Burt 144
Peabody College 94
Peabody Fund 117
Peabody, George 117
Pearles, Town 59
Peed Family 44
Peed, John 41
Pelham, Ga. 94
Pendall, Sarah 147
Penland, Buster L. 75
    Carl 75
Pensacola, Fla. 141
Pentecostal Holiness Ch. 45
Peoples Bank, Jacksonville 42
Perdieu, William 22
Perkinson, Levin 32
Perryman, Clinton J. 45,73,92
    E.R. estate 135
    Edwin R. 94, 139
    George B. 96
    Martha 94, 139
    Minnie Thaddeus 94, 139
    T. Leland 34, 66, 89, 94
Peteet, Richard 147
Petersburg 4, 8, 30, 31
Petersburg-Augusta Rd. 48
Petersburg Battle 56
Pharr, Samuel 23, 147
Pharr's Chapel Meth. Ch. 46
Phi Beta Kappa 118
Phi Sigma 118
Philadelphia, Pa. 127
Phillippine Islands 73
Phillips, Rev. A.A. 39
Pickens, Andrew 8-10, 15
Pickens Co., SC 93
Pickens, Gen. 119
Pierce's Chapel 141
Pilcher, Rev. T.J. 34
Pine Grove Meth. Ch. 37, 142
Pine Grove School Dist. 65
Pine Grove Settlement 99
Pistol Creek 4,5, 145-47
Pitt, H.B. 70, 71
Plant System of Railroads 112
Pleasant Grove Meth. Ch. 46
Plexico, Rev. J.C. 45
Plum Branch, SC 69
Plum Branch-Double Branches
    Mail Route 69
Pope, David H. 92

Populists 69
Porter, Rev. W.H. 45
Poss, M.C. 59
Powell, B.F. 59
   Francis 152
Powell (Green) Hotel 34
Powell, Joe Grimsley 76
   Richard 23, 150
   Mrs. T.R. 126
   W.C. 91
Powell's Academy 67
Prather, A.M. 59
   Richard 50
Prattville, Ala. 94
Preacher, G. Loyd 67
Preston, Ga. 112
Price, John 84
Price, John M. 69, 85, 91
   Julius J. 75
   Miss Loudell 85
Price's Grove Bapt. Ch. 46
Prickett, Rev. B.C. 40
Prince Edward Co., Va. 138
Prince, Rev. Mark B. 92
Provisional Confederate
   Congress 116
Provost General 19
Psalmonds, Thomas L. 152
Pugh, Jesse 4
Pulaski 19
Pullen, George 74, 80
Purysburgh 10
Putnam Co., Ga. 143
Quachita College 144
Quarles, Robert 75
Quillian, Rev. W.F. 38
Quinn Dallas Home 61
Quinn, John 87
   William 22, 152
Quitman, Georgia 111
Rabun, Willram 52
Rae's Mill 17
Ramsay, Dr. 108
Ramsey, Caleb R. 96
   I.N. 59
   John 147
   William W. 96
Randall, Joe Henry 79
Ratliff, Hezekiah 151, 152
   Richard 151
   Robert 147
   Samuel 151
   Thomas 151
   William 23, 147
Ray, Jonathan 59
Ray's Water-Mill 30
Red Hill, S.C. 94
Red Lick Creek 107

Reed, Alexander 79
   Fletcher L. 75
Reese, Albert G. 75
   Rev. F. B. 37
   J. J. 59
   Seaborn 142
   Judge William M. 141
Rehoboth Church 129
Reid, A. J. 56
   Griffin 56
   Grover C. 76
   Jabe M. 57
   James K. 33
   John 51
   Mell J. 66, 76
   R. R. 56
   W. A. 32, 36
   W. M. 59
   William 56
   Rev. William A. 92
REMINISCENSES OF FAMOUS
   GEORGIANS 142
Remson, James 57
   N. P. 73
   Rem 23, 48, 57, 73,
      86, 89, 150
   Jr., Rem 86
   Sr., Rem 96
   T. H. 57, 88
   Jr., Thomas H. 92
   Sr., Thomas H. 69, 70
Revier, J. G. 59
   John 56
   J. H. 41
Rhodes, Eustern 152
   J. M. 34
Rice, Judge Samuel F. 116
Richardson, Walker 147
Richland, Ga. 94
Richmond College 117
Richmond Co. 93
Richmond, Va. 54, 61, 62, 115,
   116
Roberts, A. Q. 56
   Jesse 58
   R. E. 59
   T. H. 56
Robertson, Augustus 59
   Frank 59
   Mrs. W. G. 128
Robnson, R. L. 33
Rochester Univ., N.Y. 118
Rock Hill Meth. Ch. 35, 42
Rockmart, Ga. 95
Rockmart High School
Rocky Spring Church 32
Rome, Ga. 93, 126, 131
Roquamore, James 147

Ross, M. C. 59
Rumbley, Rad W. 57
Runnells, Robert 50
Russell, John 22,23
    Thomas C. 21,22, 23, 85
    Rev. W.J.A. 45
Rutland, Rev. T. L. 37, 39
St. Joseph's Academy 95
St. Louis, City of 113
St. Luke Bapt. Ch. (Col'd) 46
St. Marie Cemetery (LeHavre) 74, 134
Saint Paul Meth. Ch. 40
Sale, Annie 95
    Miss Frances Ann 136
    H. M. 57
    Rev. J. M. 34
    P. Wyatt 95
    Miss Ruth 95
    Thomas 57
Salem Academy 50
Salem Bapt. Ch. 34, 42
Salem Community 18
Sale's Gold Mines 82
Samuel, Benjamen 22
Samuels, Anthony 88
    Benjamin 51
    E. L. 56
Samuels Family 37
Sanders, B. M. 34, 35
    Rev. Britton 38
    Rev. E. N. 34
Sandwich, Dr. Thomas 149
Sanford, Fla. 92
Sanford, Jordan 67
Santiago 73
Saturday Evening Post 114
Savannah, Co. of 101
Savannah River 1,3,4,5,9,10, 11,17,30,31,37,61,63,70,81, 108,110,119,121,145,146,147, 148
Savannah, Town of 7,10,11,12, 16,18,19,50,99,100,101,102, 108,123,129
Scaggs, William 22
Scott, Alexander 147
Scott, Charlie 74, 80
    George W. 76
    Jack 79
    Noah 59
    Samuel 147
Seaggo, William 150
Seal, Anthony 148, 149
    Jarvis 148
    John (Seale) 22, 23
    Pressley N. 42

Seals, Anthony 23
    Richard 22
Searcy, Rev. B. P. 37, 40
Searles, Arges 79
    John 59
    Robert 33
    T. C. 58
    Will 79
Sears, Rev. A. J. 37, 40
Selles, Jacob 22
Semore, - 4
Senders, Robert 148
Senoia, Ga. 143
Seven Days Battle 54
Seven Pines, Battle of 54,56
Shady Hill 18
Shank, Rev. J. A. 32,33,34,36
Shannon, Thomas 22
Sharon Church 129
Shay's Rebellion 20
Sherman, General 55
Shiloh, Battle of 54
Shorter College 126,129,131
Shreveport, La. 131
Sibert, Frederick 152
    John 151
Siloam Bapt. Ch. 34
Simmons, Fess 79
Simmons Home 84
Simmons, Miss Mary A. 136
    Stern (Sterne) 5, 23, 84, 152
Simms, George 23
Simpson, Rev. F. T. 45
    Hester 66
Sims, Alex B. 99
    G. S. 59
    George L. 40
    John 91
    John A. 94
    Dr. John L. 66, 93
    Leonard 39, 86
    Lucile 126
    Marjorie 126
    Miss Mildred 126
    Mrs. Rachel 39
    William F. 91, 152
Singleton, Rev. W. L. 37,40
Sisson (Ga.) School 131
Sistrunk, Goshen 152
Slater Fund 117
Slaton, W. A. 3
Slaughter, Samuel 148
Sloan, Fred 79
Smalley, Allison Kent 141
    B. N. 42
    Benjamin 76
    Charles D. 141

Smalley, Edward 73
    Edward W. 76
Smalley Family 42
Smalley, James 58
    Mary E. (Hogan) 141
    Mary June 141
    Michael B. 89
    W. N. 41
    Welcome Talmadge 91, 141
Smart, Ezekiel 150
    James 23
Smith, Rev. A. M. 37
    Augustus 23
    Austin 150
    B. 110
    Benajah 147
Smith College 127
Smith, David 147
    Drew 147
    Edward 23, 90
    Francis 23
    Gabriel 147
    D.D., George G. 37
    Rev. H. A. 45
    Henry 147
    James Esq. 22, 150
    Lewis 149
    M. E. 41
    Nathaniel 147
    Peter 32, 147
    Dr. Racy H. 93
    Reuben C. 76
    William 21, 147
Smith's Chapel Meth. Ch. 46
Smithsonia, Ga. 96
Snead, James 22
Snow, Delila 151
    Jamesw P. 151
Soap Creek 4,5,12,21,82,145-148
Soap Creek Church 32
Soffold, Andrew 79
Solly, Michael 23
Soperton, Ga. 95
S. Lincoln Cir. 39-42
Southern Bapt. Conv. 130
Southern Bapt. Theo. Seminary 128
Southern Norman Univ. 94
THE SOUTHERN STATES OF THE AMERICAN UNION 118
Spain, Ambassador 117
Spanish-American War 73
Speer, Rev. W.H. 37
    Rev. Z. 37
Spinks, John 23
Spires, Carter 56

Spires, Edgar 96
Spires Family 37, 41
Spires, Hezekiah 23, 150
    J.N. 58
    James 58
    Luther B. 76
Spires Place 99
    Sim 59
    W.B. 58
    W.J. 56
    W.N. 42
    William 41
Spottsylvania Battle 55
Spratlin, Clark T. 76, 93
Sprayberry, Rev. A.N. 37
Stanford, Kimbus 23
Stanley, Rev. Carl 39
Starkville, Ga. 136
State Bapt. Convention 118
State Demo. Ex. Com. 105,113
State Med. College 126, 127
State Normal Sch. 95,127,139, 142
State Senate 105,128,135,142
Statham, Charles 91
    Rev. J.E. 39
Statom, Willie 79
Steal, Cuthbert 22
Steamship Geo. Washington 74
Steed, E.A. 32
Steel, Cuthbert 22, 23
Stephens, Alex. H. 101, 142
    Rev. L.W. 34
    Linton 137
Stevenson, N.W. 57
    T.O. 66
Stewart, James 151
Stockton, Rev. J.H. 34
Stokes, Henry 79
    Rev. W.H. 33, 34
    William 147, 150
    William C. 48
    Willie H. 79
    William Jr. 22, 23
Stone, J.D. 57
Stono Ferry 19
Story, Sam 79
Stovall, Charles 23, 88
    Drury 149
    John 88
    Josiah 21, 22
    Lewis 48
    Ralph 150
    Stephen 33,50,87,88,151
    Thomas 88
    Wade 76
Stribbling, Anthony 152
    Thomas 152

Strickland, Bessie A. 39
Strother, Aldolphus E. 59,
   89, 91, 140, 141
   Alan-Del 140
   C.A. 59
   C.R. 91
   Chapley R. 91
   Clara H. 140
   Rev. H.J. 40
   J.E. 59
   J. Sidney 140
   Jeremiah 76
   Joseph 89, 91
   Josephus A. 140
   Josephus E. 91
   Maude O. 140
   Nancy 140
   William Francis 140
   William J. 140
Sturkey, Edgar L. 76
Sturkey Family 37
Sturkey, James P. 65
   M.L.B. 96
   Pickens L. 99
   W.O. 96
Suddith, James 22
   Laurence 23
Sumter, General 108
Superior Ct. of Lincoln 135
Supreme Ct. of Ga. 137
Sussett, Leonard 23
Sutton, Joel B. 42
Swindler, Rev. D.W. 34
Swords, James 23
Sybert District 18, 21
Sybert Post Office 69
Tait, Judge Charles 52,
   123, 124
Talbott, John 148
   John Jr. 148
   Thomas 148
Talledega Co. 115, 116
Tampa, Fla. 94
Tannery 51
Tarleton, Col. 19
Tate 10
Tate High Sch. 95
Tate, Pearl 79
Tatom, Abel 23, 148-49
   Abner 88, 148-49
   John 21, 23, 148
   Wiley G. 152
   William 21
Tatum, B. Franklin 88
   Hon. B.F. 63, 67, 88
Tatum Family 37
Tatum, J.H. 59, 91
   J.W. 59

Tatum, Wiley G. 57, 86
   William P. 37, 57
Taylor, Rev. F.L. 35
   Rev. Francis 35, 36
   John 22
   Milledge 79
   Thomas 79
   Rev. W.R. 34
   Ward 5
Teaseley, Rev. G.A. 37,39,40
Teasley, J.A. 40
   L.P. 40
Tebow, John 57
Telfair Academy 102
Telfair, Benjamin 21, 23
Tenth Cong. Dist. Sch. 127
Tenth Dist. Agri. Sch. 95
Tenth Dist. Athletic Meet 84
Texas Rangers 116
Thankful Bapt. Ch. 46
Thomas, Charlie 79
   Elisha 23
   Jake 79
   Johnnie 79
Thompson, Furman 59
   Jesse 110
   Samuel 22, 148, 149
Thomson, Ga. 142, 143
Thurmand, James 22
Thurmond Family 37
Thurmond, Felix 57
   Roy C. 76
Tignall, Ga. 82
Tillery, Thomas 35
Todd, James E. 50, 86, 88
   John 148
Tom Watson Mem. Assoc. 106
Toole, Rev. Jonathon 34
Tories 107-08, 119-121
Tory Pond 11, 120
Trammell, David 58
   J.W. 56
   Sam W. 76
   Rev. W.H. 37
   William Jr. 152
Trans-Oconee Republic 110
Traveller's Rest 136
Triplett, William 148
Troup, George M. 52
Troup, Governor 123
Troy, John 148
Tucker, Wm. H. 74, 80
Tulane Univ. 133
Tulley, Moses 22
Tullis, Miller C. 76
   Moses 148
Tunnage, James 56
Turman, George 79

Turman, Roy 79
Turner, Shadrack 22,49,91
  Rev. W.D. 37
Turpin, John B. 116
  Manly B. 116
Tutt, Benjamin 141
  Carl 141
  George 59, 79
  Henry 59
  Jackson 79
  Lucien W. 141
  Mary A. Fleming 141
  Col. Wm. Duncan 59,91,
    92, 141, 142
  Willie 79
Twiggs, General 108, 110
Twitty, George 150
Tyler, A.H. 40, 41
  C.H. 41
  Edwin 56
  Francis 42
Ullum, Francis 152
Ulm, Asbury 59
Ulm Family 37
Union Bapt. Church (Old)
  34, 38
Union Church 38,44,66,135
Union Hill Sch. Dist. 65
Union Theo. Seminary 131
Union Univ. 131
U.S. Dist. Court 72
Upper Trading Path 5
Upton, Gen. 61
Upton's Creek 32
Valhalla, NY 127
Valley Campaign, Va. 54
Veal, Rev. W.C. 34
Veasey, William 148
Verdery, W.M. 33
Villa Rica, Ga. 143
Villers-Gouslains 133
Waddell, Moses (Sch.) 138
Wadsmouth, William 23
Wadsworth, Angus 22
  James 86, 151
  Thomas 22, 148
Wakefield, Ben 79
Walker, Augustus 60
  Henry G. 152
  Rev. I.R. 35
  J. 38
  Rev. John H. 32,35,36,
    86, 90, 150
  John W. 34
  Lawrence Jehu 76
  Malcom T. 152
  Miss 115
  Moses 148

Walker, Sanders 148
  V.M. 37
Wallace, Dave 56
  James 150, 152
  Jerry 56
  Marjery 148
  Ollie 60
  Robert 150
  T.A. 56
  William 22,23,148,149
Walton, Benton 150
  Edward 79
  Elizabeth 121
  J. 110
  John 23, 148
  John H. 150
  Lewis 79
  Newell 22, 23, 148
  Newell, Jr. 85, 86
  Robert 22,85,89,150
  Thomas 22
  Thomas Sr. 22
  William 22
Ward, Dr. B. Harvey H. 93
  Bryan 4
  Lavilla A. 94,142,143
  Dr. Pelham C. 93
  Rosa Hawes 142
  T.C. 41
  Mrs. T.C. 41
  W. Cleveland 142
Ware, Rev. Cleo B. 42
Ware Co. 128
Ware Family 39, 41
Ware, Dr. Fritz L. 93
  Henry 148
  Henry Jr. 148
  Henry B. 76, 85
  Rev. J. Lane 42, 92
  James 22,33,86,149,150
  Joseph 39
  Leonard 79
  Mary Long 143
  N.C. 39
  Nannie 94, 143
  Nicholas 128, 148
  Robert A. 39
  Robert 23,86,90,148
  Robert A. 143
  Robert W. 92
Warren, Bennie 79
  Collie 79
Warren Co., Ga. 93
Warren, Lot 149
  Lott 22
Warrenton, Ga. 84, 93
Warrenton, Va. 54, 136
Washington Co. 93

Washington, D.C. 103
Washington, George 18-20
Washington High Sch. 95
Washington, Lt. Gov. 20
Washington, Ga. 3,4,17,48,
   61-63, 70-72, 94-96, 101,
   121, 126, 130, 141
Washington & Lincolnton RR
   48, 69, 71, 72
Water's Plantation 8
Waters, Lt. Thomas 4
Watkins, Benjamin 148
Watkins Chapel 42
Watkins, Garland 92
   Rev. J.W.G. 37
   John 22, 148
Watson, Bob 79
   Senator 129
   Thomas E. 142
   Tom 106
Wattauga River 13
Waycross, Ga. 112
Wayne, Gen. 16, 108
Weathers, John 23
   Samuel 23
Webster's Blue Back 37
Weeks, Ollie 37
Weems, George 79
Welborn, Arthur 152
Wellborn, Wilkes R. 87
Wellmaker, W.L. 36
Wells, Clarence W. 76
Well's Creek 146
Well's Creek Bapt. Ch. 36
Welton, Noah 50
Wesleyan Female College 42
West, Rev. J.C. 35
   J.Q. 32, 33
   James E. 76
   R.F. 37
   Rev. T.B. 34
   Rev. W.F. 35
Western Cir. Judge 121
Whatley, Michael Jr. 148
Wheat's Campground 36,38,
   42, 43
Wheat, Harvey 42, 49
Wheatley, Leonard 57
Whitaker, Samuel 22
White 20
White, Edgar Henry 76
   H.E. 40
White House 12
White, J.L. 41
   Rev. Miller D. 38
White Plains 18
White Rock Bapt. Ch. 46
Whitfield, Rev. A.L. 45

Who's Who in America 103
Wilde, Gen. 62, 63
Wilderness, Battle 55
Wilheit, Thomas T. 89
Wilkes Co., Ga. 1,2,4,6-8,
   10-12,14,16-18,32,61,70,
   82,83,92,93,101,107,110,
   111,119-121,125,128,131,
   132,138,139,141,143,145,
   150
Wilkes, Dr. John L. 91, 92
   Lt. John L. 55,87,88
   John M. 94
   Judge 68
   Nathan C. 76
   Samuel Dorsey 76
   Dr. Samuel L. 67,87,93
   Judge S.L. 114
Wilkinson, Georgia Murray 94
   Tell H. 94
   Thomas P.
WILLIAM EWART GLADSTONE 118
Williams, Calvin 80
   Charles 148
   Col. 107
   Eddie 80
   Elizabeth 148
   Ezehiel 22
   George E. 76
   Jake 80
   Dr. Joseph W. 93
   Lee 80
   Roy 74, 80
   Simmie, 76
   Susannah 148
   Tom 80
   William 23
   Winifred 114
Williamson, Micajah 14, 148
   Polly 110
   William 23
Willingham Family 38, 41
   Frank 76
   Isaac 88
   James 150
   John 41, 60
   Zack S. 66, 88, 89
Willington, SC 138
Wilson, Rev. John 35
Wilson, President 74
Wing, John 151
Winn, Dorothy Wright 115
   Jefferson 91
   John 21, 85, 115
   Prudence Lamar 115
   Richard 22, 150
   Richard F. 115, 150
Winne, John 47

Wood, Johnnie R. 76
Woods, William 36, 56
Woolridge, Gibson 22,23,149
Wooten, Thomas 148
Worth Co., Ga. 92
Wortham, Marty 116
Wright, B.S. 57
    F.M. 58
    George W. 96
    Gustavus T. 89
    Guy H. 76
    James (Gov.) 5
    John 35,50,86,90
    Otis Wright Place 47
    Rev. Samuel P. 92
    Thomas B. 76
    W.M. 58
    William 151, 152
Wright's Academy 67
Wrightsboro 4, 9, 10
Wyatt, Peyton 21-23,85,111
Wynn, Steve 80
    Willie 80
Yarbrough, Rev. J.F. 37,40

York, Burwell 90
    David 152
    John 150
Yorkshire, England 134
Yorktown Va. 16, 19
Young Harris College 42
Zachery, William 148
Zellars, I.N. 60
    Jacob 23, 150
    John 60, 80, 143
    John Thomas 144
    Macie Pete 144
    Mary Florence 143
    P. 66
    Peter 66,70,94,143
    Reid Nash 144
    Robert L. 80
Zellenor, John 42
Zimmerman, Phillip 17,22,23, 86, 90, 148
Zoellner, George 32

www.ingramcontent.com/pod-product-compliance
Lightning Source LLC
Chambersburg PA
CBHW060354080526
44583CB00012B/303